CLEATS & EATS
ISLANDS

boater's restaurant guide to the
San Juan Islands and Gulf Islands

To: Jean

Lorena Landon

By Lorena Landon

Printed and bound in United States of America.

Warnings/Disclaimers/Cautions

All locator maps, diagrams, and drawings, including but not limited to islands, bays, docks, landings, streets, and restaurants in this publication should NOT be used for navigation. Boaters are responsible for carrying all appropriate charts and maps for purposes of navigation along with timely tide tables and charts of currents and all necessary equipment and supplies. Boat owners and operators need to make their own determination as to the suitability of docks, buoys, and anchorage pertaining to their own vessel's length, weight, type, and other factors.

Information and comments in this publication regarding restaurants, facilities, and other businesses are for information purposes only and do NOT constitute an endorsement or recommendation of any kind. Information in this publication has been included as provided by restaurants, marinas, park departments, municipalities, fisheries, private organizations, visitor centers, and historical records. Although the author and publisher have made every effort to ensure the accuracy and completeness of information contained in this publication, we assume no responsibility for errors, inaccuracies, omissions, or any inconsistency herein. Any slights of people, places, or organizations are unintentional.

The author and publisher disclaim liability and responsibility to any person or entity with respect to any loss or damage caused or alleged to be caused, directly or indirectly, by the use and/or interpretation of any of the information contained in this publication. The author and publisher do NOT warrant the fitness, quality, security, or accessibility of the places, facilities, or businesses referenced herein. The reader should verify the information by contacting the restaurant, marine facility, docks, and other business establishments in this publication to make their own determination. This publication is about restaurants accessible by water and related information as we know or believe them to be and are subject to change without notice.

Published by
Woodland Cove Press   **ISBN-13: 978-0-9741380-4-6**
9805 NE 116th Street, PMB 7346
Kirkland, WA 98034 USA
425-894-6016
www.CleatsandEats.com

Table of Contents

About the Author _____ iii

Cleats & Eats Overview _____ iv

Navigating this Book _____ v

Wineries, Spas, and Museums _____ vi

List of *Cleats & Eats* by Island _____ vii

   Gulf Islands 2
       Gabriola Island......................................3
       Galiano Island..7
       Mayne Island 21
       North Pender Island 31
       South Pender Island 45
       Saltspring Island 49
       Saturna Island 75
       Thetis Island 81
       Vancouver Island 85

   San Juan Islands 174
       Blakely Island 175
       Lopez Island 177
       Orcas Island 187
       San Juan Island 225
       Shaw Island..247

Index _____ **251**

About the Author

Lorena Landon is a noted author of nautical guide books as well as a contributing writer for boating magazines. She has written books and articles for the boating community for over seven years with a focus on the Pacific Northwest from Portland, Oregon through the inland waterways of Washington State and British Columbia. She has become an established author of boating destinations in the Northwest and serves the boating community as a member of the Boating Programs Advisory Committee for the State of Washington.

Lorena Landon and her husband, Leonard, have cruised the Gulf and San Juan Islands since the early 1980's. While raising their two sons, it was a family tradition to spend a portion of the summer exploring, cruising, and hiking in this Island paradise. The Landon's were first inspired by reading the Gunkholing books written by Jo Bailey and Al Cummings, which led to many adventures and life-long memories.

Today, Lorena and Leonard cruise the Islands as a couple or with their grandchildren and extended family. The Landon's continue to find hidden treasures that boaters love and appreciate.

Lorena and Leonard would like to extend special appreciation to Robert (Bob) Hale, author of the Waggoner Cruising Guide, and his team at Robert Hale & Co., Inc., nautical book distributors, including Oscar Lind and others, for their words of encouragement.

Cleats & Eats Overview

"Cleats & Eats" directs boaters to unique eateries and hidden gems located upland from community docks, exclusive restaurant docks, public wharves, and marinas, ranging from fine dining and winery bistros to nautical restaurants and pubs in the San Juan and Gulf Islands with portions of Vancouver Island from Sidney to Nanaimo. You won't be left rudderless once you reach land thanks to "Cleats & Eats," the must have restaurant and activities guide specifically written for boaters. "Cleats & Eats" includes fun breakfast and lunch stops for planning your cruise and things to do and see once you reach your destination, including casual and fine dining venues. All the research and leg work has been done for the boater's convenience in mind.

"Cleats & Eats," a boater's restaurant guide, is well organized for easy reference. Restaurant information includes décor, cuisine, hours, and contact information in the "Eats" section of this guide along with basic landing information in the "Cleats" section, including transient hourly and overnight procedures, location, fees, and contact information. Dollar amounts are expressed in Canadian and U.S. dollars respectively. Locator maps are included in this unique guide directing the captain and crew to docks, wharves, and marinas in the "Cleats" section along with town maps and restaurant locations in the "Eats" section. Restaurants are generally within 1 km or a half mile or less from each landing.

Landing descriptions include interesting historic notes and points of interest like wineries, museums, spas, unique shops, and local events. "Cleats & Eats" even gives taxi information and bicycle, moped, and car rental information where appropriate to reach those points of interest and additional restaurant gems.

Navigating this Book

Information within this guide is organized into sections by harbor or bay which are grouped by island. Information within each harbor/bay section is conveniently organized into four elements, described below. Photos of landing destinations and restaurants are included throughout this guide.

Harbor / Bay : A general description of each bay or harbor begins each section of this guide and includes a description of surroundings, points of interest, and nearby restaurants.

Landing "Cleats": Details including short term and overnight stays for each dock, wharf, or marina are included in a tabular

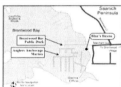

description (right) and related annotated diagram (left) of the harbor/bay locating each landing. Additionally, these diagrams locate area eateries.

Restaurant "Eats": Select individual restaurants are described including décor, cuisine, and hours of operation in a tabular format (right).

Towns of significant size contain a listing (left) of restaurants along with selected restaurants described individually.

Street diagrams: For towns of significant size, street diagrams are included in this section showing the location of restaurants to help the reader find their restaurant of choice.

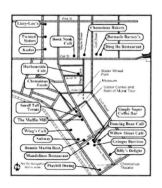

Wineries, Spas, and Museums

Wineries & Vineyards

Glenterra Vineyards, pg 101
Cherry Point Vineyards, pg 108
Lopez Island Vineyards, pg 177
Morning Bay Vineyards & Winery, pgs 39, 45
Muse Winery, pg 153
San Juan Vineyards, pg 225
Saturna Island Winery & Vineyards, pg 75
Westcott Bay Orchards, pg 239

Spas

Afterglow Spa, pg 239
Brentwood Lodge & Spa, pg 85
Galiano Inn & Spa, pg 15
Ganges Message Therapy, pg 57
Hastings House, pg 66
Haven Spa, pg 157
Lavendera Spa, pg 225
Mayne Inn Spa, pg 21
Skin Sensations Spa, pg 57
Susurrus Spa, pg 45

Museums

B.C. Aviation Museum, pg 157
Chemainus Valley Museum, pg 93
Gabriola Museum, pg 3
Lopez Historical Museum, pg 177
Maritime Museum, pg 101
Maritime Society Museum, pg 123
Miners Bay Museum, pg 25
Moran Mansion, pg 213
Nanaimo Bastion, pg 139
Nanaimo Museum, pg 139
Orcas Island Historical Museum, pg 195
Pender Island Museum, Pg 35
Sidney Historical Museum, pg 157
Whale Museum, pg 225

List of *Cleats* & *Eats* by Island

GABRIOLA ISLAND 3

Silva Bay...............................3
Page's Resort Marina___4
Silva Bay Marina ___5
Silva Bay Inn Dock ___5
Silva Bay Bar & Grill 6

GALIANO ISLAND 7

Montague Harbour...........7
Montague Provincial Park __ 9
Montague Harbour Marina__9
Montague Harbour Wharf__9
Harbour Grill 11
Hummingbird Pub 11
La Berengerie 13
Atrevida Bakery Boat 14

Sturdies Bay......................15

Whaler Bay 15
Galiano Inn Dock___17
Sturdies Bay Public Dock __17
Whaler Bay Public Dock __17
Sturdies Bay restaurants 18
'eat' Restaurant 19
Grand Central Emporium 20

MAYNE ISLAND 21

Bennett Bay......................21
Mayne Inn Dock___22
Brickworks on the Bay 23

Miners Bay......................25
Miners Bay Dock___26
Miners Bay Restaurants 27
Springwater Lodge 28
Sunny Mayne Bakery 29
Wild Fennel 30

NORTH PENDER ISLAND 31

Hope Bay..........................31
Hope Bay Wharf___32
Hope Bay Cafe 33
Sharkie's Pizza 33

Otter Bay..........................35
Otter Bay Marina___36
Otter Bay Bistro 37
The Stand 38

Port Browning 39
Port Browning Marina___40
Port Browning Public Wharf40
Port Browning Café & Pub 41
Pender Island Bakery 43

SOUTH PENDER ISLAND 45

Bedwell Harbour 45
Poets Cove Marina___46
Aurora Restaurant 47
Syrens Lounge 48
Moorings Café 48

SALTSPRING ISLAND 49

Fernwood Point................49
Fernwood Public Wharf___50
Raven Market Cafe 51
North Island Coffee Co. 52

Fulford Harbour 53
Fulford Outer Public Wharf 53
Fulford Harbour Marina __ 54
Fulford Harbour Wharf___54
Fulford Inn Pub 55
Morningside Bakery 56
Rock Salt 56

Ganges Harbour 57
Breakwater Public Dock __ 59
Ganges Centennial Wharf_ 59
Ganges Marina ___ 59
Kanaka Public Dock ___ 59
Rotary Dinghy Dock & Park 60
Salt Spring Marina ___ 60
Ganges Restaurants 61
Auntie Pesto's 65
Bocados Bistro 65
Hastings House 66
House Piccolo 67
Moby's Pub 68
SaltSpring Inn 69
Tree House Café 70

Vesuvius Bay 71
Seaside Restaurant Dock___ 72
Vesuvius Public Wharf ___ 72
Seaside Restaurant 73
Vesuvius Village Store 74

SATURNA ISLAND 75

Breezy Bay.........................75
Saturna Island Winery 75
Breezy Bay Dock ___ 75

Lyall Harbour 77
Lyall Harbour Public Wharf 77
Lighthouse Pub 79
Saturna Cafe 80

THETIS ISLAND 81

Preedy Harbour 81

Telegraph Harbour..........81
Telegraph Harbour Marina 81
Thetis Community Dock __ 82
Thetis Island Marina ___ 83
Thetis Island Restaurants 83
Burgees Café 84
Thetis Island Pub 84

VANCOUVER ISLAND 85

Brentwood Bay................85
Butchart Gardens Dock ___ 86
Seahorses Café Dock___ 87
Brentwood Bay Lodge ___ 87
Anglers Anchorage Marina 87
Brentwood Public Dock __ 87
Port Side Marina ___ 87
Blue's Bayou Cafe 89

Seagrille 90
Seahorses Cafe 91

Chemainus Bay................ 93
Chemainus Municipal Dock 94
Chemainus Restaurants 95
Chemainus restaurants
Continued 96
Dancing Bean Café 97
Kudo's 98
Willow Street Café 99

Cowichan Bay................ 101
Bluenose Marina ___ 101
Dungeness Marina ___ 102
Fishermen's Wharf___ 102
Oceanfront Grand Resort 103
Pier 66 Marina ___ 103
Cowichan Bay Restaurants 105
Masthead Restaurant 107
Cherry Point Vineyards 108
Rock Cod Café 108
Thistle's Café 109
The Grand 109
Schooners 110

Genoa Bay...................... 111
Genoa Bay Marina ___ 112
Genoa Bay Cafe 113

Birds Eye Cove 115
Birds Eye Cove Marina __ 115
Maple Bay Marina ___ 115
Shipyard Pub & Restaurant 117
Quamichan Inn 118

Maple Bay 119
Brigantine Inn Pub Dock _ 119
Maple Bay Public Wharf _ 119
Brigantine Inn Pub 121
Grapevine On The Bay 122

Ladysmith Harbour 123
Ladysmith Fisherman's __ 125
Ladysmith Marina ___ 125
Page Point Marina ___ 125
Maritime Society Docks _ 125
Ladysmith Restaurants 127
Printingdun Beanery 129
Royal Dar Restaurant 129
Transfer Beach Grill 130
Jimmy O's Grill 131

Nanaimo Harbour......... 133
Newcastle Marine Park Docks
___ 134

Nanaimo - Brechin Point__135
Stones Marina ___ 135
Beefeaters ChopHouse & Grill 137
Nauticals Seafood Bar & Grill 138
Muddy Waters Pub 138

Nanaimo- Port 139
Dinghy Dock Pub___ 139
Nanaimo Port ___ 140
Nanaimo Downtown Restaurants 141
Nanaimo Island Restaurants 142
Nanaimo Old Quarter Restaurants 143

List of *Cleats & Eats* by Island

Dinghy Dock Pub 145
LightHouse Bistro & Pub ... 146
Modern Café 147
Wesley Street Café 148

Sidney – Canoe Cove 149
Canoe Cove Marina _____ 149
Swartz Bay Wharf _____ 149
Sofie's Cafe 151
Stonehouse Pub 152

Sidney – Deep Cove 153
Chalet Beach Access 153
Deep Cove Chalet 155

Sidney - Port 157
Port Sidney Marina 158
Sidney restaurants 159
Sidney restaurants 161
Beacon Landing Restaurant &
Pub 163
Bistro Suisse 164
Boondocks 164
Haro's 165
Pier Bistro 166
The Rumrunner 166

Sidney – Tsehum Harbour . 167
Van Isle Marina _____ 167
Blue Peter Dock _____ 167
Blue Peter Pub & Restaurant 169
Dockside Grill 170
The Latch 171

BLAKELY ISLAND   175

Blakely Island Marina ... 175
Blakely Island Store & Fountain 175
Blakely Island Marina ___ 176

LOPEZ ISLAND   177

Fisherman Bay 177
Lopez Village Beach ____ 179
Island Marine Center ____ 179
Lopez Islander Marina ___ 179
The Galley Dock & Buoys 179
Lopez Village restaurants 181

Fisherman Bay restaurants 182
Bay Café 183
Islander Restaurant 184
Love Dog Café 185
The Galley 185
Vita's Wildly Delicious 186

ORCAS ISLAND   187

Deer Harbor 187
Deer Harbor Marina 188
Deer Harbor Inn 189
Deer Harbor Store & Grill 190

Doe Bay 191
Doe Island Marine State Park
_____ 191
Doe Bay Resort _____ 191
Doe Bay Café 193

East Sound 195
Eastsound Public Beach __ 195
Eastsound Public Dock ___ 195
Eastsound restaurants 197
Eastsound restaurants
Continued 198
Christina's 199
Ecotopian 200
New Leaf Café 201
Rose's Café 202

Olga 203
Olga Public Dock 204
Café Olga 205
Olga Store & Deli 206

Orcas Landing 207
Orcas Landing 208
Russells 209
Mamie's Restaurant 210
Octavia's 211
Orcas Village Store 212

Rosario 213
Rosario Resort Marina 214
Cascade Bay Grill 215

West Beach 217
West Beach Resort 218
West Beach Store 219

West Sound 221
West Sound Marina _____ 221
Boddington Public Dock ... 222
Westsound Cafe 223

SAN JUAN ISLAND   225

Friday Harbor 225
Friday Harbor Port Marina 227
Friday Harbor restaurants 229
Friday Harbor restaurants 231
Backdoor Kitchen 233
Market Chef 234
Coho Restaurant 234
Bluff Restaurant 235
Steps Wine Bar & Café 236
The Place Bar & Grill 237
Vinny's Ristorante 238

Roche Harbor 239
Roche Harbor Marina 241
San Juan Co. Dock - Roche 241
Beechtree Espresso Bar 243
Lime Kiln Cafe 243
Madrona Bar & Grill 244
McMillin's 245
Duck Soup Inn 246

SHAW ISLAND   247

Blind Bay 247
Shaw General Store Dock 248
Shaw General Store 249

Cleats – Marina/Dock Name, page #   *Eats* – Restaurant Name, page #

Gabriola Island.............................. **3**
   Silva Bay...3

Galiano Island **7**
   Montague Harbour....................................7
   Sturdies Bay...15
   Whaler Bay...15

Mayne Island **21**
   Bennett Bay 21
   Miners Bay 25

North Pender Island **31**
   Hope Bay...31
   Otter Bay...35
   Port Browning..39

South Pender Island..................... **45**
   Bedwell Harbour.....................................45

Saltspring Island **49**
   Fernwood Point.......................................49
   Fulford Harbour 53
   Ganges Harbour 57
   Vesuvius Bay 71

Saturna Island **75**
   Breezy Bay 75
   Lyall Harbour 77

Thetis Island **81**
   Preedy Harbour......................................81
   Telegraph Harbour..................................81

Vancouver Island **85**
   Brentwood Bay 85
   Chemainus Bay 93
   Cowichan Bay..101
   Genoa Bay 111
   Birds Eye Cove 115
   Maple Bay...119
   Ladysmith Harbour 123
   Nanaimo Harbour 133
   Nanaimo - Brechin Point 135
   Nanaimo- Port.......................................139
   Sidney – Canoe Cove.............................149
   Sidney – Deep Cove 153
   Sidney - Port 157
   Sidney – Tsehum Harbour 167

Gulf Islands

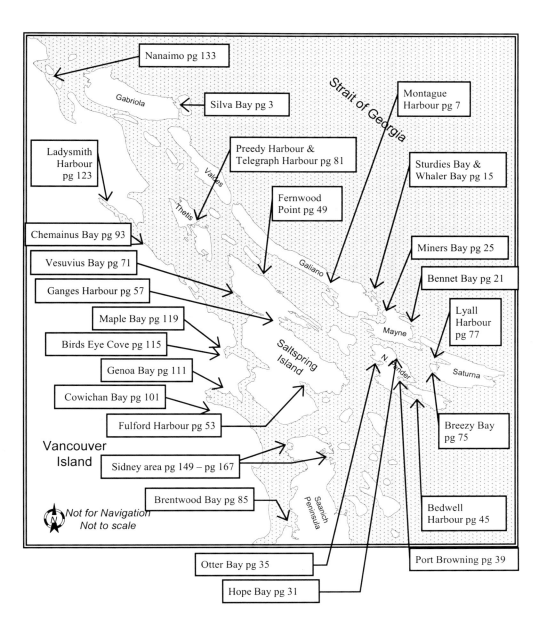

Nanaimo pg 133

Silva Bay pg 3

Gabriola

Strait of Georgia

Montague Harbour pg 7

Preedy Harbour & Telegraph Harbour pg 81

Ladysmith Harbour pg 123

Sturdies Bay & Whaler Bay pg 15

Valdes

Fernwood Point pg 49

Thetis

Chemainus Bay pg 93

Miners Bay pg 25

Vesuvius Bay pg 71

Galiano

Bennet Bay pg 21

Ganges Harbour pg 57

Maple Bay pg 119

Lyall Harbour pg 77

Birds Eye Cove pg 115

Mayne

Saltspring Island

Genoa Bay pg 111

N. Pender

Saturna

Cowichan Bay pg 101

Fulford Harbour pg 53

Breezy Bay pg 75

Vancouver Island

Sidney area pg 149 – pg 167

Not for Navigation
Not to scale

Brentwood Bay pg 85

Saanich Peninsula

Bedwell Harbour pg 45

Otter Bay pg 35

Port Browning pg 39

Hope Bay pg 31

GABRIOLA ISLAND
Silva Bay

Beautiful Silva Bay offers boaters two marinas for short term and overnight stays as well as anchorage in the Bay. Boaters may tie-up at a 40-foot float on the south side of the Silva Bay Inn docks, while shopping at the Silva Bay General Store (250-247-8703) and the Artworks Shop (250-247-7432), both located just upland. The Silva Bay Bar & Grill located at Silva Bay Marina is one of several pubs on the Island and currently the only eatery in Silva Bay. Silva Bay has two fuel docks and serves many boaters as a first or last fueling stop before crossing the Strait of Georgia and serves as an alternative to Nanaimo.

Pages Marina has an excellent book shop where you can purchase Canadian Hydrographic service charts, tide tables, and nautical books. Silva Bay Marina hosts the Annual Maritime Festival in April when wooden boats make the pilgrimage to Silva Bay for the event. Students of the Silva Bay Shipyard School (250-247-8809) launch their boats at this event as part of their graduation ceremony. The school is the only fulltime traditional wooden boatbuilding school in Canada and is located next to the Silva Bay Marina. Don't miss the Sunday Farmers Market held in the open field behind the Marina, which normally runs 10am to 2pm July and August.

Gabriola is known as the Petroglyph Island and is well suited for exploration by dinghy. Nearby Drumbeg Bay, Taylor Bay, Lock Bay, and Degnen Bay offer the opportunity to see interesting rock formations and petroglyphs. More than 50 petroglyphs can be found at Petroglyph Park located behind the United Church at the intersection of Price Road and South Road, east of Degnen Bay.

For Island transportation, contact the "Gabriola Taxi" (250-247-0049). Bicycles, scooters, and car rentals are available from CC Rentals/Cliff Cottage (250-247-0247) and can be delivered to the marina(s), a popular option for boaters. Car rentals require advanced reservations. There are about a dozen Bed & Breakfast accommodations located on the Island, see www.gabriolabb.com

The Gabriola Museum (250-247-9987) showcasing Island history, First Nations history, and petroglyph reproductions is of interest on the Island. The Museum is located at Lochinvar Lane & South Road near the Folklife Village and is open Wednesday through Sunday from 1 pm to 4 pm June – August, and open on Sat & Sun only during the off season. Events on Grabriola include the Farmers' Market from 10 am to noon on Saturdays at Agi Hall on South Road (just up the hill from the Descanso Bay Ferry Landing) held from May to early October. For more information about Island events, contact the Gabriola Visitor Centre (250-247-9332).

Page's Resort Marina   250-247-8931
www.pagesresort.com

Mostly permanent moorage marina with some guest moorage slips including power, fuel, restrooms, showers, and laundry. The Resort has cute cottages, tent sites, and an excellent Book & Chart Store.

Short-Term: Boaters anchored in the Bay may tie-up at Page's Dinghy Dock; check in at the marina office located in the Book & Chart Store.

Overnight: Moorage for most all size craft at $1.25 per foot plus power ($1/ft off season), call ahead for slip assignment and availability. Anchorage in Bay.

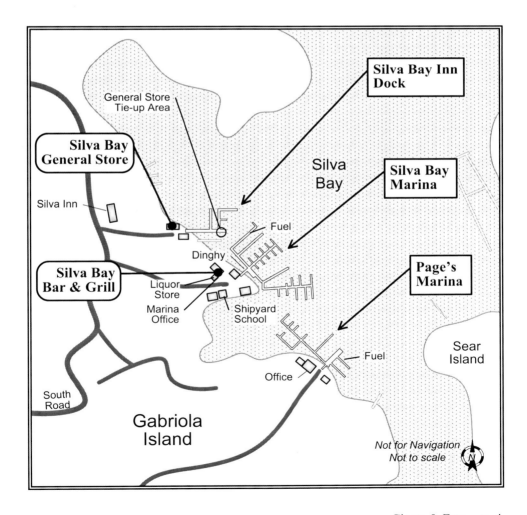

GABRIOLA ISLAND
Silva Bay

Silva Bay Inn Dock
250-247-9351
www.silvabayinn.ca

Private docks belonging to the Silva Bay Inn with power and restrooms. Silva Bay food market at head of docks. Several gift galleries on site.

Short-Term: Dinghy and runabout tie-up permitted for 30 minutes at red-painted 40 foot dinghy dock without charge while shopping at the Silva Bay General Store.

Overnight: Some overnight spaces as available at $1.25/ft plus GST, call ahead. Anchorage in Bay.

Silva Bay Marina
250-247-8662   VHF 66A
www.silvabaymarina.com

Full service marina with power, fuel, restrooms, showers, laundry, liquor store, and Pub on-site. Coffee Shack mid-May through Aug. open Sat & Sun.

Short-Term: Short term stays permitted on the transient Dinghy Dock without charge with a max 2-hour stay daylight hours, and max 5-hour stay evenings.

Overnight: Moorage available for most all size craft at $1.30 per foot plus power, call ahead for slip assignment. Anchorage in Bay.

Silva Bay Marina

SILVA BAY BAR & GRILL

The Silva Bay Bar & Grill is located at the Silva Bay Marina offering great views of the Bay and the Flattop Islands. The Pub & Grill serves sandwiches, burgers, mussels, crab cakes, and other seafood dishes. Dinner entrees include Wild Salmon and Halibut served with new potatoes and greens; or try the oven roasted Lamb T-Bones with couscous and goat cheese emulsion shallots. Be sure to ask about the daily specials and that favorite beer on tap or favorite glass of wine. Visitors enjoy live music at the Bar & Grill held on Friday and Saturday nights June through August.

Lunch/ Dinner	11:30am – 9pm Sun–Thur 11:30am – 10pm Fri & Sat Pub open till "Late" Hours Vary Off Season
Price	Moderate
Outdoor Seating	Yes, Patio, Summer Months
Contact	250-247-8662 #1

The attractive dining room separate from the bar area is a perfect gathering spot for families. During the summer months, the Coffee Shack at the Marina is open on weekends so boaters can pick up morning coffee and fresh baked goods.

Silva Bay Bar & Grill

GALIANO ISLAND
Montague Harbour

Scenic Montague Harbour has several short-term and overnight options for boaters: Montague Harbour Marina, the Montague Harbour Public Wharf, and the Montague Harbour Provincial Park Dock and buoys. Additionally, the Harbour can hold a large number of boats for those who prefer to anchor out in the bay.

The Montague Harbour Marina offers a casual dining venue, and the charming La Berengerie is within easy walking distance of the Marina. Visiting boaters look forward to buying baked goods from the Atrevida Bakery Boat, which anchors in the Harbour each year from May to mid-September. The popular Hummingbird Pub (located inland) has Pub Bus pickup service near the Marina and at the entrance to the Provincial Park. The Market Deli (250-539-2505), also located inland, is accessible via moped. Moped rentals are available from the Galiano Moped & Boat Rentals Co. (250-539-3443 or 0233), which is located behind the Marina. The Marina Store carries groceries, ice, charts, and gift items. Events on Galiano include the Galiano Wine Festival held in August at Lions Park. For more information about the festival, go to www.Galianoisland.com/winefestival/.

The beautiful Montague Harbour Marine Park at the north end of the bay was the first provincial marine park established in British Columbia and offers hiking trails, beaches, a guest dock, and lovely camp sites with beautiful views of the Harbour and Trincomali Channel.

Montague Harbour Marina

Montague Harbour Provincial Park Dock

GALIANO ISLAND
Montague Harbour

Montague Harbour Marina
250-539-5733   VHF 66A
www.montagueharbour.com

Montague Harbour Marina is open May through September and offers guest moorage with restrooms (no showers), a store, and café. Fuel dock hours are reduced during the winter months.

Short-Term: Short-term stays are available at the dinghy dock located in front of the marina office on a first-come basis at no charge for patrons of the Marina only.

Overnight: Overnight moorage is available for runabouts and cruisers on the docks and slips as assigned. Rates are based on vessel length. Use the self-pay station after office hours. Anchorage in Montague Harbour.

Montague Harbour Wharf
250-222-0124
Wharfinger

The Montague Harbour Public Wharf is located adjacent to the Marina and offers a 160 foot guest dock for short-term and overnight stays.

Short-Term: Short-term stays are available without charge up to 4 hours. Rates are posted for additional hours. Use self-pay station.

Overnight: Overnight stays are charged as posted. Use the self-registration, payment box at the head of the dock. Anchorage in Montague Harbour.

Montague Provincial Park
www.bcparks.com

The Montague Provincial Park offers a 300 foot dock for short-term and overnight stays for vessels under 36 feet (11 meters). Numerous Park buoys are available at the north end of the Harbour.

Short-Term: Short term stays are available at the Provincial Park Dock without charge for dinghies and vessels under 36 feet.

Overnight: Overnight rates/charges take effect after 6 pm for stays at the Provincial Park Dock and on the Park's Buoys. Use the self-registration payment box at the head of the stairs, rates are posted. Anchorage in Montague Harbour.

Montague Harbour Marina

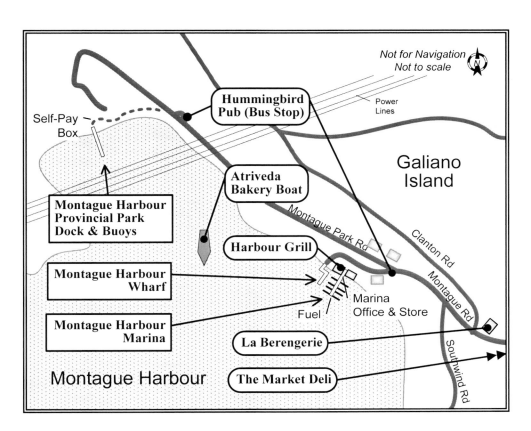

GALIANO ISLAND
Montague Harbour

HARBOUR GRILL

The Harbour Grill is managed by the Marina and is open during the summer months, hours vary. The Store & Grill's large deck has great views overlooking the Marina and Montague Harbour, a great place to enjoy the morning with a cup of coffee and muffin. Lunch and dinner menu selections include salads, burgers, and appetizer platters like the smoked Salmon Pate, Garlic Prawns & Spring Greens, and the Hummus Platter with pita bread. Burgers are always a favorite like the Salmon Burger, Curried Chicken Burger, Garden Burger, and the Montague Burger.

Breakfast/ Lunch	9:30am – 4:30pm Daily May – September
Dinner	5pm – 9pm Thur-Sat June – Labor Day
Price	Moderate
Outdoor Seating	Yes, Deck, Summer Months
Contact	250-539-5733 (Marina)

HUMMINGBIRD PUB

The Hummingbird Pub is located several kilometers inland and the Pub Bus makes regular stops upland from the Marina at Montague Rd. & Montague Park Rd. for lunch and dinner guests; pickup hours are posted at the Marina. Riding the vintage Hummingbird Bus is an adventure in itself and you can purchase a "survivor sweatshirt" on the Bus or at the Pub to mark the experience.   The Pub, like the hummingbird, is feisty and full of activity with its varied floor levels, separate bar & pool table area, outdoor barbeque patio, and the large backyard with picnic tables.

Lunch / Dinner	11am – 12am Sun-Thur 11am – 1am Fri & Sat
Price	Moderate
Outdoor Seating	Yes, Patio, Summer Months
Contact	250-539-5472

The interior sports a combination of tile and wood floors, stucco walls, wood beams, and half-timbers; and of course, you can watch the hummingbirds feed mid-March to mid-July. The food and drink is fun too, offering starters, coolers, ciders, beer on tap, wine, and other drinks. The extensive Pub menu includes burgers, pizza, quesadillas, sandwiches, soups, salads, and seafood dishes. Be sure to check the blackboard for daily specials like the Shellfish Bowl, a heaping bowl of tender oysters, mussels, and clams in a tasty herb broth. The Hummingbird Pub is an all-around fun adventure not to be missed.

Harbour Grill

Hummingbird Pub

LA BERENGERIE

The La Berengerie is located upland from Montague Marina. Walk southeast on Montague Road for about .6 km (1/3 mile), passing Southwind Road until you come to Clanton Road. The La Berengerie is on the left at the y-intersection in a charming lap-board cottage. A set of stairs leads through the trees and to the cottage, or you can walk down the driveway. This French-style restaurant has an attractive dining room with flower-patterned linen tablecloths, tile floors, area rugs, and country-style furnishings. The La Berengerie serves a predetermined four-course meal, including soup, salad, an entrée, and dessert. Entrees vary and may include duck breast with apricot chutney, wild salmon with pesto sauce, or meat balls in a tomato-olive sauce.

Dinner	6pm – 9pm Thur-Mon August – July
	6pm – 9pm Weekends Spring and Fall
	Closed Nov – mid-April
Price	Moderate - Expensive
Outdoor Seating	Yes, Porch Summer Months
Contact	250-539-5392

Entrée selections change daily and are served with local organic vegetables, rice, or potatoes. Fresh fish is used from the Island when possible and local organic greens are used in salads. Soups are made fresh, as well, like the leek & potato soup. Desserts provide the finishing touch and include crème caramel, or the raspberry cake. The La Berengerie is a hidden gem, conveniently located for boaters near Montague Harbour, reservations are a must.

La Berengerie

ATREVIDA BAKERY BOAT

A special treat for boaters in Montague Harbour is the seasonal "Atrevida Bakery Boat" where folks can purchase baked goods directly from this re-furbished car ferry including scones, cinnamon rolls, breads, cakes, pies, and sweets. The Bakery Boat is normally stationed in the Harbour from May through mid-September and is open 8 am till close; hours may vary as weather and demand dictate. The Bakery Boat has a dinghy float along side the vessel for patrons to pick up and place orders; look for the "open" sign when approaching the ship.

Breakfast/ Lunch	8am – Close Weather/Demand Dictates May till mid-September
Price	Moderate
Outdoor Seating	N/A
Contact	Visit the Atrevida vessel in Montague Harbour

It is customary for boaters to place their order the night before, which helps the owner plan for the 4 am baking routine. "Homemade pricing" is based on the "homemade sizing." Visiting the Bakery Boat is a unique experience and provides a close up look at this vessel that was commissioned in 1928 and served as a car ferry from Gabriola Island to Nanaimo. The friendly owners have enjoyed meeting and serving their customers for over ten years.

Atrevida Bakery Boat

GALIANO ISLAND
Sturdies Bay & Whaler Bay

The Sturdies Bay Public Dock, located next to the Ferry Landing, offers short-term and overnight guest space. If the Sturdies Bay Public Dock is full, there may be space available at Whaler Bay Public Dock, which is located northwest in Whaler Bay behind Gossip Island. It is approximately a .8 km (1/2 mile) walk from the dock at Whaler Bay to the Sturdies Bay restaurants.

A variety of eateries are within a short walk of the Sturdies Bay Public Dock ranging from take-out and casual eats to fine dining. The elegant Galiano Inn & Spa, located on the waterfront next to the Public Dock, now offers its own guest dock accommodating runabouts, cruisers, and small yachts for guests of the Inn and for visitors to the Inn's "eat Restaurant."

Most of the eateries at Sturdies Bay are located along Sturdies Bay Road, where you will also find the Garage Grocery store and Galiano Island Books. Continue further west and you will come to the Sturdies Bay Bakery along with several boutiques and art galleries. The popular Grand Central diner is located next door.

Dining at the restaurants in Sturdies Bay is a great way to get a feel for island life on Galiano. You will meet locals who are eager to share their stories and are interested in your adventures as well. Before you know it, you start to feel like a local yourself. Residents on Galiano include retired teachers, boat captains, artists, musicians, and a large number of famous authors.

Galiano Island is named after Commander Galiano of the Spanish vessel Sutil, a schooner which explored the Strait of Georgia in 1792. Settlers arrived in the mid to late 1800's and built homes mostly on the southeast end of the Island. Today, Galiano retains an undeveloped character and the community has purchased several areas as ecological reserves, including Mt. Galiano, Mt. Sutil, and Bodega Ridge with its unique rocky bluff. Community events on Galiano include the Seafood Fest in April, the Canada Day Jamboree on July 1st, and a Wine Festival in August.

Sturdies Bay Public Dock

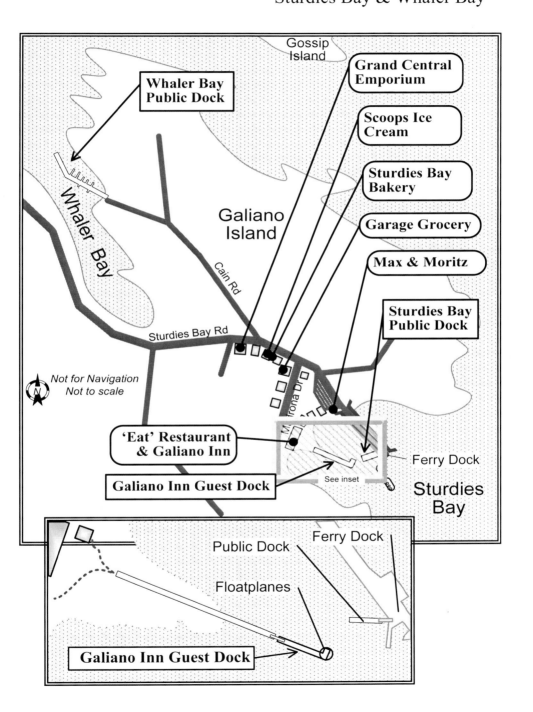

GALIANO ISLAND
Sturdies Bay & Whaler Bay

Gossip Island

Whaler Bay Public Dock

Grand Central Emporium

Scoops Ice Cream

Sturdies Bay Bakery

Garage Grocery

Max & Moritz

Galiano Island

Whaler Bay

Cain Rd

Sturdies Bay Rd

Sturdies Bay Public Dock

Not for Navigation
Not to scale

'Eat' Restaurant & Galiano Inn

Galiano Inn Guest Dock

See inset

Ferry Dock

Sturdies Bay

Public Dock

Ferry Dock

Floatplanes

Galiano Inn Guest Dock

GALIANO ISLAND
Sturdies Bay & Whaler Bay

Galiano Inn Dock   250-539-3388

A private dock 125' x 14' belonging to the Galiano Inn may be used by guests dining at the Inn and/or staying overnight in a room at the Inn. Call ahead for availability. Dock accommodates runabouts, cruisers, and small yachts (8ft draft). Additional 25' x 18' dock for float planes only.

Short-Term: Short term stays, while dining at the Inn.

Overnight: Overnight stays permitted if staying in a room at the Inn.

Sturdies Bay Public Dock   250-539-5053
Wharfinger

The Public Dock at Sturdies Bay is located next to the Ferry Landing and is approximately 80 feet long serving runabouts and small cruisers for short-term and overnight stays. Limited space during the busy summer season.

Short-Term: Short-term stays are permitted up to 4 hours at no charge. Rates for additional hours are posted. Use the self-pay station.

Overnight: Rates for overnight stays are posted. Use the self-registration payment box at the head of the ramp.

Whaler Bay Public Dock   250-539-2264
Wharfinger

A public dock with permanent moorage for the local fishing fleet. The dock has power but no other facilities. Limited guest space is located on the southeast side of the dock only in any open space that is not marked as reserved/private except for the three (3) finger docks shoreward, which are continuous private spaces. Spaces are best suited for runabouts and small cruisers.

Short-Term: Short-term stays are permitted up to 4 hrs at no charge. On-site Wharfinger collects cash payment for stays over 4 hrs as posted.

Overnight: Overnight stays with rates as posted. Wharfinger collects payment, cash only. Some anchorage in Bay.

STURDIES BAY RESTAURANTS			🍽
'eat' Restaurant	Beef, Duck, Lamb, Seafood	134 Madrona Dr.	250-539-3388
Garage Grocery	Groceries	14 Madrona Dr.	250-539-5500
Grand Central Emporium	Breakfast, Burgers, Soups, Salads	2470 Sturdies Bay Road	250-539-9885
Max & Moritz	Burgers, Dogs, and Indonesian	Ferry Terminal (orders to go)	250-539-5888
Scoops Ice Cream	Burgers, Ice Cream	2540 Sturdies Bay Road	250-539-2388 June - Sept
Sturdies Bay Bakery	Deli Sandwiches, Soups, Baked Goods	2540 Sturdies Bay Road	250-539-2004

Scoops Ice Cream

GALIANO ISLAND
Sturdies Bay & Whaler Bay

'EAT' RESTAURANT

The stylish 'eat' Restaurant is located in the elegant Galiano Inn along the water's edge with beautiful views overlooking Sturdies Bay offering fine dining, formal service, and pampering at the Inn's Madrona del Mar Spa. For casual eats, guests can enjoy the lovely Italian-style patio for salads and wood-fired oven pizzas along with local and internation beers, ciders, and wine by the glass, or the signature Blackberry Martini. Evening entrees include seafood, duck, and lamb dishes as well as free-range beef, bison, and chicken. Meals are carefully prepared and beautifully presented using fresh local meats and produce like the

Lunch	Noon – 4pm Daily June - September
Dinner	6pm – 9:30pm Daily Wed-Sun Off Season
Price	Moderate - Expensive
Outdoor Seating	Yes, Patio, Summer Months
Contact	250-539-3388

Herb Crusted Maple Farms Chicken Breast, or try the Pan Seared Okanagon Beef Medallions, or perhaps the Fraser Valley Rack of Lamb with sweet garlic lamb sausage, purple potatoes, and green beans with crème fraiche and rosemary jus paired with a Cabernet Sauvignon. Don't forget to ask about the special desserts.

Eat Restaurant

GRAND CENTRAL EMPORIUM

This fun, old-fashioned diner is located about .4 km (1/4 mile) from the Sturdies Public Dock and about .8 km (1/2 mile) from the Whaler Bay Public Dock. This historic building was built in 1903 and served as the Burrill Brothers General Store and local gathering place. It was moved to its current location in the 1940's and continues to be a popular gathering place with an eclectic mix of tables and chairs, old-fashioned couches, and old wood and linoleum floors. The Grand Central Diner serves quality pub food starting with breakfast, including homemade muffins, French toast, eggs, omelettes, pancakes, hashbrowns, and bacon & sausage among other selections.

Breakfast	7am – 3pm Daily June – August
Lunch/ Dinner	11am – 9:30pm June – August Hrs. Vary Off Season
Price	Moderate
Outdoor Seating	Yes, Patio, Summer Months
Contact	250-539-9885

In the afternoon, stop for a lamb, steak, or tuna sandwiches with homemade soups & salads followed by an ice cream sundae, root beer float, or banana split. The Diner also serves a variety of burgers and pasta dishes along with homemade cookies and seasonal fresh fruit pie. The Bar serves sodas, wine, and domestic, premium, and imported beers with "lite bites" to get you started for the night's entertainment offered during the summer months on Fridays and Saturdays with a small cover charge. The Grand Central Diner hosts well-known musicians from all over the country.

Grand Central Emporium

MAYNE ISLAND
Bennett Bay

Bennett Bay is intriguing with its rock outcroppings, rippled patterns on the rocky shoreline, and the beautiful views of Campbell Point, Georgeson Island and beyond. This beautiful bay and the east shoreline of Mayne Island are popular among kayakers. Keep an eye out for the Western Purple Martins using nest boxes mounted on pilings in the water. Purple Martins spend the winter in the southern hemisphere and return to North America to breed in late spring. The nest boxes were erected by Island volunteers in support of the BC Purple Martin Stewardship and Recovery Program.

The Mayne Inn in Bennett Bay is located upland from the private dock. Boaters normally tie up at the buoy marked "Mayne Inn" and dinghy ashore or tie up at the dock; call ahead for availability and prior permission. Be careful to use only the buoy belonging to the Inn. The historic Mayne Inn, built in 1912, has been expanded to include additional dining space and a spa is planned for the near future. The large outdoor deck provides commanding views of the Bay and is an ideal stop for lunch. The newly constructed cottages on the shoreline are available for sale as time-share ownership.

Mayne Inn Dock

Mayne Inn Dock	250-539-3122	
	ebiz.netopia.com/mayneinn	

Government dock leased to the Mayne Inn (approximately 50 feet) suitable for runabouts and dinghies.

Short-Term: Short term stays permitted on the buoy marked "Mayne Inn" while dining at the restaurant. Short term stays permitted with prior permission on the dock while dining at the Inn's restaurant.

Overnight: No overnight stays. Anchorage in Bennett Bay.

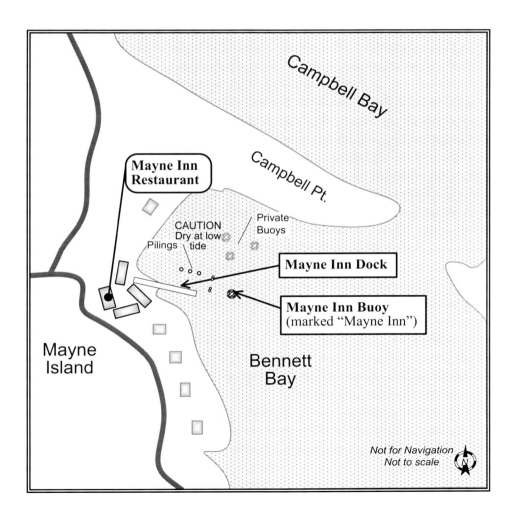

MAYNE ISLAND
Bennett Bay

BRICKWORKS ON THE BAY

"Brickworks on the Bay" is located in the historic Mayne Inn on beautiful Bennet Bay. The Inn's attractive dining room and outdoor patio have enchanting views of the Bay and Georgeson Island, the perfect stop to enjoy lunch favorites like fish n' chips, sandwiches, or burgers including the Char-broiled Chicken, the Mammoth Beef Burger, and the Salmon Burger, or the lightly grilled Vegetarian. Dinner mains include pasta and seafood dishes with weekly dessert specials. Look for new additions to the menu upon completion of the extended dining room in 2010.

Lunch	11am – 5pm Tue-Sun
Dinner	5pm – 9pm Tue-Sun Hours Vary Off Season
Price	Moderate
Outdoor Seating	Yes, Patio, Summer Months
Contact	250-539-3122

Brickworks on the Bay

Brickworks on the Bay

Mayne Inn Dock

MAYNE ISLAND
Miners Bay

Mayne Island was the commercial and social centre of the Gulf Islands in the late 1800's due to the marine traffic through Active Pass. The Pass was named after the American steam vessel, U.S.S. Active and the Island was named in honor of Lieutenant Richard C. Mayne of the Royal Navy, whose captain (George Richards) began surveying the area in the 1850's aboard the H.M.S. Plumber.

Boaters can find short-term and overnight stays at Miners Bay Dock; however, due to the strong current and wakes from passing ferries in Active Pass, boaters need to secure their vessels with additional lines and fenders. Some boaters prefer finding anchorage close by and coming to the Dock by dinghy.

The historic Springwater Lodge is just upland from the Dock and has both a restaurant and a pub overlooking Miners Bay and Active Pass. Additional B&B accommodations are nearby. East of the Springwater Lodge at the corner of Fernhill Rd. and Village Bay Rd. are a couple of art shops, a market, and Miners Bay Books. The Village Centre, housing the Sunny Mayne Bakery Café and a grocery-deli, is beyond the book store on Village Bay Rd. and is about a .4 km (1/4 mile) walk from Miners Bay Dock. A little further south on Village Bay Road is an old farmhouse, which was once owned by a Japanese farmer, Kumozo Nagata, who grew hothouse tomatoes. Many Japanese lost their greenhouse businesses when taken to war camps during World War II.

A Farmers' Market is held on Saturdays from 10am to 1pm, July through Thanksgiving weekend, showcasing musicians, artisans, baked goods, and fresh produce at the Agricultural Hall grounds, located at Fernhill Rd. and Dixon, a short walk from the dock(s). Plays and art showings are held in the hall from time to time. The Miners Bay Museum is across the street from the Hall and is housed in the old 1896 jail, once known as the Plumper Pass Lock-up, which held rabble-rousing prospectors.

Miners Bay Dock

Miners Bay Dock

250-539-5808
Wharfinger (Larry Barker)

The docks at Miners Bay are a combination of permanently moored boats with a guest dock(s) for short-term and overnight stays. The two 45 foot guest docks are marked with "float plane" and "load-unload/emergency" section(s). Fuel is available on the west dock. Tie securely due to wind, current, and ferry wash.

Short-Term: Short-term stays are permitted without charge up to 4 hours. Rates are posted for additional hours. Use the self-pay station.

Overnight: Rates for overnight stays are posted by vessel length. Use the self-registration, payment box located on the wharf. NOT RECOMMENDED FOR OVERNIGHT, due to ferry wash.

MAYNE ISLAND
Miners Bay

MINERS BAY RESTAURANTS			🍴
Miners Bay Trading Post	Market Groceries	413 Fernhill Rd.	250-539-2214
Springwater Lodge	Seafood, Burgers	400 Fernhill Rd.	250-539-5521
Sunny Mayne Bakery Café	Breakfast, Lunch, Pastries, Sweets	472 Village Bay Road	250-539-2323
Tru Value Foods	Groceries, Deli Foods	472 Village Bay Road	Unlisted
Wild Fennel	Duck, Lamb, Beef, Seafood	574 Fernhill Rd Fernhill Centre	250-539-5987

Springwater Lodge

SPRINGWATER LODGE

Overlooking Active Pass, the Springwater Lodge is within steps of the Miners Bay Public Dock and is the oldest continuously operated hotel in British Columbia. The original portion of the Lodge dates back to 1892 and was a favorite stopover for miners during the Fraser River and Caribou Gold Rush. In 1895, the original owner began offering rooms for lodgers. The Springwater Lodge is still a popular gathering place for breakfast, lunch, and dinner, offering a variety of overnight accommodations. The large outdoor deck is especially popular in the summer months with beautiful flowers, umbrella covered tables, and great views of Miners Bay. The dining room maintains the ambiance of yesteryear with wainscoting, wall paper,

Breakfast	9am – 11am Daily Summer Months
Lunch/ Dinner	11:30am – 9pm Daily Summer Months Days Vary Off Season
Price	Moderate
Outdoor Seating	Yes, Deck, Summer Months
Contact	250-539-5521

warm woods, and coffered wood ceilings. The separate pub is a full-service bar offering the lunch menu along with wine, coolers, sparkling drinks, and draft, domestic, and premium beers. The lunch menu includes burgers, sandwiches, ribs, fish, and soups & salads and is available during dinner hours. Try the Smoked Salmon Bagel with cream cheese, capers, and red onions served with a Caesar salad; or try the Tuscan Chicken Sandwich with artichoke hearts, mozzarella, pesto mayo, and lettuce & tomato. In the evenings, you can enjoy the beautiful sunset with special entrée dishes like the Ahi Tuna, B.C. Wild Salmon, New York Steak, and the Teriyaki Lamb Chops. The Springwater Lodge is a charming island setting anytime of day.

Springwater Lodge Deck

MAYNE ISLAND
Miners Bay

SUNNY MAYNE BAKERY

The Sunny Mayne Bakery is located a short walk from the Miners Bay Dock, follow Fernhill Rd. and turn right on Village Bay Rd., the Bakery will be on the left in the Village Bay Centre. You can enjoy delicious fresh baked breakfast and lunch pastries on the courtyard patio with filtered views of Miners Bay or sit inside the cozy Bakery Café. Breakfast items include croissants, muffins, scones, turnovers, and cinnamon rolls, all freshly baked. The muffin and scone selections vary based on seasonal fruit; or you may wish to choose from the traditional breakfast

Breakfast/ Lunch	7am – 5pm Daily Summer Months Hrs Vary Off Season
Price	Moderate
Outdoor Seating	Yes, Plaza Patio, Summer Months
Contact	250-539-2323

menu including scrambles, eggs, bacon, and toast or try the breakfast sandwich. Lunch is also a treat at Sunny Mayne, offering delicious homemade soups, sandwiches, and pizza. The savory rolls and pies are especially popular like the Beef Roll, Salmon Roll, and the Veggie Roll, handmade mild or spicy and filled with carrots, beans, and potatoes. And of course, like all good bakeries, the Sunny Mayne offers tempting sweets, including pies, tarts, and cookies.

Sunny Mayne Bakery

WILD FENNEL 🍽

The Wild Fennel is located at 574 Fernhill Road. For those boaters who carry bicycles, the Wild Fennel is a 1.6 km (1 mile) ride from the Miners Bay Public Dock. This casual, fine dining bistro is definitely worth the trip. The Wild Fennel first opened on Valentine's Day and is an Islanders' favorite. Art pieces created by the Bistro's owner showcasing human caricatures adorn the walls and complement the modern furnishings with a candle-lit ambiance. Menu selections change regularly throughout the seasons for freshness, creativity, and variety.

Lunch	11:30am – 3pm Wed-Sun
Dinner	5pm – 8:30pm Wed-Sun
Price	Moderate
Outdoor Seating	Yes, Patio, Summer Months
Contact	250-539-5987

Small plates may include the Smoked Tuna Salad, the Thai Style Crab Cakes, and the Seared Scallops with fennel & mango curry cream. Big Plates include the Ribeye Steak, the Vegetable Lasagna, and the Prawn & Scallop Pasta with a light curry cream and pepper sauce; or try the Lamb Chops with blackberry cumberland jus. Appetizers, fine wines, and desserts are all apart of the fine culinary experience at the Wild Fennel.

Wild Fennel

NORTH PENDER ISLAND
Hope Bay

Hope Bay has got to be one of the most charming stops for boaters looking to enjoy a little shopping and some good eats in pleasant surroundings with great views. The Wharf docks offer both short-term and overnight stays for most any size boat. Larger vessels can use the orange buoys (marked private), which are intended to be used by visitors of Hope Bay merchants. The group of buildings next to the Wharf along with a lovely courtyard consists of the Hope Bay Café, Red Tree Gallery, Sladen's Home Décor, and The Goldsmith Shop, where you will also find the Wharfinger. If you are in need of a hair cut, visit the Hope Bay Hair Salon (250-629-6911) in the complex.

In 1905, Robert Corbett established a store next to the Wharf. Up until that time, Pender residents received their provisions through mail order delivered by boat at the Wharf. In addition to managing the store, Robert served as post master and his son Percy, served as assistant post master. The Corbett & Son business continued to grow over the years and additional buildings were added over time. Robert retired in 1931 and Percy along with his son continued the family business until 1956, after which ownership changed a number of times and was once known as the "Smith Brothers" store. Unfortunately, these buildings were destroyed by fire in 1998. The Hope Bay Rising Company, with support from local residents, has brought this site back to its original charm.

A Farmers' Market is held early spring to late fall on Saturday mornings in the Community Hall (250-629-3669) on Bedwell Harbour Road, a 1 km (.6 mile) walk or bike ride southwest of Hope Bay, or you can call the Pender Island Cab (250-629-2222) for island transportation. Children enjoy movies at the Community Hall as well as picnic tables and play structures. You will pass several home based art shops on the way to the Hall as well as the MacDonald Farm Store (250-629-3817) offering farm fresh eggs. Couples looking for a romantic getaway in an oceanfront suite can contact the Morning Moon Guest House (250-629-6579) for reservations. The Morning Moon is located a short walk north from Hope Bay on Clam Bay Road.

Hope Bay Wharf

Hope Bay Wharf	250-629-9990	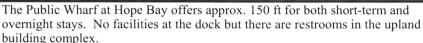
	Wharfinger (Goldsmith Shop)	

The Public Wharf at Hope Bay offers approx. 150 ft for both short-term and overnight stays. No facilities at the dock but there are restrooms in the upland building complex.

Short-Term: Short term stays are without charge up to 4 hours. Rates are posted for stays over 4 hours. Two orange buoys marked "private" can be used while visiting the shops at Hope Bay.

Overnight: Overnight stays are permitted on the docks with rates as posted. Use the self-registration, payment box at the head of the dock. No overnight stays on buoys.

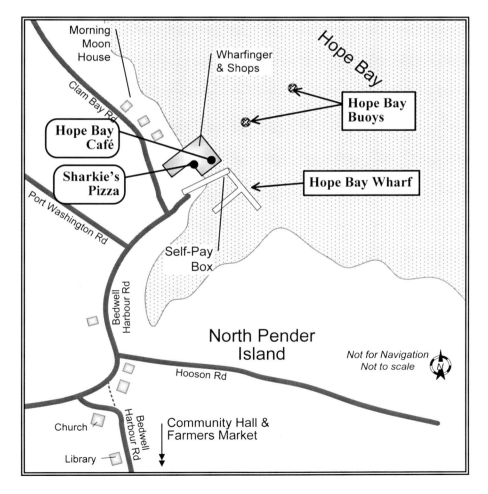

NORTH PENDER ISLAND
Hope Bay

HOPE BAY CAFE

This attractive Café perched over the water, with its yellow and orange walls, attractive art work, wood plank floors, and east facing windows, captures the beautiful views of Hope Bay and Plumper Sound. The Café serves espresso, pastries, and frittatas during the morning hours and Eggs Benny. Sandwiches, grilled vegetables, and delicious soups and salads are offered at lunch. A more formal fare is offered at dinner including the Baked Wild Coho Salmon served with a warm fennel, orange, & grainy mustard salad; or try the Curried Mussels and Prawns in a coconut curry broth with baby corn and peppers. Other choices include Linguine Clams, Pistachio Crusted Halibut, and the Pork Loin Chop served with a fruit-chutney. Don't forget to check the fine wine offerings and the excellent dessert menu.

Brunch	10am – 3pm Sat & Sun
Lunch	11am – 3:30pm Daily Days Vary Off Season
Dinner	5pm – 9pm Daily Hours Vary Off Season
Price	Moderate
Outdoor Seating	Yes, Patio & Courtyard Summer Months
Contact	250-629-6668

SHARKIE'S PIZZA

Owned and operated by the Hope Bay Café, Sharkie's is a convenient stop for take-out pizza and drinks. A variety of tasty pizzas include the Salmon Tidal Wave, the Double Pepperoni, the Maui Waui, and the Godfather to name a few. You can relax at the umbrella covered tables in the courtyard at this charming centre overlooking Hope Bay or enjoy your pizza dockside aboard your boat.

Take-Out	5pm – Close Wed-Sun Deliveries Fri & Sat
Price	Moderate
Outdoor Seating	Yes, Courtyard, Summer Months
Contact	250-629-6618

Hope Bay Wharf & Hope Bay Café

Hope Bay Cafe

NORTH PENDER ISLAND
Otter Bay

Pretty Otter Bay Marina is tucked in the bay around a point from the Otter Bay Ferry Landing. The Marina offers a gift shop and bistro bar, a lovely picnic area, and swimming pools. The Marina's Bistro Bar includes a full breakfast and lunch menu open from mid-April through September. The cute "Stand" eatery, located next to the Ferry Terminal, is within easy walking distance of the Marina. For an additional dining adventure, visit the Fairway Restaurant (250-629-6665) open from 8am to 6pm at the Pender Is. Golf & Country Club (250-629-6659). The Otter Bay Marina provides a shuttle service to and from the nine-hole golf course for a nominal fee. Set in the hillside surrounding the Marina is the attractive "Currents" development, offering quarter ownership in seaside dwellings with great views of Otter Bay.

The Pender Islands are named after Daniel Pender, who surveyed the coast from 1857-1870 aboard the H.M.S. Plumper and later the H.M.S. Hecate. Early settlers, who had arrived by the 1870's, rowed or sailed to Mayne Island for mail and supplies since wharves were not built on the Pender's until the early part of the 20th Century.

If you wish to explore the Island, moped and bicycle rentals are available through the Marina Office during the summer months. Of local interest is the adorable Pender Island Museum (250-629-6935) at 2408 South Otter Bay Road. The Museum is open on weekends and is located in The Roe House on the Roesland Pioneer Farm about 4 ½ km (2 ¾ miles) from the Marina.

Otter Bay Marina

Otter Bay Marina

Otter Bay Marina

250-629-3579   VHF 66A

A full service marina with power, restrooms, showers, laundry, swimming pools, playground, and gift shop along with moped and bicycle rentals.

Short-Term: Half day stays are charged $1.25/ft divided by two. Smaller craft, use inside docks. Check in at the marina office. Dinghies may use the dinghy dock for a $5 fee.

Overnight: Guest moorage is available for all size craft at $1.25 per foot, call ahead for space or slip assignment. Reservations are a must during the busy summer months.

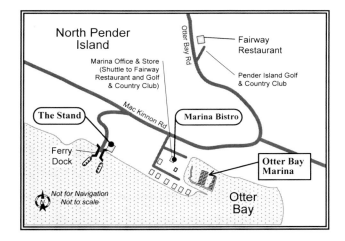

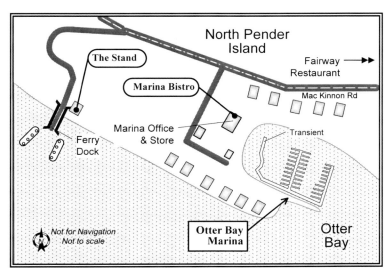

OTTER BAY BISTRO

The Otter Bay Bistro bar is located in the attractive Marina gift shop, offering indoor seating and summer outdoor seating on the lovely patio. Boaters can enjoy a morning cup of espresso and baked goods, or a hearty omelette with cubed potatoes, onions, peppers, and chopped ham. A nice variety of curry dishes, salads, and past dishes are offered for lunch and early evening meals. For lunch, try the Souvlaki and Greek Salad, or perhaps the Kashmir Lamb Curry slow cooked with curry and other spices finished with chopped spinach and cream. Other lunch favorites include Quesadillas,

Breakfast/ Lunch	9am – 5pm Sun-Thur 9am – 6pm Fri & Sat mid-April - September
Price	Moderate
Outdoor Seating	Yes, Patio, Summer Months
Contact	250-629-3579

Quiche, and the Tuna Bell Pepper Salad. The Otter Bay Bistro is a great place to relax and visit with other boaters while enjoying a late afternoon meal like the Prawns & Wild Salmon Pasta, or a bowl of hearty Chuck Wagon Chili.

Otter Bay Bistro

THE STAND 🍽

The Stand is located next to the Otter Bay Ferry Landing off MacKinnon Road, a short walk west of the Marina. From the Marina, walk up the drive and turn left on MacKinnon Road, once you see the entrance and ticket kiosk for the Ferry, follow the entrance around to The Stand. A converted RV with added outdoor patio seating serves as a creative stand, offering sandwiches, hot dogs, and burgers along with "thirst quenchers" and ice cream cones. The Wild Coho Salmon Burger, the Smokie Bavarian Sausage, and the Breaky Bun with egg, bacon, and cheese are a few of the local favorites.

Breakfast/ Lunch	7am – 5pm Mon-Fri 7:30am – 7:30pm Saturday 9am – 7:20pm Sundays Hours Vary Seasonally with Ferry Schedule
Price	Moderate
Outdoor Seating	Yes, Patio, Summer Months
Contact	250-629-3292

The Stand

NORTH PENDER ISLAND
Port Browning

Boaters come to Port Browning for its fun family atmosphere and to visit the attractive Driftwood Centre, which is within walking distance of both the Port Browning Marina and the Port Browning Public Wharf. Short-term and overnight moorage is available at both facilities. The Marina has a cute café and pub that has recently been remodeled. Tent sites are located on the Marina grounds and children love exploring the area and fishing from the docks. Overnight guests of the Marina may use the swimming pool without charge.

The Driftwood Centre is within a .5 km (1/3 mile) walk of the Marina docks and has a nice bakery/cafe, gift shops, and a grocery store that carries deli items and offers outdoor seating for deli eats.

The Morning Bay Vineyards & Winery (250-629-8351), located northeast of Port Browning on Harbour Hill Road offers wine tasting from 10am to 5pm, Wednesday through Sunday during the summer months, and on a reduced schedule during the off season. The Winery offers pick up service for boaters from the Public Wharf and from the Marina in Port Browning as their schedule permits; more often than not, Winery staff will meet you part way along the road as you walk to the Vineyards. The Winery is a 2.25 km (1.4 miles) walk or bike ride up hill from the Public Wharf. For walking directions, see the map on the following pages. You can book tours of the Winery through Poets Cove Resort, see under Bedwell Harbour and Poets Cove in this publication.

Port Browning Marina

Port Browning Public Wharf

Port Browning Marina

250-629-3493   VHF 66A
www.portbrowning.com

Full service marina with power, restrooms, laundry, pool, pub & cafe.

Short-Term: Short term stays are without charge up to 3 hours at the docks and in slips as available. Rates for additional hours are posted. Check in at the marina office or the café.

Overnight: Moorage is available for most all size vessels at a $1.25 per foot. Check in at the marina office. Anchorage in the harbour.

Port Browning Public Wharf

250-881-2019
Wharfinger

Public wharf offering two floats totaling 120 ft; mostly taken by permanent moorage. Rafting permitted. No facilities at the dock.

Short-Term: Short term stays are without charge up to 4 hours. Rates for additional hours are posted. Use the self-pay box on the wharf.

Overnight: Moorage as available for all size craft, rates vary. Use the self-registration, payment box on the wharf at the head of the ramp.

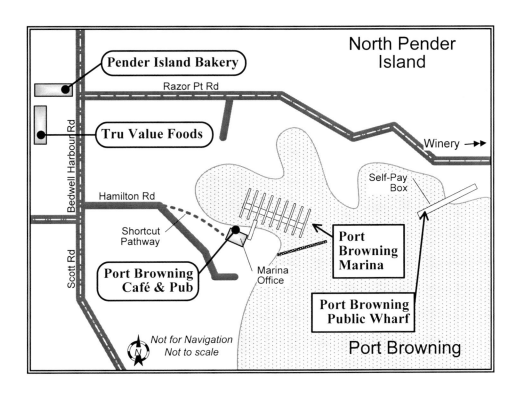

PORT BROWNING CAFÉ & PUB

The charming Port Browning Café has a country-style kitchen appeal and a cute side patio overlooking the Marina, while the recently refurbished Pub offers outstanding views of the harbour and a large deck for summer dining. Both venues offer the same menu, including tapas and unique entrees. For a tapa, try the Smoked Wild Salmon Cornucopia, a crepe cone with lox-style smoked salmon, lemon dill cream cheese, capers, and red onion. Entrée choices include the Organic-fed Chicken Breast with herb goat cheese and cranberry jus, or try the Lamb shanks, or perhaps the Spicy Seafood Linguine. Burgers, sandwiches, and salads are available for lunch and don't forget about breakfast with family and friends at the Prot Browning Café.

Breakfast	7am – Noon Daily Winter Hours Vary
Lunch/ Dinner	12pm – 9pm Daily Winter Hours Vary
Pub	Noon – 11pm Mon-Thur Noon – 1am Fri & Sat
Price	Moderate
Outdoor Seating	Yes, Patio, Café Yes, Deck, Pub
Contact	250-629-3493

Port Browning Café

Port Browning Pub

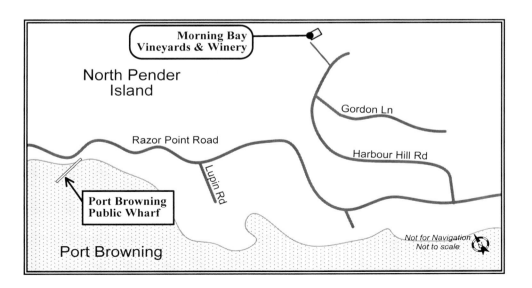

NORTH PENDER ISLAND
Port Browning

PENDER ISLAND BAKERY

The Pender Island Bakery is located a short .5 km (1/3 mile) walk from Port Browning marina. Follow the well-worn path through the shrubs, continue up the road and turn right; you will see the cute village of Driftwood Centre just down the road on the left. The Bakery has delicious pastries for breakfast and lunch along with dessert pastries, cookies, and other sweets. The Bakery also serves salads, panini, and quesadillas. You can relax at tables inside or outside, while enjoying your baked goods, espresso, or smoothie.

Breakfast/ Lunch	7:30am – 5pm Mon-Fri 8am – 5pm Saturdays 10am – 4pm Sundays Hours Vary Off Season
Price	Moderate
Outdoor Seating	Yes, Patio, Summer Months
Contact	250-629-6453

Driftwood Center

Driftwood Center Grocery Deli

Morning Bay Vineyards & Winery

SOUTH PENDER ISLAND
Bedwell Harbour

Poets Cove Resort & Marina (250-629-2100) in Bedwell Harbour on South Pender Island is known as the classy, nautical destination of the Gulf Islands. This beautiful resort offers fine dining, classy casual dining, a wine shop, and coffee shop. Overnight guests can enjoy the Fitness Centre, play tennis, use the outdoor swimming pool and hot tub, or relax at the indoor Susurrus Spa (250-629-2113).

Short-term moorage is located on the breakwater with shuttle service to the main docks and in shore-side slips as available. Overnight stays are available on the breakwater as well as in the main dock moorage slips. The Canada customs dock has signage at the Marina.

Accommodations at the Resort include the beautiful Poets Cove Lodge and private Villas (888-512-7638). The Resort offers tours of local art galleries and a tour of Morning Bay Vineyards & Winery on North Pender Island. To book tours, call the Activities Centre (250-629-2116). If you wish to explore on your own, you can rent bicycles at the Centre or get your exercise through one of the fitness classes or perhaps take a short walk up the hill to the adorable 1938 "Church of the Good Shepherd" and read the historic markers about the church and Bedwell Harbour.

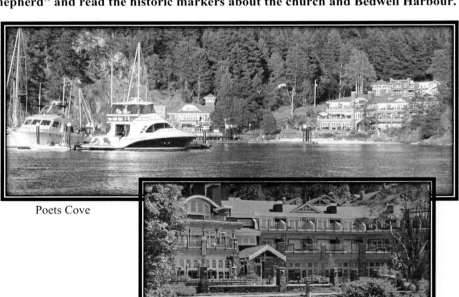

Poets Cove

Poets Cove Marina	250-629-2111 VHF 66A
	www.poetscove.com

Full service marina with power, fuel, restrooms, showers, laundry, pub, restaurant, pool, fitness room, spa. Customs clearance.

Short-Term: Short term stays permitted during the day on the breakwater dock without charge and in shore-side slips as available. Tender service from breakwater.

Overnight: Moorage for all size craft, rates vary seasonally. Call ahead for reservations and slip assignment. Overnights on breakwater dock do not include power or water. Overnight stays include access to pool and hot tub. Other amenities with additional fee.

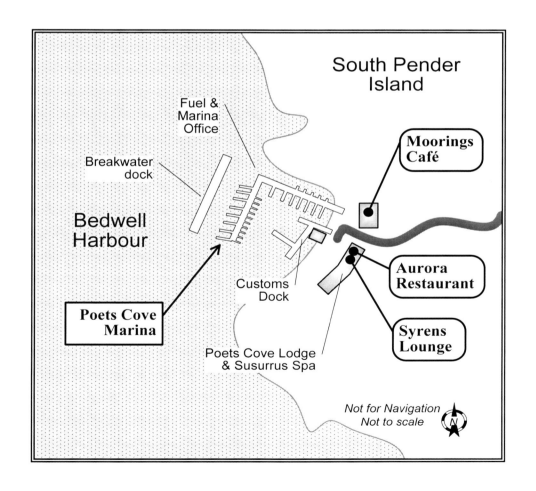

South Pender Island

Fuel & Marina Office

Moorings Café

Breakwater dock

Bedwell Harbour

Aurora Restaurant

Poets Cove Marina

Customs Dock

Syrens Lounge

Poets Cove Lodge & Susurrus Spa

Not for Navigation
Not to scale

SOUTH PENDER ISLAND
Bedwell Harbour

AURORA RESTAURANT

The Poets Cove Resort is a destination for boaters looking to relax, be pampered, and enjoy some excellent eats. The Aurora dining room, located upstairs at the waterfront lodge accommodations, serves breakfast and dinner. This elegant dining venue with its stone fireplace, warm woods, and beautiful fixtures and furnishings has wonderful views of Bedwell Harbour and the Marina. The tables are set with wine goblets, linens, and sea-blue place-settings. Beautiful draperies soften the French doors that open to the lovely outdoor dining patio.

Breakfast	8am – 11:30am Daily
Dinner	6pm – 9pm Daily Hours Vary Off Season
Price	Expensive
Outdoor Seating	Yes, Patio Deck, Summer Months
Contact	250-629-2115

The meals are elegant too, like the pan seared Beef Tenderloin with sweet potato rosti, port wine sauce, and seasonal baby vegetables; or you might try the Poets Cove Seafood, a selection of shellfish and seafood with reduction of passion fruit, grapefruit, orange, and coconut milk. The Aurora Restaurant is a nice venue for breakfast as well, including a full buffet option.

Aurora Restaurant Deck

SYRENS LOUNGE

The casual but classy Syrens Lounge is located downstairs from the Aurora Restaurant and serves soups, salads, sandwiches, burgers, and thin-crust pizza. Special features include Slow Roasted Prime Rib, Chicken Stir Fry, and Mushroom Ravioli. There is even a fun children's menu for the "little one's." The lovely outdoor, waterfront patio is a great place to enjoy appetizers and mixed drinks or on-tap lagers and ale's. The classy interior has coffered ceilings, warm woods, and beautiful light fixtures. Seating is available at several bar areas and at tall bar-style tables and chairs. The deep warm colours along with comfortable lounge furniture and a stone fireplace create a cozy ambiance.

Lunch/ Dinner	11:30am – 9pm Daily Hours Vary Off Season
Price	Moderate
Outdoor Seating	Yes, Patio, Summer Months
Contact	250-629-2114

MOORINGS CAFÉ

The Moorings Cafe, located next to the swimming pool, carries logo shirts and jackets. You can purchase lattes and deli sandwiches to enjoy on the store's deck overlooking the pool and beautiful Bedwell Harbour. The adjacent Beer and Wine Store window is open for cold drink sales to accompany your deli sandwich and snacks. If the spirits window happens to be closed, just ask for assistance at the Café.

Deli Items	8am – 6pm Daily Hours Vary Off Season
Beer/Wine Store	10am – 6pm Mon-Thur 10am – 8pm Fri/Sat
Price	Store Pricing
Outdoor Seating	Yes, Store Deck, Summer Months
Contact	250-629-2112

Syrens Lounge

SALTSPRING ISLAND
Fernwood Point

Fernwood Public Wharf, located west of Walker Hook, is a world apart from the busy shops and streets of Ganges. Fernwood offers a peaceful country setting and an adorable café located in the Raven Street Market with a coffee shop next door just upland from the Public Wharf. The Market carries groceries, books, and gift items. The separate Café is homey and comfortable. The adjacent coffee shop has picnic tables and great views of Houston Passage and the Fernwood Wharf.

Fernwood Point was the site of the first general store in the late 1800's on Salt Spring Island. Farmers had begun to settle on the Island to raise livestock and plant orchards. The Island was named by officers of the Hudson's Bay Company for the cold and briny saltwater springs on the north end of the Island.

Fernwood Public Wharf

Fernwood Public Wharf — Under Local Management

A 45 foot dock at the Fernwood Public Wharf is maintained under local management and is available to the public for short-term stays. One buoy is currently available for larger vessels with additional buoys planned for the future. Donations for maintenance are gladly accepted at the Raven Market Café.

Short-Term: Short term stays without charge while visiting the area.

Overnight: Overnight stays are permitted without charge for a maximum of 24 hours. Donations accepted at the Raven Market Café.

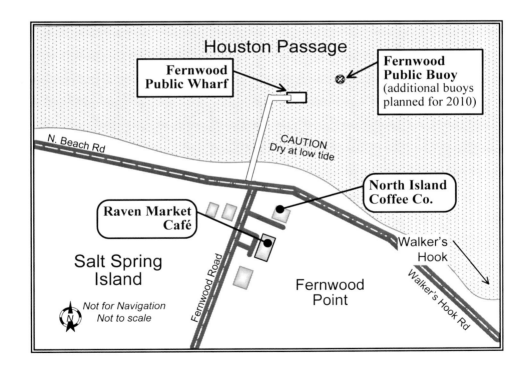

SALTSPRING ISLAND
Fernwood Point

RAVEN MARKET CAFE

Visiting the Fernwood Wharf and the Raven Market Café is a true Island experience with its rural, peaceful setting. The charming Market and Café located upland from the Wharf has a surprisingly extensive menu, including the Teriyaki Salmon in a white ginger homemade teriyaki sauce served with greens and Indian rice, or try the Chipotle Chili with lamb, chorizo sausage, jalapenos, and potatoes. For a lighter meal, order the Wood-Fired Mussels or the West Coast Crab Cakes. Sandwiches like the Deli Roast Beef and the Baked Salmon Burger are also available along with unique wood-fired pizzas, including the Spicy Greek Vegetarian and the Peppered Shrimp.

Lunch/ Dinner	Noon – 8pm Daily
Market	Noon – 8pm Daily
Price	Moderate
Outdoor Seating	No (Indoor Patio)
Contact	250-537-2273 Delivery Service

Dining space is located in an enclosed patio at the front of the Market with beautiful area rugs, a wood-burning stove, and wood patio furnishings all of which creates a very homey ambiance in this country-style grocery.

Raven Market Café

NORTH ISLAND COFFEE CO.

This attractive coffee shop at Fernwood is located just upland from the wharf, an ideal spot to enjoy the views of Houston Passage and observe your boat dockside. The coffee shop offers outdoor picnic tables or you can enjoy the comfortable couch and furnishings indoors. The coffee shop, owned by the Raven Market Café, serves espresso drinks, pastries, sweets, and deli sandwiches, including Black Forest Ham, BBQ Chicken, and the California Club. Ferwood is definitely a relaxing seaside venue not to be missed.

Hours	8am – 4pm Daily
Price	Moderate
Outdoor Seating	Yes, Lawn Area, Picnic Tables
Contact	250-931-7207

North Island Coffee Co.

SALTSPRING ISLAND
Fulford Harbour

The village at Fulford Harbour has an eclectic mix, offering a bakery, café, pub, art gallery, clothing shops, and the historic Patterson's Market grocery (250-653-4321). The historic Fulford Inn Pub is located on the northwest end of the Harbour. Fulford Harbour was named after Captain John Fulford, commanding officer of the flagship "H.M.S. Ganges" of the Royal Navy Pacific Station.

There are several short-term and overnight options for boaters visiting Fulford Harbour. The Fulford Harbour Wharf (inner wharf) and Roamers Landing (outer wharf) are both within steps of the Village. Located between the two wharves is the Swartz Bay/Fulford Ferry Landing. At the northeast end of Fulford Harbour is the Fulford Harbour Marina with overnight and short-term moorage as available.

Don't miss seeing the old St. Paul's stone church near the Marina on Fulford-Ganges Road, which you will pass on your walk or bicycle ride to the Fulford Pub. If you have bikes on board, you may wish to visit the Cheese Farm Shop (250-653-2300) at 285 Reynolds Road, a 4 km (2 ½ mile) bike ride from Fulford Harbour via Beaver Point Road or call the Silver Shadow Taxi (250-537-3030). The Farm offers sales and tastings of their fresh handmade goat cheeses, which are absolutely delicious and attractively presented. Tastings include a wide variety of cheeses along with chutneys, crackers, and an olive bar. Visitors can go on a self-guided tour of the cheese-making process and enjoy snacks and cheeses in the lovely courtyard.

Fulford Outer Public Wharf	250-537-5711 VHF 09
	Saltspring Harbour Authority

Roamers Landing, the outer wharf at Fulford Harbour with short-term and overnight stays on a 50 foot dock. No power or water.

Short-Term: Short-term stays from 8am to 4pm are at no charge up to 2 hours. Half-rates apply over 2 hours as posted. Payment box at dock.

Overnight: Rates are posted for stays after 4pm and overnight stays with a 48 hour limit. Use the self-pay box at the building on the Roamers Landing Wharf. Be aware of ferry wash.

Fulford Outer Wharf

<u>Fulford Harbour Marina</u>   250-653-4467   VHF 66A

www.saltspring.com/fulfordmarina/

Full service marina with power, restrooms, and showers offering short-term and overnight moorage.

Short-Term: Short term stays up to 2 hrs located on the outside area of the main dock for $5 under 30 ft and $10 larger vessels. Check in at the marina office.

Overnight: Moorage for all size craft at $1 per foot, call for reservations and space assignment during the busy summer months.

<u>Fulford Harbour Public Wharf</u> 250-537-5711   VHF 09

Saltspring Harbour Authority

The Fulford Wharf is the inner harbour wharf and has short-term and overnight moorage on the outside of the 120 foot dock and has power and water.

Short-Term: Short-term stays from 8am to 4pm are at no charge up to 2 hours. Half-rates apply over 2 hours as posted. Payment box at dock.

Overnight: Rates are posted for stays after 4pm and overnight stays. Guest space is located on the outside of the 120 foot dock with a 48 hour maximum stay. Use self-pay station at the head of the dock.

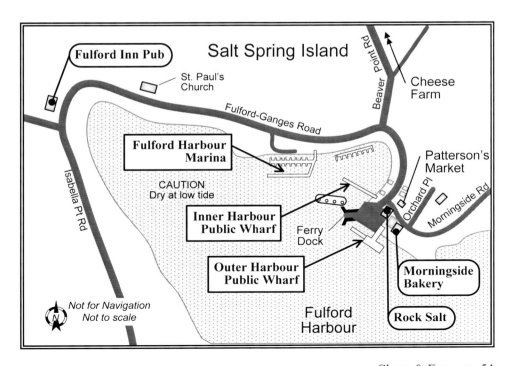

SALTSPRING ISLAND
Fulford Harbour

FULFORD INN PUB

The Fulford Inn Pub, located at the northwest end of Fulford Harbour, can be reached by bicycle from the village of Fulford, a 1.2 km (3/4 mile) ride or a .8 km (1/2 mile) walk from Fulford Harbour Marina. Boaters can also opt for the Pub's delivery service. The Pub has a rustic character with an attractive atrium and an outdoor deck sporting a fire pit and lovely views of Fulford Harbour. A welcoming brick fireplace and a variety of conversational seating creates the indoor scene. The Pub serves salads, sandwiches, burgers, pasta, and pizzas. Try the Grilled Chicken Foccacia with chicken breast, roasted red peppers, lettuce, and pesto mayo served with pan-fried potatoes or create your own pizza with a variety of topping selections. Appetizers are always a great choice along with the Pub's eleven individually crafted brews. Don't miss the homemade baked pies, including apple, chocolate pecan, and strawberry rhubarb.

Lunch/ Dinner	11am – 9pm Daily Till 10pm Thur & Fri Winter Hours Vary
Pub	11am – Midnight Hours Vary Off Season
Price	Moderate
Outdoor Seating	Yes, Deck, Summer Months
Contact	250-653-4432
Note	Delivery Service and Fulford Liquor Store

Fulford Pub Deck

MORNINGSIDE BAKERY

The Morningside Bakery & Café is definitely worth a visit for its unique architecture as well as for the unique organic goodies and espresso. Check out the wooden airplane wings used as a cover over the patio of this hacienda-style building which was made from downed trees and found wood on the Island. The patio with its intriguing outdoor fireplace has ample seating for visitors. The Morningside serves baked organic goods for breakfast and smoked tofu sandwiches and veggie burgers for lunch; or you might want to stop by for cookies and a cup of tea or coffee. The Morningside is the only all-organic restaurant on the Island.

Breakfast/ Lunch	9am – 6pm Daily
Price	Moderate
Outdoor Seating	Yes, Covered Patio
Contact	250-653-4414

ROCK SALT

The Rock Salt is a high-energy restaurant and café with brightly coloured walls and coloured glass partitions along with a display of local art. The separate café is popular with folks riding the ferry, who wish to enjoy a quick meal or take-out services. The Rock Salt offers comfort food with a varied blend of Mexican, Asian, mid-Eastern, and Italian dishes like the Roasted Yam Quesadilla, the Seafood Pesto Penne, and the Linguini Pescatore with mussels, prawns, and wild coho salmon. Burgers are served on grilled ciabatta and include the Caribbean Lamb, the Lemon Salmon, and the BBQ Chicken. Classic main dishes include Grilled Halibut, Wild Coho Salmon, Monk's Curry, and the Beer Broth Pork Ribs with tangy tamarind sauce.

Breakfast	7am – 11am Daily
Lunch	11am – 4:30pm Daily
Dinner	4:30pm – 9pm Daily
Brunch	7am – 3pm Sat & Sun
Price	Moderate
Outdoor Seating	Yes, Lanai, Summer Months
Contact	250-653-4833

SALTSPRING ISLAND
Ganges Harbour

Ganges is the largest town in the Gulf Islands with numerous shops, restaurants, and art galleries. You may find it hard to decide where to dine with so many good restaurants, some of which host professional musicians for your dining pleasure during the summer months. For a great cup of coffee, visit Saltspring Is. Roasting, a local's favorite lunch stop. Saltspring (Salt Spring) Island is the most densely populated of the Gulf Islands with numerous amenities, services, and B&B's. Accommodations in town include The Harbour House Inn (250-537-4700) located across the road from Salt Spring Marina and the SaltSpring Inn (250-537-9339) located near the Kanaka Public dock on Lower Ganges Road.

Ganges is definitely a destination for boaters with two Marinas, a Public Wharf, two Public Docks, and a Dinghy Dock; even so, you will want to make reservations where possible during the busy summer months. The marinas and docks are all within easy walking distance for restaurants and shops in Ganges. Good anchorage can be found in the Harbour.

Entrepreneurs of every kind live on Salt Spring Island, including well known artists, musicians, and authors. The "ArtSpring" Centre at 100 Jackson Avenue, houses a theatre and gallery spaces. For programs and events, call the ticket office (250-537-2102). Many products are grown or produced on the Island like fruits, vegetables, cheeses, wine, beer, and seafood products, and of course the world-famous Salt Spring Island lamb. Some of these products can be purchased at the Saturday Market, operating from April to October in the Centennial Park (next to the Centennial Wharf). Be sure to visit Mouats (a pioneer family name) located in front of the Kanaka Public Dock. Mouats (250-537-5551) carries everything from marine supplies and hardware to clothing, gifts, furniture, and kitchenware. For those in need of a little pampering and relaxation, visit Skin Sensations Day Spa (250-537-8807) or Ganges Massage Therapy (250-537-9433).

If you want to explore outside Ganges, you can rent cars and scooters from the Salt Spring Marina (250-537-5810) and bicycles can be rented from the Salt Spring Adventures Co. (250-537-2764) located next to Moby's Restaurant & Pub. During your travels through the Island, you might pass signs on the road featuring a black sheep and a painted number. These signs indicate participating art studios, which are open to the public during "Studio Tour" held mid-May to the end of September. You can pick up tour maps from the Visitors Centre (250-537-5252) in Ganges, located at the corner of Lower Ganges Rd. and Purvis lane. Don't forget to purchase "Salt Spring Dollars" at the Visitor Centre. Most Island businesses accept these dollars and they also serve as great keepsakes.

Centennial Wharf

Breakwater Public Dock

SALTSPRING ISLAND
Ganges Harbour

Breakwater Public Dock
250-537-5711   VHF 09
Saltspring Harbour Authority

Public wharf with ample short-term and overnight guest space with power. Space reserved for seaplanes. Coast Guard Station on site. Anchorage in Harbour.

Short-Term: Short-term stays from 8am to 4pm are at no charge up to 2 hours. Half-rates apply over 2 hours as posted. Payment box at dock.

Overnight: Rates are posted for stays after 4pm and overnight stays. There is approximately 180 feet plus 3 fingers for guest space. Use the self-registration payment box at the head of the dock.

Ganges Centennial Wharf
250-537-5711   VHF 09
Saltspring Harbour Authority

The Centennial Wharf is mainly used for commercial and permanent vessels. Transient space as available, rafting permitted, approximately 150 feet.

Short-Term: Short term stays permitted at no charge as available. Check in at the Saltspring Harbour Authority Office just upland.

Overnight: Overnight as available, register at Harbour Authority Office, rates vary by vessel length.

Ganges Marina
250-537-5242   VHF 66A
www.gangesmarina.com

A full service marina with power, restrooms, showers, laundry, fuel dock, and short-term and overnight moorage. Pool & hot tub for overnight guests.

Short-Term: Short term hourly stays available on the breakwater for $10

Overnight: Moorage available for all size craft at $1.45/ft. Reservations are a must during the busy summer months. Anchorage in Harbour.

Kanaka Public Dock
250-537-5711   VHF 09
Saltspring Harbour Authority

Public dock with ample short-term and overnight guest space with power and water, approximately 800 feet of guest space.

Short-Term: Short-term stays from 8am to 4pm are at no charge up to 2 hours. Half-rates apply over 2 hours as posted. Payment box at dock.

Overnight: Rates are posted for stays after 4pm and overnight stays. Use the self-registration payment box at the head of the dock. Anchorage in Harbour.

Rotary Dinghy Dock & Park   Supported by Rotary

The dingy dock (supported by the Rotary Club, Thrifty Foods, and Mouats) is located between the Kanaka Public Dock and Ganges Marina. No usage charge.

Short-Term: Short term stays for dinghies while visiting in town. (10' x 15')

Overnight: No overnight stays. Anchorage in Ganges Harbour

Salt Spring Marina   250-537-5810   VHF 66A
www.saltspringmarina.com

A full service marina with power, restrooms, showers, and laundry with short-term and overnight guest moorage. Moby's Pub and Rogue Cafe upland.

Short-Term: Short stays as available; 10 dollars for 2-hr maximum.

Overnight: Moorage available for all size craft at $1.25 per foot summer rates. Reservations are a must during the busy summer months.

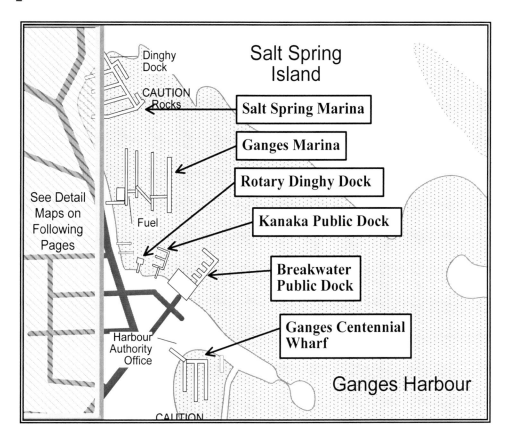

SALTSPRING ISLAND
Ganges Harbour

GANGES RESTAURANTS			🍽
Arigado Sushi	Sushi, Teriyaki	102 Gasoline Alley	250-538-1881
Auntie Pesto's	Pasta, Sandwiches	Grace Point Square	250-537-4181
Barb's Buns	Breads, Pastries, Sandwiches, Soups	#1 Creekside McPhillips Ave.	250-537-4491
Bocados Bistro	Lamb, Seafood	Grace Point Square	250-538-1622
Bruce's Kitchen	Soups, Sandwiches	106 Gasoline Alley	250-931-3399
Café Talia	Espresso, Sweets, Sandwiches	122 Herford Ave.	250-931-4441
Calvin's Bistro	Chicken, Lamb, Steak, Seafood	133 Lower Ganges Road	250-538-5551
Embe Bakery Embe Too Cafe	Breakfast/Lunch Pastries	174 Fulford/ Ganges Road	250-537-5611
Glads Ice Cream	Candy, Ice Cream	101 Purvis Lane	250-537-4211
Harbour House Inn	Breakfast, Burgers, Pasta, Seafood	121 Upper Ganges Road	250-537-4700
Harlan's Chocolates	Chocolates, Gelato	100 Lower Ganges	250-537-4434
Hastings House	Beef, Lamb, Fish	160 Upper Ganges	250-537-2362
House Piccolo	Beef, Duck, Lamb, Seafood	108 Hereford Ave.	250-537-1844
Local Bar & Bistro	Beer/Wine Lounge	Gasoline Alley	250-537-9463

Café Talia

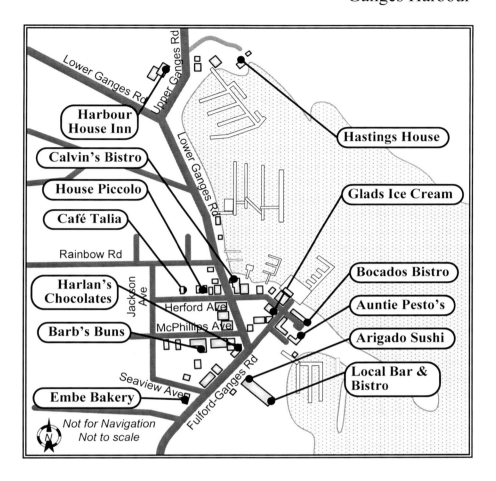

Harbour House Inn
- Calvin's Bistro
- House Piccolo
- Café Talia
- Harbour House Inn

Lower Ganges Rd
Upper Ganges Rd
Lower Ganges Rd
Rainbow Rd
Jackson Ave
Herford Ave
McPhillips Ave
Seaview Ave
Fulford-Ganges Rd

- Hastings House
- Glads Ice Cream
- Bocados Bistro
- Auntie Pesto's
- Arigado Sushi
- Local Bar & Bistro

- Harlan's Chocolates
- Barb's Buns
- Embe Bakery

Not for Navigation
Not to scale
N

Harbour House Inn

SALTSPRING ISLAND
Ganges Harbour

GANGES RESTAURANTS CONTINUED			🍽
Market Place Café	Breakfast, Seafood, Lamb, Veggie	103 Gasoline Alley	250-537-9911
Mexico Café	Mexican Cuisine	Dockside Mouats Landing	250-537-5747
Moby's Pub	Breakfast, Burgers, Seafood	120 Upper Ganges Road	250-537-5559
Oystercatcher Bar & Grill	Breakfast, Burgers, Seafood	Harbour Building	250-537-5041
Pasta Fresca	Fresh Pasta, Sauce, take-out to cook	101 Gasoline Alley	250-537-8588
Pomodoro Pizza	Pizza, Wraps, Salads	142 Fulford/ Ganges Road	250-537-5660
Rendezvous	French Patisserie	126 Upper Ganges	250-537-8400
Saltspring I. Roasting	Coffee, Pastries	109 McPhillips Avenue	250-537-0825
Teddy Bear's	Take-Out Burgers, Fish 'n Chips	170 Fulford/ Ganges Road	250-537-4062
Thrifty Foods Dockside Delivery	Groceries, Deli (by 2pm delivery)	114 Purvis Lane	250-537-1522
TJ Beans	Coffee, Pastries	110 Lower Ganges Road	250-537-1216
Tree House Café	Breakfast, Mexican & Caribbean	Next to Mouats	250-537-5379
Salt Spring Noodle Bar	Indian and Asian Cuisine	149 Fulford/ Ganges Road	250-537-1234
SaltSpring Inn Restaurant	Fish, Sandwiches, Pizza, Burgers	132 Lower Ganges Road	250-537-9339

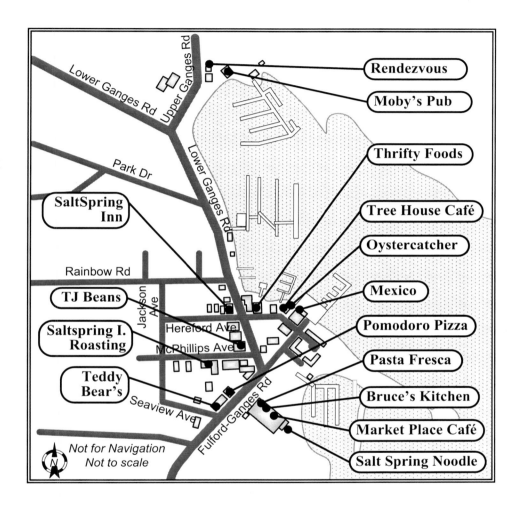

Lower Ganges Rd

Upper Ganges Rd

Lower Ganges Rd

Park Dr

Rainbow Rd

Jackson Ave

Hereford Ave

McPhillips Ave

Seaview Ave

Fulford-Ganges Rd

SaltSpring Inn

TJ Beans

Saltspring I. Roasting

Teddy Bear's

Rendezvous

Moby's Pub

Thrifty Foods

Tree House Café

Oystercatcher

Mexico

Pomodoro Pizza

Pasta Fresca

Bruce's Kitchen

Market Place Café

Salt Spring Noodle

Not for Navigation
Not to scale

N

SALTSPRING ISLAND
Ganges Harbour

AUNTIE PESTO'S

Auntie Pesto's is located at 115 Fulford Ganges Rd. in Grace Point Square overlooking Ganges Centennial Wharf. Aunti Pesto's is a great place for any meal. The meat & deli cheese tray with roasted vegetables is a real treat, or try one of the deli sandwiches like the Chicken Breast with roasted peppers, provolone, and pesto or black olive paste. The Roasted Beef Sandwich with caramelized onions and brie grilled on ciabatta with stone ground mustard is also good. Tasty pasta dishes are available at dinner or come by for breakfast and enjoy the Fresh Fruit Salad with wedges of brie and gruyere served with a fresh baked scone while you relax on the nice deck overlooking the Harbour.

Breakfast	8am – 11am Mon-Sat
Lunch	11am – 4pm Mon-Sat
Dinner	5pm – 9pm Mon-Sat
Price	Moderate
Outdoor Seating	Yes, Deck, Summer Months
Contact	250-537-4181

BOCADOS BISTRO

Bocados Bistro is located at Grace Point Square near Centennial Wharf sporting French doors that open to a small patio overlooking the Harbour. This lovely bistro has beautiful coffered ceilings, cane-backed chairs, and colourful art work adorning the yellow pastel walls. Bocados is the perfect choice for a casual intimate meal; the tables are set with fresh cut flowers, wine goblets, and pretty dual tablecloths. Tapas, soups, salads, and burgers are offered at lunch, including the Saltspring Island Lamb Burger and the BC Wild Salmon Burger. A variety of Kabobs are also a nice choice for lunch or dinner. Dinner entrees include the Seared Ahi Tuna, the Lamb Curry,

Lunch	11:30am – 3pm Mon-Sat
Dinner	5pm – 9pm Mon-Thur 5pm – 10pm Fri & Sat
Price	Moderate - Expensive
Outdoor Seating	Yes, Patio, Summer Months
Contact	250-538-1622

and the Bocados AAA Beef Tenderloin; or try the Free Range Chicken Breast stuffed with goat cheese, spinach, and sundried tomatoes. Don't forget about the Chocolate Eruption Cake or the Apple Cinnamon Crepe for dessert.

HASTINGS HOUSE 🍽

The Hastings House is one of those once in a life-time experiences not to be missed and is truly a place to nurture both the body and the soul. The Hastings House is located within walking distance of Ganges and the Salt Spring Marina yet a world apart in its peaceful forested hill-top setting. The grounds are beautiful with numerous flower gardens, historic buildings, and an English Manor House. Guests can choose from various accommodations, including The Post, the original Hudson Bay Post on Saltspring Island, and The Manor built in 1938, where Warren Hastings designed the WWII naval landing craft. The ladies will appreciate the special Spa services with body wraps, massages, and steam showers.

Dinner	5:30pm – 8pm Daily Winter Hours Vary
Price	Expensive – Very Expensive
Outdoor Seating	Yes, Cocktail Patio
Contact	250-537-2362

Visitors as well as guests can make dinner reservations for the Manor Dining Room or you can ask for the more casual Verandah. Space is as available for drop-in visitors. Dinner can be requested from the three-course Ala Carte menu or the six-course Chef's Menu, which changes daily. The meals are superb with exquisite presentation and include herbs and produce from the Hastings House garden, fresh seafood, Salt Spring Island lamb, and Alberta beef. You might begin your meal with an appetizer like the local goat cheese with red and golden beets with balsamic syrup followed by the Peppered Filet of Alberta Beef with parmesan polenta, braised red cabbage and Port wine jus finished with a special dessert like the White Chocolate Mousse Lemon Lavender Shortcake. No matter what, you will feel like royalty at the Hastings House. Sunday Brunch is usually offered on Easter and Mother's Day.

Hastings House

SALTSPRING ISLAND
Ganges Harbour

HOUSE PICCOLO

The House Piccolo is a real gem and is off the beaten path from the tourists, located at 108 Hereford Avenue within easy walking distance of the marinas. Look for the blue house with white trim and large umbrellas on the front porch. The dining tables in this intimate restaurant are set with blue and white double tablecloths, candles, and wine goblets. Copper pots and tea kettles are displayed on shelves under which hang lovely watercolours on the heavy-textured white walls. Finnish Chef, Piccolo Lyytikainen, creates wonderful European and Scandinavian meals and offers 250 international wines from his wine cellar.

Dinner	5pm – Close Daily Hours Vary Off Season
Price	Expensive
Outdoor Seating	Yes, Patio, Summer Months
Contact	250-537-1844

For starters, try the pacific Cold Smoked Salmon, locally smoked wild salmon with capers served with a lemon and crème fraiche. Main courses come with a house salad and fresh baked bread and include the Roasted Muscovy Duck, a crispy breast with tangy orange and green peppercorn demi-glace; or try the Charbroiled Beef Filet with a rich, smooth Gorgonzola sauce, or perhaps the Roasted Vegetable & Saffron Risotto. Don't miss the warm Lingonberry Crepes for dessert served with homemade vanilla ice cream and filled with lingonberry compote moistened with Finlandia Vodka.

House Piccolo

MOBY'S PUB

Located upland from Salt Spring Marina, Moby's is a favorite pub destination popular among boaters. Moby's has fabulous views of the Marina and Ganges Harbour from the outdoor deck and from the interior through the large ocean-side windows. It's the friendly service, camaraderie, and good home cooking that bring folks to Moby's. Moby's offers an ever changing assortment of fresh oysters and other appetizers, including Avocado Prawns sauteed in a sambal hot sauce with fresh cilantro and avocado served with fresh baguette. You won't want to miss the nice selection of local beers on tap and the extensive wine list to accompany a favorite main like the

Lunch/ Dinner	11am – 11pm Daily Drinks till 1am Fri & Sat
Brunch	11am – 3pm Sat & Sun
Price	Moderate
Outdoor Seating	Yes, Deck, Summer Months
Contact	250-537-5559

Veggie Stack, the Steak Sandwich, or perhaps the Seafood Melange, a bowl of delicious fresh seafood in a tomato port broth with fresh herbs. Live jazz is hosted on Sunday nights along with occassional live band performances as scheduled.

Moby's

SALTSPRING ISLAND
Ganges Harbour

SALTSPRING INN

The SaltSpring Inn in the heart of Ganges offers nice accommodations and a modern restaurant and bar. The menu includes tapas, soups & salads, sandwiches, specialty entrees, and thin crust pizzas. Start with one of the tapas like the Pan Seared Tuna with chipotle crème fraiche or the Baked Herbed Goat Cheese served with apple chutney and garlic crostini, or perhaps the Curried Butternut Squash Soup. For the main event, try the Southern BBQ Chicken Pizza or the Grilled Cajun Halibut Burger, or a Crab Quesadilla. Other excellent choices include the Split Roasted Chicken

Breakfast	8am – 11pm Mon-Sat
Lunch/Dinner	11am – 10pm Daily
Brunch	8am – 2pm Sundays
Price	Moderate
Outdoor Seating	Yes, Porch, Summer Months
Contact	250-537-9339

and the West Coast Fish Pot. The Inn's front porch is available during the summer months from which you can watch all the activity of this popular destination, and you won't want to miss the special Sunday night jazz performances by renowned muscians.

SaltSpring Inn

TREE HOUSE CAFÉ

This adorable café is unique to Ganges, located literally under a large plum tree. The cute house serves as the kitchen where meals are prepared from scratch and also provides indoor seating during the cooler months. The house once served as the Island's first electrical generating station and later as the home of Aunt Margaret, a member of the Mouats family of Mouats hardware store located next door. The Café is open daily during the summer months and serves sandwiches, wraps, and burgers for lunch along with seafood and meat dishes added to the dinner menu. Lunch favorites include the Lamb Gyro, the Roasted Yam Burrito, and the Butternut Squash Stew.

Breakfast	8am – 11:30am Daily
Lunch	11am - 4:30pm Daily
Dinner	4:30pm – 9pm Daily Hours Vary Off Season
Price	Moderate
Outdoor Seating	Yes, Under Plum Tree Summer Months
Contact	250-537-5379

For an evening meal, try the Salmon & Prawn Dinner with a six ounce fillet of wild salmon served in ginger teriyaki sauce combined with a skewer of large grilled lemon garlic prawns. Live evening performances by professional musicians are held nightly throughout the summer months creating a special evening under the stars at the Tree House Cafe.

Tree House Cafe

SALTSPRING ISLAND
Vesuvius Bay

Vesuvius is an enchanting tiny village perched on the hillside overlooking Stuart Channel. A small ferry runs between Vesuvius and Crofton on Vancouver Island. Because of the warmer waters around Vesuvius, this area is a popular swimming destination. A flight of stairs off Langley Street takes you down to the beach. Be sure to take note of the deeply inclined rock strata.

The Vesuvius Public Wharf offers short-term and overnight moorage. Adjacent to the Wharf is the Seaside Restaurant with its own Private Dock available to visiting boaters dining at the restaurant. Groceries, espresso, and baked goods are available at the Vesuvius Village Store (250-537-1515) located a short distance east on Vesuvius Bay Road. The Meredith Studio Gallery (250-537-9876 or 1502), located across the street from the Village Store, displays beautiful watercolours and pottery by Jacqueline and Mark Meredith for viewing and sales.

Vesuvius Bay was the home of the first settlers of 1859 on Salt Spring Island, many of whom were African Americans from California, who wanted to escape the harsh laws of the state. Island land was not surveyed at the time and virtually free to the settlers. The village of Vesuvius takes its name from the Royal Navy sloop, "Vesuvius," which served in the Crimean War (1853-1856) in the Black Sea.

Seaside Restaurant Dock

Vesuvius Public Wharf

Seaside Restaurant Dock

250-537-2249
Private Dock

The Seaside Restaurant Dock (8' x 35') is located just east of the Ferry Landing and is open to boaters dining at the Seaside Restaurant.

Short-Term: Short term stays are permitted while dining at the Seaside Restaurant.

Overnight: No overnight stays.

Vesuvius Public Wharf

250-537-5711   VHF 09
Saltspring Harbour Authority

Adjacent to the Ferry Landing is the Vesuvius Wharf with a 10' x 60' float for short-term and overnight stays. Wharfinger periodically on site.

Short-Term: Short term stays are without charge up to 2 hours. Half rates apply for stays over 2 hours as posted. Payment box on the dock.

Overnight: Rates are posted for stays after 4pm and overnight stays. Use the self-registration payment box at the head of the dock.

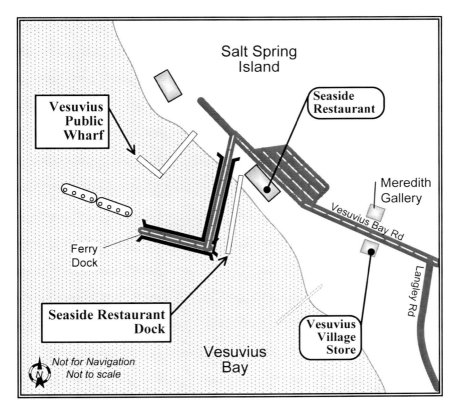

SEASIDE RESTAURANT

If you are looking for beautiful views and great food, the Seaside Restaurant overlooking Vesuvius Bay towards Vancouver Island is the perfect stop and has its own guest dock. The entrance to the restaurant is accessed on the street side down a narrow set of stairs. There are several seating options, the main level near the prep-kitchen and wine racks; the outdoor deck; or the upper more formal area, all of which have great views.

Lunch / Dinner	11am – 9pm Daily Winter Hours Vary
Price	Moderate
Outdoor Seating	Yes, Deck, Summer Months
Contact	250-537-2249

The food is nicely prepared and presented like the oriental Salad with chicken, veggies, and greens with oriental dressing and The Seaside Creation with greens, roasted nuts, and mandarin oranges in honey-mustard vinaigrette. The burgers are big and juicy and the seafood dinner dishes are equally good, like the Grilled Fresh Halibut with a roasted red pepper & basil sauce, roasted potatoes, and fresh vegetables; or try the Linguini Di Mare Pasta with digby scallops, tiger prawns, and Newfoundland ice shrimp sautéed in olive oil, basil, white wine, and garlic. Fish n' chips and Baby Back Ribs are also available along with beer, ciders, and fine wines.

Seaside Restaurant

VESUVIUS VILLAGE STORE

The old-fashioned Village Store at Vesuvius is housed in a cute blue and yellow cottage and offers fresh produce, sandwiches to-order, groceries, and gift items. Sandwich choices include a variety of meats and cheeses; or you can enjoy an espresso along with delicious sweets while you relax on the Village Store patio adorned with planter boxes and flower baskets. The delightful Vesuvius Village Store is located a short walk southeast of the Public Wharf at 735 Vesuvius Bay Road.

Hours	9am – 6pm Mon-Sat 11am – 4pm Sundays
Price	Moderate
Outdoor Seating	Yes, Patio, Summer Months
Contact	250-537-1515

Vesuvius Store

SATURNA ISLAND
Breezy Bay

Although Breezy Bay is not conducive for overnight anchorage, it is the perfect afternoon stop and offers the unique experience of visiting the Saturna Island Winery and Vineyards, offering wine tasting and an excellent bistro. The Saturna Island Winery recently added its own guest dock next to the community dock in Breezy Bay. Guests of the Winery and Bistro may tie-up at this 60 foot guest dock, which is clearly marked with signage. Large vessels can make use of the Winery guest buoys, also clearly marked. The number of buoys may vary due to the maintenance schedule. Boaters should stay clear of the community dock and the Campbell Farm dock in front of Thompson Park, both of which are private.

The trail up to the Vineyards is marked and the 1 km (.6 mile) hike is definitely worth the walk for the beautiful Tuscany-like scenery. This winery and vineyard setting is absolutely breathtaking with huge sandstone and granite cliff walls embracing the north side with sixty acres of vineyards in the valley below overlooking Plumper Sound to the south. Breezy Bay with its sandy beaches and Saturna Island Winery and Bistro is truly a hidden gem.

Breezy Bay Dock   250-539-5139 or 3521

Private 10' x 60' dock and several buoys open to guests of the Saturna Island Winery.

Short-Term: Short term stays are permitted at the winery dock up to 2 hours and on the orange buoys (marked "winery guests") while visiting the vineyards.

Overnight: No overnight stays on dock. No overnight stays on buoys.

SATURNA ISLAND WINERY

To locate the Vineyards and Winery Bistro, walk up the road from the dock and take a left at the inter-section, signs are posted along the way. When you reach the sign "end of public road," turn right. The walk is about .8 km (1/2 mile) to the Bistro. This unique, fully operational winery grows specific grape varieties for Pinot Gris, Chardonnay, Gewurztraminer, Pinot Noir, and Merlot among other varieties which have won numerous medals of excellence. The Winery's chef creates exceptional seafood dishes like the Wild Spring Salmon Trio with tataki, tartare, and house-smoked candied salmon; or try the Albacore Tuna with charred cherry tomatoes and Nicoise olive tapenade. Be sure to ask about dessert while enjoying your wine and the great views from the lovely outdoor patio.

Lunch	11am – 3pm Daily May – mid Sept
Wine Tasting	11am – 4pm Daily May – mid Sept
Price	Moderate
Outdoor Seating	Yes, Patio, Summer Months
Contact	250-539-5139 877-918-3388

Saturna Island Winery

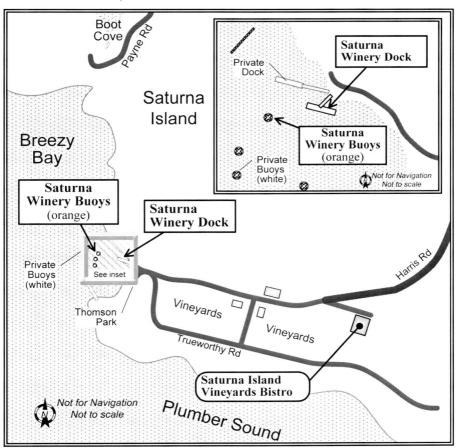

SATURNA ISLAND
Lyall Harbour

The Lyall Harbour Wharf, adjacent to the Ferry landing, offers short-term and overnight moorage. The Saturna Point Store & Lighthouse Pub are within a few steps of the Wharf. The Store (250-539-5726) stocks groceries, fresh produce, ice, spirits, hardware, locally baked goods, clothing, books, and other items. The Pub serves as a gathering point for locals to relax, play some pool, and enjoy the views with a cool drink and pub fare. The Saturna Café, located in the Saturna General Store at 101 Narvaez Bay Road, is worth a visit and provides a glimpse into this rural and remote Island.

The Island was named after a Spanish schooner, "The Saturnina," captained by Jose Maria Narvaez, who explored this southern Gulf Island in 1791. Settlers arrived in the mid to late 1800's and started orchards and raised sheep and later goats. You might spot some feral goats that went wild in the 1920's.

Sheep farming still prospers on the Island and Saturna hosts the popular July 1st Canada Day Lamb BBQ in Winter Cove at the Winter Cove Marine Park in Hunter Field. The BBQ is popular among boaters, who anchor in the Cove and are shuttled to shore to enjoy the live entertainment, numerous games, the beverage garden, and the lamb, which is cooked on upright iron crosses over a fire pit. A brief Canada Day Ceremony is included in the festivities. Entrance to the site is free; but if you wish to partake in the BBQ, you will need to purchase tickets at the booth near the site entrance. Meals are served in the order of tickets purchased. The Grounds open at 9:30 am. Boaters (guests) are asked to leave their own drinks and any pets aboard their vessel.

Other community events include the Gallery Tour in August, when Saturna artists at various locations open their studios for special viewing and sales; and the Saturday Crafts Fair held July through August from 10am to 1pm at the Saturna Café.

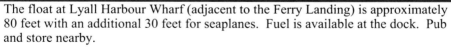

Lyall Harbour Public Wharf	250-539-2229
	Harbour Manager

The float at Lyall Harbour Wharf (adjacent to the Ferry Landing) is approximately 80 feet with an additional 30 feet for seaplanes. Fuel is available at the dock. Pub and store nearby.

Short-Term: Short term stays are without charge up to 2 hours. Rates are .50/ft for additional hours. Wharfinger on site to collect payment.

Overnight: Wharfinger collects cash payment of .50/ft for overnight stays.

Lyall Harbour Wharf

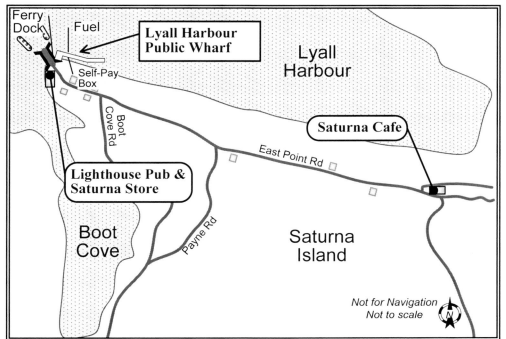

SATURNA ISLAND
Lyall Harbour

LIGHTHOUSE PUB

Located next to the Public Wharf and Ferry landing in Lyall Harbour, the Lighthouse Pub has fabulous views of the Harbour with Mayne and North Pender Islands in the distance. To access the Pub, walk down a flight of stairs around back from the Saturna Point Store. To blend in with the locals, place your order at the bar and seat yourself. The Pub serves up sandwiches, burgers, and fish, including the Marinated Prawns topped with grilled peppers and mixed greens, or try the Open-Faced Eggplant Sandwich, or perhaps the New York

Lunch/ Dinner	Noon – 8:30pm Daily Hours Vary Off Season
Price	Moderate
Outdoor Seating	Yes, Deck, Summer Months
Contact	250-539-5725

Steak Sandwich topped with fried onions, mushrooms, and Swiss cheese. Dinner selections include the Grilled Breast of Chicken, Grilled Halibut Steak, and the Grilled Sirloin Steak. The Lighthouse Pub is always a great place to just stop and relax, play a game of pool, or enjoy the views with a glass of wine, cider, or one of several draft beers.

Lighthouse Pub

SATURNA CAFE

If you want to stretch your legs and go for a country walk, or have bicycles aboard your vessel, the Saturna Café is a pleasant l.6 km (1 mile) walk or bike ride from the Lyall Harbour Public Wharf. The Café is located at the junction of East Point Rd. and Narvaez Rd. inside the Saturna General Store and is definitely worth the effort. The Store is well stocked with groceries, wines, and deli meats and cheeses. The Café with its separate dining space has attractive furnishings, nice art work, and fresh flowers on the tables. Menu items include deli salads, soups, and seafood dishes like the Dungeness Crab Cakes, Fish Stew, and the Seared Haida Gwaii Halibut with olive tapenade and ratatouille. Don't miss the Haggis Farm Dessert, King figs in season poached in white wine, or choose one of the seasonal berry desserts. The Saturna Café, in its country island setting, is a fun place to meet, greet, and eat.

Breakfast	9:30am – 11:30am Wednesday – Sunday
Lunch	Noon – 2pm Wednesday – Sunday
Dinner	6pm – 8pm Fri & Sat Winter Hours Vary
Price	Moderate
Outdoor Seating	Yes, Patio & Deck, Summer Months
Contact	250-539-5177

Saturna Café

THETIS ISLAND
Preedy Harbour & Telegraph Harbour

Thetis Island is ideal for walking about, offering beautiful pastoral views, ocean views, and forested country roads. This small Island of about 400 permanent residents is so peaceful and special that boaters come here for that very reason. The few commercial enterprises that are on the Island are located on farms and in private homes in addition to the two marinas in Telegraph Harbour. Burgees Café at Telegraph Harbour Marina, and Thetis Island Pub at Thetis Island Marina are the two main dining venues on the Island.

In addition to the two marinas in Telegraph Harbour, boaters can tie-up during the day at the Thetis Island Community Dock, which is in Preedy Harbour next to the Thetis Island Ferry Landing. It is an easy .8 km (1/2 mile) walk from the Community Dock to Telegraph Harbour. From the Community Dock, turn left and walk along Foster Pt. Rd., you will pass the beautiful Capernwray Farm & Bible Centre. Continue around to the right on Foster Pt. Rd. which becomes Pilkey Road with views of Telegraph Harbour. Be sure to stop at Capernwray Farm (250-246-9440) to take in one of the most picturesque settings in the Islands or to buy farm fresh eggs (closed Sundays).

Unique stops in Telegraph Harbour include the Pot of Gold Coffee Roasting Company (look for the Gold Pot shingle) along Pilkey Pt. Rd. east of Telegraph Marina, where you can purchase fresh roasted coffee by the pound. The Howling Wolf Farm at the corner of Pilkey Pt. Rd. and Marina Dr. is a great stop to purchase jams, pies, vegetables, and breads. In the morning after waking up to chirping birds and crowing roosters, stop by Doe's Eats & Treats (250-416-6736) for donuts and baked goods that can be ordered the night before. You can pick up your orders at the "farm gate" located at 90 Pilkey Pt. Road; a ½ km (1/3 mile) walk or bike ride from Telegraph Harbour. This site includes the Thetis Island Vineyards, which are being re-established by the new owners.

Telegraph Harbour Marina	250-246-9511 VHF 66A
	www.telegraphharbour.com

Full service marina with power, fuel, restrooms, showers, laundry, and café & store. Picnic tables, bbq's, and field games. Facilities open mid April – Sept; moorage available year-round.

Short-Term:	Short term 2-hr stays available without charge, while shopping or dining at the Burgees Café, call ahead for space assignment (800-246-6011).
Overnight:	Moorage for most all size vessels at $1.10 per foot plus power, reservations a must during the busy summer months. Anchorage in Harbour.

Thetis Island Community Dock

A public community dock in Preedy Harbour next to the Ferry Landing. Approximately 140 feet of space on an octagon-shaped dock.

Short-Term: Short term stays are permitted for day-use without charge.

Overnight: No overnight stays. Anchorage in Preedy Harbour, Telegraph Harbour, and Clam Bay.

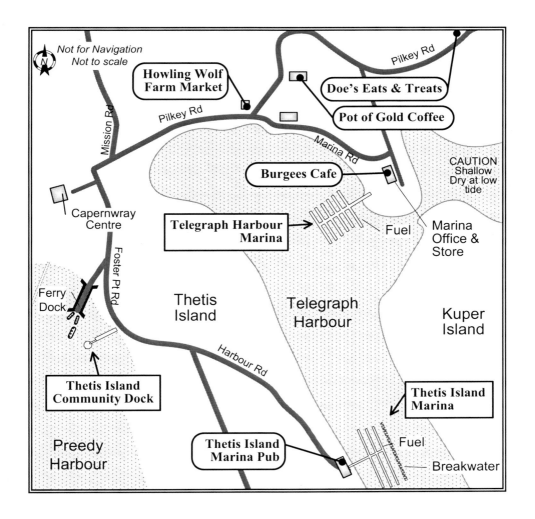

Thetis Island Marina	250-246-3464 VHF 66A	
	www.thetisisland.com	

Full service marina with power, fuel, restrooms, showers, and laundry facilities. Pub, store, liquor store, and post office on site.

Short-Term: Short term stays permitted without charge, while shopping or dining at the Thetis Island Pub, call ahead for space assignment or check in at the fuel dock. Several dinghy docks shore-side.

Overnight: Moorage for all size craft at $1.15 per foot, reservations a must during the busy summer months. Anchorage in Harbour. End of docks "g" and "h" for float planes.

THETIS ISLAND RESTAURANTS

Burgees Café	Soups, Pizza, Ice Cream, Sandwiches	Telegraph Harbour Road	250-246-9511
Capernwray Centre	Fresh Farm Eggs	298 Foster Pt. Rd	250-246-9440
Doe's Eats & Treats	Donuts, Coffee, Baked Goods	90 Pilkey Pt. Rd. "farm gate"	250-416-6736
Howling Wolf Farm	Vegetables, Jams, Pies, Breads	Marina Drive and Pilkey Pt. Rd	250-246-2650
Pot of Gold Coffee	Coffee by the Pound	73 Pilkey Pt. Rd	250-246-4944
Thetis Island Pub	Burgers, Chicken, Seafood	Thetis Island Marina	250-246-3464

Burgees Cafe

BURGEES CAFÉ

The Burgees By The Bay Café is located upland at Telegraph Harbour Marina. The Café & Store is full of colourful Burgee flags and has a 50's style soda fountain along with groceries, gifts, clothing, books, and charts. To get you started in the morning, the Café offers muffins, scones, and "Pot of Gold" coffee. Bacon & eggs are offered seasonally, June through August. Throughout the day, the Café serves soups, salads, sandwiches, and homemade pizzas. Pies and pizzas can be delivered directly to your boat. The Burgees Café has gained a reputation for its fresh baked pies, and irresistible ice cream treats like shakes, sundaes, hard ice cream, and banana splits.

Breakfast/ Lunch	8:30am – 8pm Daily June – Sept Days/Hrs Vary Off Season
Price	Moderate
Outdoor Seating	Yes, Patio, Summer Months
Contact	250-246-9511

Don't miss the Farmers' Market held on the Marina grounds on Sundays from 10 am to noon, May through mid September where you can purchase local produce, baked goods, canned goods, crafts, and Native carvings.

THETIS ISLAND PUB

The Thetis Island Marina recently completed upgrades to the Pub and other upland buildings. The menu includes Halibut filet and BC Sockeye Salmon with tarragon lemon sauce on a bed of basmati rice served with steamed broccoli, or try the half Broiled Chicken served with garlic mashed potatoes. Burgers and Fish & Chips continue to be favorites; the burgers are hand-made and the Fish & Chips are available grilled or battered along with fresh cut potato French fries. Homemade meat pies, quiches, pasta dishes, and shell fish are also offered along with daily specials throughout the summer months.

Lunch/ Dinner	11:30am – 8pm Daily mid May – Sept. Pub open till 11pm Days/Hours Vary Off Season
Price	Moderate
Outdoor Seating	Yes, Deck, Summer Months
Contact	250-246-3464

Boaters are within steps of the Pub from the Marina docks and can enjoy the deck overlooking the Marina and Telegraph Harbour. A covered BBQ picnic area is available for groups and boat clubs and is a popular venue for pig roasts and barbecued meals prepared by the Marina and include all the fixings like corn on the cob, baked potatoes, and salads.

VANCOUVER ISLAND
Brentwood Bay

Pretty Brentwood Bay, located on the southeast bank of Saanich Inlet, draws boaters, who want to visit the world famous Butchart Gardens, relax at the five-star Brentwood Lodge & Spa, or visit the waterfront cafes.

Boaters have several options for short term and overnight stays in Brentwood Bay, including the Brentwood Public Dock, the Brentwood Bay Lodge Marina, and Anglers Anchorage Marina. The Port Side Marina (250-652-2211) also located in Brentwood Bay has a dinghy dock with a $5 usage fee. Anchorage is available in nearby Tod Inlet, be sure to check the tide tables. Short-term stays for dinghies are permitted at the Seahorses Café docks, while dining at the Café located next to the Ferry Landing. The docks in front of the Café belong to Compass Rose Cabins (250-544-1441) with overnight stays as available. Located upland is the Moodyville Store & Gift Shop (250-652-2081) and the Orient Restaurant (250-652-2203). The adorable Blue's Bayou Café is located next to the Brentwood Public Dock, which is south of the Ferry Landing.

Don't miss visiting the beautiful Brentwood Lodge & Spa offering a classy Pub & Café and the fine dining Seagrille venue with fabulous views. The romantic suite accommodations are first class, designed with adults and couples in mind. Overnight stays include use of the pool, spa, and the fitness room. Brentwood Lodge Marina offers kayak rentals and scuba diving classes located on the south side of the Ferry Landing. Visitors can take the glass-domed water shuttle to Butchart Gardens from the Lodge for a fee, which includes tickets to the Gardens and a half-hour ecological tour; the water shuttle leaves at 10:30am and 1:30pm May-October. Call the Brentwood Lodge Marina for reservations (250-652-3151) or (888-544-2079).

Butchart Gardens (250-652-5256 or 888-824-7314), located in Butchart Cove, close to Brentwood Bay, has four buoys and a 45 foot dinghy dock for boaters visiting the Gardens. Upon arrival, buzz in at the gate to purchase tickets and receive a map of the grounds. Don't miss visiting these beautiful Gardens (22 ha or 55 acres), where you can have Afternoon Tea from noon to 3 pm in the historic Butchart home or enjoy lunch or dinner offered seasonally (250-652-8222). You can also dine at the Blue Poppy cafeteria or visit the Coffee Shop for sandwiches and pastries. During the months of July and August, low profile fireworks in the Gardens are presented at the Totem Pole location.

The Gardens began as an idea by Jennie Butchart to beautify a worked-out limestone quarry, which had supplied her husband's nearby Portland Cement Plant. The Gardens showcase beautiful plants, trees, lawns, fountains, and flowers, including Japanese, Italian, and Sunken gardens. The Gardens are lit at night with a last entrance time of 10:30 pm, off season hours vary.

Butchart Gardens Dinghy Dock 250-652-5256
www.butchartgardens.com

Dinghy dock approx. 45 ft and four buoys in Tod Inlet (Butchart Cove) for visitors of Butchart Gardens only. Upon arrival, buzz in at the gate for tickets and a grounds map.

Short-Term: Short term stays for tenders permitted at the dinghy dock while visiting the Gardens. No overnights at dinghy dock.

Overnight: Overnight stays are permitted without charge on any of the four buoys on a first come basis for purposes of visiting the Gardens.

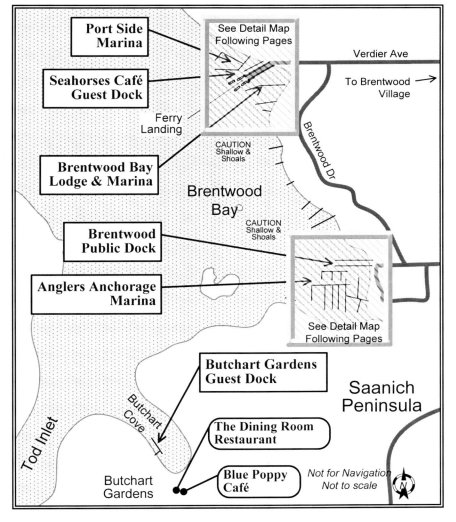

VANCOUVER ISLAND
Brentwood Bay

Anglers Anchorage Marina   250-652-3531
250-217-7494 Les

Marina with mostly permanent moorage with 600 ft of overnight transient moorage slips and side-tie as available. South of Brentwood Public Dock.
Short-Term: Call ahead for hourly stays.
Overnight: Overnight as available at $1 per foot with reservations.

Brentwood Bay Lodge Marina   250-652-3151
888-544-2079

A private 40 slip marina with restrooms, showers, laundry, fitness room, and restaurants.
Short-Term: Short term stays available without charge while dining at the Lodge.
Overnight: Moorage for most all size craft at $1.50/ft and $1.65/ft on holidays, call for reservations and slip assignment.

Brentwood Public Dock   250-652-4444
District of Central Saanich

Public dock with 70 feet of dock space, vessels limited to 32.8 feet. Rafting up to two (2) boats. Anchorage in nearby Tod Inlet, check tide tables.
Short-Term: Short term stays permitted up to 9 pm without charge.
Overnight: No overnight stays (no stays between 9 pm and 7 am).

Port Side Marina   250-652-2211
250-886-6323

Private marina with new upgrades; restrooms, showers, and laundry; power and water. Rail lift on site.
Short-Term: Short term stays permitted for dinghies with a $5 docking fee.
Overnight: Moorage for vessels 8 ft to 60 ft at $1.25/ft

Seahorses Café Dock   250-544-1565 Cafe
(Compass Rose Cabins)   250-544-1441 Compass Rose

Private docks belonging to the Compass Rose Cabins located in front of the Seahorses Café adjacent to the Ferry Landing.
Short-Term: Short term stays for dinghies permitted without charge while dining at the Café
Overnight: Overnight stays permitted as available at $1.25/ft, check in at the Café or call Compass Rose. Anchorage in nearby Tod Inlet.

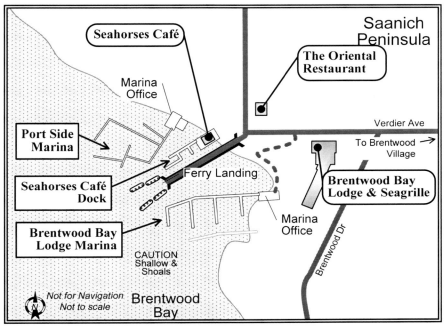

Brentwood Bay - North

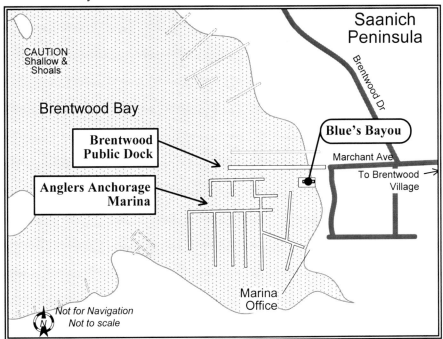

Brentwood Bay - South

BLUE'S BAYOU CAFE

The Blue's Bayou Café is adjacent to the Brentwood Public Wharf on Marchant Street. The Café is absolutely adorable filled with a vibrant décor of hot chili peppers, crocodiles, Mardi-Gras masks, and jazz scene posters. Check out the crocodile on top of the Café building at the main entrance. The large deck overlooking Brentwood Bay is very popular during the summer months. The menu is vibrant too, offering Cajun style dishes and appetizers like the New Orleans Classic Jambalaya with jumbo shrimp, chicken, and Andouille sausage tossed in a hearty creole sauce served over steamed rice with warm cornbread. Other dinner entrees include the Mississippi Seafood Cannelloni and the Hickory Smoked Cracked Pepper Ribs. For lunch, try the Gator Gumbo with

Lunch	11:30am – 4:30pm Mon – Sat
Dinner	5pm – Close Mon-Sat
	Closed Sundays Closed Mon Oct-May
Price	Moderate
Outdoor Seating	Yes, Deck, Summer Months
Contact	250-544-1194

chicken, okra, and rice in a rich broth topped with corn tortillas; or perhaps the Bourbon Street Club sandwich with Cajun chicken, Capicoli ham, lettuce, sprouts, tomatoes, and Creole mayo wrapped in a Cajun tortilla. Don't miss this Cajun experience complete with lemonade, wine, beer, and other refreshing drinks.

Blue's Bayou Cafe

SEAGRILLE

The Seagrille is located in the five-star Brentwood Lodge with fabulous mountain and ocean Bay views. The dining space has a modern appeal with stylish furnishings, large colourful paintings, and striking wood paneling. Seafood is the main focus, including Seared Tuna, Roasted Ling Cod, and Queen Charlotte Halibut studded with pancetta on sweet potato flan with cane sugar, fresh basil, and roasted peppers. Quality meat dishes are also available like the triple-A Alberta Beef Tenderloin and the hazelnut crusted Rack of Lamb. Starters include the Roasted Squash Soup and the Ashened Brie & Beet Salad to name a few; and don't forget to ask about the special desserts. The Classy Pub & Café is located next to the Coffee Bar and serves wood-oven pizzas, sandwiches, seafood, and hearty burgers. For a lighter fare, visitors can enjoy the Sushi & Sake Bar located next to the SeaGrille, offering local seafood and fresh ingredients flown in daily from Japan.

Breakfast	8am – 10:30am Daily
Dinner	5:30pm – 11pm Daily
Lunch/ Dinner	Pub & Café 11:30am – 11pm Sun-Thur 11:30am – 12am Fri & Sat
Price	Moderate – Expensive Moderate Pub & Cafe
Outdoor Seating	Yes, Patio(s), Summer Months
Contact	250-544-5100 Seagrille & Wine Bar 250-544-5102 Pub & Cafe

Seagrille at Brentwood Lodge

VANCOUVER ISLAND
Brentwood Bay

SEAHORSES CAFE

Seahorses Café, adjacent to the Ferry Landing at Brentwood Bay, is a fun eatery located right on the docks. There is ample outdoor seating with great views of the Bay. This cute Café serves burgers, sandwiches, wraps, and quesadillas for lunch along with soups, salads, and lighter fare like crab cakes and garlic prawns; or try the Baked Brie on Baguette with roasted garlic, spinach, and house made raspberry coulis. Main courses include steak, chicken, and seafood dishes like the Red Snapper or the Maple Glazed Salmon served with rice and seasonal vegetables. Brunch is available on the weekends until noon and includes scrambles, Egg Benny's, and French Toast. For a special treat be sure to visit the Seahorses Café on Friday evenings for live music.

Lunch	11am – 5pm Daily
Dinner	5pm – 8pm Mon-Thur 5pm – 8:30pm Fri-Sun
Brunch	9am – Noon Fri-Sun
Price	Moderate
Outdoor Seating	Yes, Deck, Summer Months
Contact	250-544-1565

Seahorses Cafe

Seahorses Cafe

Seahorses Cafe

VANCOUVER ISLAND
Chemainus Bay

The community of Chemainus is a delightful town to visit, offering cute cafes, shops, and numerous outdoor murals depicting local history. Boaters appreciate the recently expanded and improved docks with power, water, restrooms, and showers. The adjacent small Ferry Landing shuttles passengers and cars to nearby Thetis and Kuper Islands. Once docked, boaters will be within steps of "Old Town" Chemainus and within a .8 km (1/2 mile) walk to the town's upper area, where you will find the Visitor Centre, the Museum, Water Wheel Park, and the Chemainus Theatre. Artistic murals and fun cafes and shops are located in both areas of town.

Thanks to the citizens of Chemainus and the Chemainus Murals Project, this small town once known for mining, fishing, and lumber industries of an earlier time, has transformed itself into a charming tourist and boater's destination. "The Little Town That Did" expresses its heritage through large murals on the sides of buildings painted by artists drawn from all over the globe and is considered the world's largest outdoor gallery. You can follow the painted footprints on the sidewalks for a self-guided tour or take the 45 minute group walking tour guided in character with Isabel Askew (1850) offered at 5 dollars per person Wednesday through Saturday at 10am, 12:30pm, and 2pm; meet at the Chemainus Visitor Information Centre (250-246-3944). Another option is to take the "Horse Drawn Mural Tours" or the "Simulated Steam Train Tour" (250-246-5055), which start from the Water Wheel Parking Lot. To view artifacts and learn more about the history of Chemainus, visit the Chemainus Valley Museum (250-246-2445) at 9799 Water Wheel Crescent.

The charm of Chemainus is due to the historic homes and buildings as well as the bakeries, cafes, art galleries, gift shops, and murals. The beautiful Chemainus Theatre (250-246-9820 or 800-565-7738) at 9737 Chemainus Road presents professional live theatre and also houses the Playbill Dining Room. For area transportation, call the Saltair Taxi (250-252-0905).

Chemainus Municipal Docks

Chemainus Municipal Dock   250-246-4655   VHF 66A
www.northcowichan.bc.ca

A public municipal dock(s) with power, water, restrooms, and showers; 360 feet of usable space. Overnight reservations accepted.

Short-Term: Short term stays permitted May-Sept. as available, $5 under 40 feet and $10 over 40 feet with a 2 hour maximum stay.

Overnight: Moorage available for all size craft, rates vary as posted. Use self-registration payment box on office door upland from ramp.

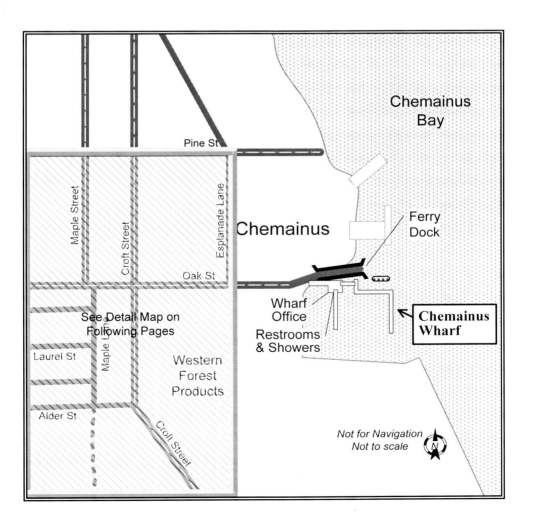

VANCOUVER ISLAND
Chemainus Bay

CHEMAINUS RESTAURANTS			🍽
49ᵗʰ Parallel Grocery	Groceries	2835 Oak Street	250-246-3551
Amineh's	Pizza, Pasta, Meats	9779 Willow Street	250-246-5335
Barnacle Barney's	Fish 'N Chips	2869 Oak Street	250-246-2710
Billy's Delight Parlor	Ice Cream, Soups, Sandwiches	9739 Willow Street	250-246-4131
Bonnie Martin Restaurant	Burgers, Steak, Sandwiches	2877 Mill Street	250-246-1068
Book Nook Café	Coffee, Muffins	2859 Oak Street	250-246-9188
Cara Vaggio Café	Coffee, Chocolate, Milkshakes	9756C Willow Street	250-246-3613
Chemainus Bakery	Pasties, Pastries	2871 Oak Street	250-246-4321
Chemainus Foods	Grocery, Deli	9790 Willow Street	250-246-9412
Chemainus Sushi	Sushi To-Go	Croft & Oak	250-324-1237
Dancing Bean Café	Espresso, Wraps, Seafood, Pasta	9752 Willow Street	250-246-5050
Ding Ho Chemainus	Chinese Cuisine	2857 Oak Street	250-416-0338
Fans Sports Grill	Pub Fare	2876 Mill Street	250-246-3486
Harbourside Café	Burgers, Chicken, Soup, Fish, Pies	2885 Laurel Street	250-416-0107
Kudo's	Japanese Cuisine	9875 Maple Street	250-246-1046
Meadowvale Farm	Gourmet Foods	9828 Unit B Croft	250-246-4608
Playbill Dining Room (Wed-Sat)	Seafood, Meats, Pasta, Salads	9737 Chemainus Road	250-246-9800 Ext 2, Ext 8
Small Tall Treats	Muffins, Sweets, Soups, Sandwiches	9780B Willow Street	250-246-3008
The Garden Eatery (outdoor, seasonal)	Greek Cuisine	9748 Willow Street	250-246-4199 (April–Sept.)
The Muffin Mill	Muffins, Coffee, Soups, Sandwiches	9772 Willow Street	250-246-1260
Twisted Sisters	Pasties, Quiche, Salads, Soups	9885 Maple Street	250-246-1541

CHEMAINUS RESTAURANTS CONTINUED			
Utopia Bakery Café	Soups, Sandwiches	9780-A Willow St.	250-246-9992
Willow Street Café	Soups, Wraps	9749 Willow Street	250-246-2434

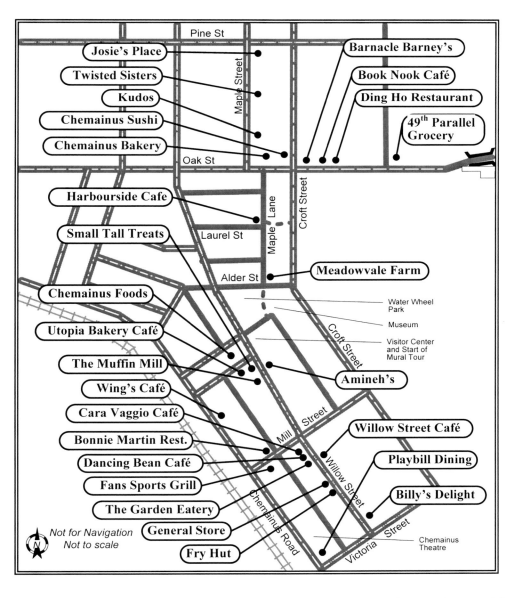

Pine St

Josie's Place

Twisted Sisters

Kudos

Chemainus Sushi

Chemainus Bakery

Oak St

Maple Street

Barnacle Barney's

Book Nook Café

Ding Ho Restaurant

49th Parallel Grocery

Harbourside Cafe

Small Tall Treats

Laurel St

Maple Lane

Croft Street

Chemainus Foods

Alder St

Meadowvale Farm

Water Wheel Park

Museum

Utopia Bakery Café

The Muffin Mill

Wing's Café

Cara Vaggio Café

Bonnie Martin Rest.

Dancing Bean Café

Fans Sports Grill

The Garden Eatery

General Store

Fry Hut

Visitor Center and Start of Mural Tour

Amineh's

Croft Street

Mill Street

Willow Street Café

Playbill Dining

Billy's Delight

Willow Street

Chemainus Road

Victoria Street

Chemainus Theatre

Not for Navigation
Not to scale

DANCING BEAN CAFÉ

This intimate café with earth tone colours and accents serves locally roasted coffee and espresso drinks. Baked goods and egg dishes are offered during the morning hours like the "Incredible Eggs" scrambled with feta cheese, sundried tomatoes, spinach, and bacon. Delicious salads and sandwiches are available for lunch, including the Chicken Breast, Thai Tuna, and the Pacific Smoked Salmon with cream cheese, artichoke hearts, and fresh spinach. Special buffets are served twice a month between 6pm and 8pm: the Pasta Bar Buffet on the first weekend of the month, and the Indian-style Curry Buffet on the third weekend of the month. Don't miss Show Nights at the Dancing Bean hosting professional musicians and featuring a selection of entrees and appetizers, which change regularly.

Breakfast	8:30am – 11am Mon-Fri 9am – 11am Sat & Sun
Lunch	11am – 4pm Daily
Dinner	5pm – 8pm Thur, Fri, Sat Show Nights Only Days may vary
Price	Moderate
Outdoor Seating	No
Contact	250-246-5050 www.dancingbean.ca

No matter what, you are sure to have fun at the Dancing Bean Café. Stop by for coffee; view the changing art work; check out the sale items like soaps, hand creams, jewelry, and coffee; or stop by to enjoy the special menu offerings and desserts like the Chocolate Pecan Pie or the Raspberry Mango Cheesecake.

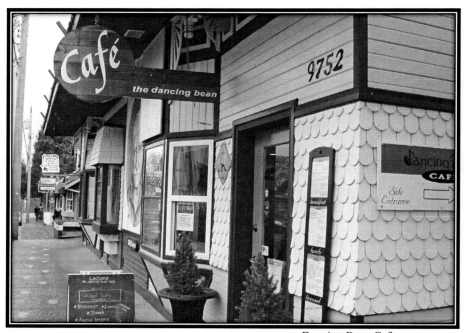

Dancing Bean Cafe

KUDO'S

Kudo's is located a short distance from the Chemainus Municipal Dock at 9875 Maple Street and has great Makis, Sushi, Donburi, and Sashimi. Kudo's also serves tempura, teriyaki, yaki udon (stir-fried thick noodles), and bento boxes with a variety of items. Don't forget the Miso soup or an appetizer like the Korokke, a breaded potato with beef or seafood. For a special treat, try the Shabu-Shabu Hot Pot for two with assorted vegetables, tofu, thick noodles, and thin sliced Shabu beef cooked at your table in a Shitake mushroom based broth, includes Sunomono Salad and Dessert of the Day. The dining space is attractive and comfortable with a beautiful side porch and lovely garden for summer enjoyment.

Lunch	11:30am – 2pm Wed-Sun Except Sun Off Season
Dinner	5pm – 9pm Wed-Sun
Price	Moderate
Outdoor Seating	Yes, Porch, Summer Months
Contact	250-246-1046

Kudo's Japanese Restaurant

VANCOUVER ISLAND
Chemainus Bay

WILLOW STREET CAFÉ

The Willow Street Café is a casual lunch venue housed in a 1920's historic building that once served as the Masonic Hall. Homemade soups come with all orders on the menu along with a green salad or pasta salad. Menu items include pizzas, quesadillas, and sandwiches like the Egg Salad Sandwich and the Curried Chicken Quesadilla, or try the Szechwan Veggie, or perhaps the Veggie Pizza. The Smoked Salmon Bagel and the Ham, Cheese, & Onion Quiche are nice choices for a late morning treat. The Café's sun porch with umbrella shaded tables is a popular gathering spot during the summer months and the perfect vantage point to watch all the activity on Willow Street.

Hours	8:30am – 6pm Daily Till 5pm Off-Season
Price	Moderate
Outdoor Seating	Yes, Porch, Summer Months
Contact	250-246-2434

Willow Street Cafe

Chemainus Mural

Horse Drawn Mural Tour

VANCOUVER ISLAND
Cowichan Bay

The Cowichan Bay Village is located in the southwest corner of Cowichan Bay. The area is popular with kayakers and bird watchers, who come to view over 200 species of migrant songbirds and shorebirds near the mouth of the Cowichan River. The Village is both fascinating and adorable, offering cafes, a bakery, cheese shop, gift shops, and fine dining venues. A large portion of the Village is built over the water on stilts creating its unique character. Don't miss visiting the Maritime Museum (250-746-4955) located on a 350 foot pier with pods housing exhibits ranging from history and boat building techniques to restored marine engines and restoration projects in progress. Children can enjoy building their own toy boats from a supply of wood pieces.

Several vineyard operations have been established in the area and are open for tours and wine tasting. Cherry Point Vineyards (250-743-1272) and Glenterra Vineyards (250-743-2330) at nearby Cobble Hill serve lunch during the summer months. For transportation call the Cobble Hill Taxi (250-743-5555).

The Village of Cowichan was founded by Samuel Harris, who later sold his property to Giovanni Baptiste Ordano, a resident in Genoa Bay. In 1863, Ordano built the Columbia Hotel which now houses The Masthead Restaurant. Around 1886, Ordano built a small shipyard to build rental boats; the building still stands and can be seen next to the Masthead Restaurant.

Today, Cowichan offers a variety of shops and eats, including a cheese shop, bread shop, and several gift shops. You will meet lots of friendly folk here too, like Bo owner of Bo's Boat Store, who is often seen wearing his colourful rainbow suspenders. Bo's Boat Store carries new and used marine supplies and can consign your marine "extras." If you are dining at the Oceanfront Grand Resort or staying in the Resort's accommodations, boaters may use the Resort's private dock. Transient moorage is available at several marinas in Cowichan Bay including Fishermen's Wharf.

The first Annual Cowichan Bay Spot Prawn Festival was held in May 2009. This new event hosts chef demonstrations, Spot prawn sampling, music, and Spot prawn sales off the boats at Fishermen's Wharf.

Bluenose Marina	250-748-2222	VHF 66A
www.bluenosemarina.com	250-715-8196 Marina Mngr.	

Full service marina offering permanent and transient moorage and one floating home rental. Power, showers, restrooms, and laundry. Transient moorage is located on concrete docks, call ahead for directions. Schooners restaurant upland.

Short-Term: Hourly stays at no charge while dining at Schooners.

Overnight: Moorage is $1.25 per foot; reservations recommended.

Dungeness Marina

250-748-6789   VHF 66A
www.dungenessmarina.com

A full service marina with power, restrooms, showers, and a café, offering 92 feet of guest space.

Short-Term: Short term stays for 2 hrs at $5 on guest dock until 2pm; call ahead for availability. Signage on transient dock.

Overnight: Moorage for all size craft at $1.25 per foot on guest dock or in unoccupied slips, call ahead for space assignment. Reservations recommended.

Fishermen's Wharf

250-746-5911   VHF 66
www.haa.bc.ca

Cowichan public wharf with short term and overnight stays during the summer months. Facilities include power, restrooms, showers, and laundry.

Short-Term: Short term stays permitted in available spaces on guest dock at no charge up to 2 pm. Rafting is encouraged.

Overnight: Moorage for most all size craft at $1 per foot plus power with rates in effect at 2 pm on guest dock. Use self-registration payment box at office on the Wharf.

Fishermen's Wharf

Oceanfront Grand Resort Dock   250-597-4280
www.thegrandresort.com

Private dock for guests of the Resort and The Grand Restaurant, 150 feet of space on an L-shaped dock. Follow pathway to pool and buzz door at pool side.

Short-Term: Short term stays permitted while dining at the Resort.

Overnight: Overnight stays for vessels of occupants staying in a hotel room.

Pier 66 Marina   250-748-8444
www.pier66marina.com

Marina with a store, fuel, and power. No restrooms or showers.

Short-Term: No hourly stays available.

Overnight: Moorage for boats up to 50 ft. by reservation at $1 per foot located on outer most dock marked "overnight moorage only."

True Grain Bread

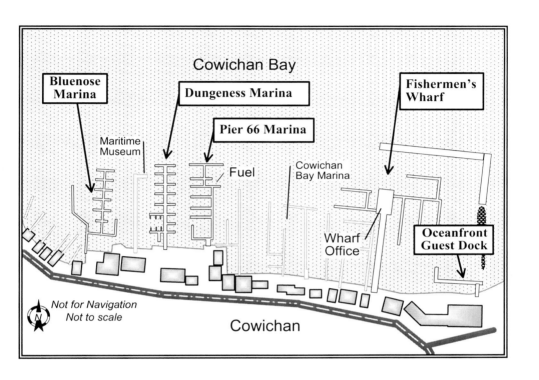

Cowichan Bay

Bluenose Marina

Dungeness Marina

Pier 66 Marina

Fishermen's Wharf

Maritime Museum

Fuel

Cowichan Bay Marina

Wharf Office

Oceanfront Guest Dock

Not for Navigation
Not to scale

Cowichan

Oceanfront Resort and Dock

COWICHAN BAY RESTAURANTS			🍽
Boathouse Café	Burgers, Panini, Sandwiches, Fish	1751 Cowichan Bay Road	250-709-9688
Bo's Boat Store	Espresso, Pastries, Marine Supplies	1725 Cowichan	250-746-1093
Cherry Point Vineyards	Seafood, Steak, Wine, Omelettes	840 Cherry Point Road	250-743-1272
Cowichan Bay Seafood Market	Fresh Fish Market	1751 Cowichan Bay Road	250-748-0020
Hilary's Cheese Co.	Specialty Chesses	1725 Cowichan Bay Road	250-746-7664
Liquid Café & Juice Bar	Espresso, Juice Drinks, Desserts	1721 Cowichan Bay Road	250-748-3800
Masthead Restaurant	Seafood, Steak, Chicken	1705 Cowichan Bay Road	250-748-3714
Rock Cod Café	Breakfast, Burgers, Fish, Sandwiches	1759 #3 Cowichan Bay Road	250-746-1550
Schooners	Seafood, Steak, Pasta, Pizza	1765 Cowichan Bay Road	250-748-2841
The Bay Pub	Specialty Burgers, Chicken, Seafood	1695 Cowichan Bay Road	250-748-2330
The Grand (Oceanfront Resort)	Breakfast, Steak, Seafood, Wraps	1681 Cowichan Bay Road	250-597-4280
Thistle's Café Glenterra Vineyards	Seafood, Salads, Wine Tasting	3897 Cobble Hill Road	250-743-2330
True Grain Bread	Hand Crafted Breads	1725 Cowichan Bay Road	250-746-7884
Udder Guy's	Ice Cream, Coffee, Candy	1721 Cowichan Bay Road	250-746-4300

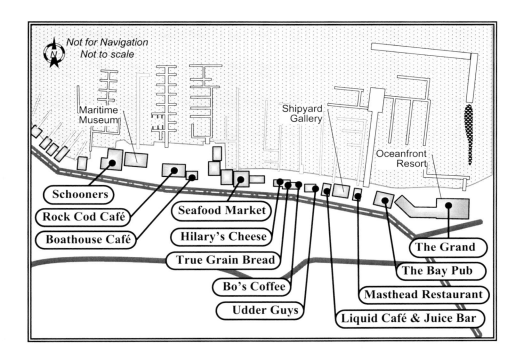

Not for Navigation
Not to scale

Maritime Museum

Shipyard Gallery

Oceanfront Resort

Schooners

Rock Cod Café

Boathouse Café

Seafood Market

Hilary's Cheese

True Grain Bread

Bo's Coffee

Udder Guys

The Grand

The Bay Pub

Masthead Restaurant

Liquid Café & Juice Bar

Rock Cod Cafe

VANCOUVER ISLAND
Cowichan Bay

MASTHEAD RESTAURANT

The Masthead Restaurant is located in a historic building once known as The Columbia Hotel built in 1863. Roadhouses were a necessity during the 1800's providing food and lodging to weary travelers along the wagon road from Victoria. Today the building serves as a fine dining venue for locals, tourists, and boaters. The meals are exquisitely prepared like the "Cowichan Bay Farm" Duck with roasted corn and goat cheese; or try the Pan Roasted BC Halibut with poached local mushrooms and smoked

Dinner	5pm – Close Daily
Price	Expensive
Outdoor Seating	Yes, Deck, Summer Months
Contact	250-748-3714

tomato and fennel sauce. The Chef's three course meal is offered each day starting with a soup or salad followed by a choice of entrees like the Rare Albacore Tuna or the Grilled Quist Farm Flank Steak with roasted red peppers, followed by a trio of desserts. Be sure to try one of the Vancouver Island Estate wines, which are purchased and reserved well in advance of each harvest for the enjoyment of restaurant patrons.

Masthead Restaurant

CHERRY POINT VINEYARDS BISTRO

The Cherry Point Vineyards located near Cowichan is worth a visit for the excellent wine tasting, the self-guided tours, and the delicious bistro food service offered outdoors on the lovely patio during the summer months and indoors during the cooler season. Cherry Point is home to the world famous Cowichan Blackberry Port. In addition, the winery has received numerous awards at the prestigious All Canadian Wine Championships and the Northwest Wine Summit. Guests can enjoy west coast cuisine with fresh local ingredients like the West Coast Seafood Platter with Dungeness crab and shrimp cakes, garlic prawns, steelhead lox, salmon cake, tuna, scallops, and roasted red pepper coulis. The Assorted Artisan Bread Platter is also nice, served with roasted red pepper hummus, red onion chutney, and garden herb whipped butter.

Lunch/ Brunch	11:30am – 4pm Wed-Sun May - September Days Vary Off Season
Wine Tasting	10am – 5pm Daily Hrs. Vary Off Season
Price	Moderate
Outdoor Seating	Yes, Patio, Bistro Months
Contact	250-743-1272
Note	Cobble Hill Taxi 250-743-5555

Waiters will help you choose the perfect wine for each menu selection. For a more casual lunch you can purchase picnic items from the wine shop and enjoy the lower patio picnic grounds. Don't forget to ask Cherry Point about the First Nations Salmon Bake and other special events.

ROCK COD CAFÉ

The Rock Cod Café is located just upland from the Dungeness Marina docks. This cute Café is a local's favorite, serving up great fish 'n chips, burgers, and salads along with lots of friendly service. Ample seating is available inside, where you will find seafaring murals and other nautical décor, or you can enjoy the outside deck overlooking the Marina. Fish 'n chip dinners are served with home-cut fries and coleslaw; choose between battered or grilled fish. Don't forget about the appetizers like the Oysters & Dip, or the Rock Cod Clam Chowder.

Lunch/ Dinner	11am – 9pm Daily Hrs. Vary Off Season
Price	Moderate
Outdoor Seating	Yes, Deck, Summer Months
Contact	250-746-1550

"Asian Bowls" are also available, including the Crispy Halibut Bowl drizzled with sweet Thai sauce served over Szechuan stir-fry with baked noodles. Weekly specials include Red Snapper Fajitas and the Shellfish Bouillabaisse to name a few. There is something for everyone at the Rod Cod, including a menu for the children.

VANCOUVER ISLAND
Cowichan Bay

THISTLE'S CAFÉ

Thistle's Café is located on the lovely grounds of the Glenterra Vineyards on Cobble Hill accessible by taxi (250-743-5555). Glenterra offers estate grown small lot wines, which can be enjoyed at the Thistle's Café with indoor and outdoor seating. The menu is seasonally inspired and may include the Roasted Mediterranean Vegetable Strudel with eggplant, zucchini, sundried tomatoes, mushrooms, olives, and feta wrapped in phyllo, served on arugula with a balsamic glaze; or try the Prawn Cakes and local organic green salad with vinaigrette and tropical salsa. Dinner specials include Shot Ribs, Fresh Halibut, and Wild Sockeye Salmon. Don't forget to ask about the fresh seasonal desserts.

Lunch/	11:30am – 5pm Thur-Sun
Dinner	5pm – Close Fri & Sat
Winery	11:30am – 6pm Daily May - December
Price	Moderate
Outdoor Seating	Yes, Patio, Summer Months
Contact	250-743-2330

THE GRAND

The Grand Restaurant is located in the Oceanfront Resort, which has its own guest dock with ample space and convenient moorage for patrons of the Resort. This fine dining venue has grand views of Cowichan Bay and Mount Tzouhalem and provides a relaxing stop any time of day. Breakfast includes French Toast, Salmon Scramble, Eggs Benedict, and other traditional breakfast items; or you can enjoy the breakfast buffet offered twice on Sundays. Lunch mains include fish, chicken, and beef sandwiches like the Blackened Halibut with chipolte aioli, sprouts, and baby spinach in a mango vinaigrette; or choose the Crab Cakes, or perhaps the West Coast Caesar Salad with salmon, shellfish, and shaved parmesan.

Breakfast	7:30am – 11am Mon-Sat till 9am Sundays
Lunch	11am – 5pm Daily
Dinner	5pm – 9pm Mon-Thur 5pm – 10pm Fri & Sat
Buffet	at 10am and Noon Sundays
Price	Moderate - Expensive
Outdoor Seating	Yes, Street-side Deck, Summer Months
Contact	250-597-4281

Dinner entrees include meat and seafood dishes like the Grilled Cajun Wild Sockey Salmon served with risotto; or try the Free Range Chicken with Burgundy demi glace and gorgonzola.

SCHOONERS

Schooners, overlooking Cowichan Bay, expresses all the character of this seaside village offering a pretty dining room, a lovely lounge, and a large outdoor deck from which to enjoy the beautiful sunsets. A Pizzeria adjoins the deck accessed through a separate entrance where you can order a variety of "take-out" pizzas. The separate restaurant and lounge serves charbroiled meats and pasta dishes along with soups and salads. Start with the Lobster Chowder or Feature Soup followed by the Beef Tenderloin or the Chargrilled Chicken Breast;

Restaurant & Lounge	11:30am – 9pm Tue-Thur & Sun 11:30am – 9:30pm Fri & Sat
Pizzeria	Same hours
Price	Moderate
Outdoor Seating	Yes, Large Deck Summer Months
Contact	250-748-2841

Or try the Salmon & Asparagus Linguine tossed in a white wine and garlic cream sauce garnished with basil and marinated cherry tomatoes. Wraps, quesadillas, and burgers are available for lunch along with yam fries and zucchini sticks. Boaters and locals alike enjoy this seaside venue, and boaters appreciate the convenience of docking at the Bluenose Marina while dining at Schooners.

Schooners Deck

VANCOUVER ISLAND
Genoa Bay

Genoa Bay is a beautiful small tranquil bay with a treed shoreline tucked in the northern portion of Cowichan Bay. Welcoming staff at Genoa Bay Marina make you feel right at home.

The Marina offers short term and overnight stays with full service, including nice restrooms and laundry facilities. The Marina Store is open till 5pm daily and carries grocery items, snacks, gifts, books, video rentals, and marine supplies. Moorage guests are invited to participate in "Music Nights" scheduled throughout the season ranging from classical and jazz to Cajun and folk. Call the Marina for dates or go to their web site for the latest schedule. Be sure to visit The Gallery (250-746-5506), located on the docks in a charming house boat, for a nice selection of pottery, sculptures, and paintings. Located upland is the Genoa Bay Café, which has excellent food and a lovely outdoor deck overlooking the Marina.

Genoa Bay received its name from the early Italian pioneer, Giovanni Baptiste Ordano, who arrived in the area in 1858 and opened the first store in the district at Tzuhalem. Ordano named this Bay after his birthplace, Genoa, Italy. If you wish to explore beyond the confines of the Marina, you can arrange for a rental car pickup through the Marina, or ask the Marina about their shuttle van service available to moorage guests. Genoa Bay Marina continues to draw the interest of independent boaters as well as boating clubs and groups who reserve the gazebo with its covered kitchen area, fire pit, and BBQ located upland near the Café. A covered picnic area is also available on the docks.

Genoa Bay Marina

Genoa Bay Marina

250-746-7621   VHF 66A
www.genoabaymarina.com

Full service marina open year-round; power, nice restrooms, showers, laundry, store, and café. 1200 feet of dock space. Fuel nearby at Cowichan.

Short-Term: Short term stays located on A Dock (as available) at no charge.

Overnight: Moorage available for most size craft at $1.30 per foot on B, C, and D docks. Reservations a must during the summer season. Anchorage in Bay.

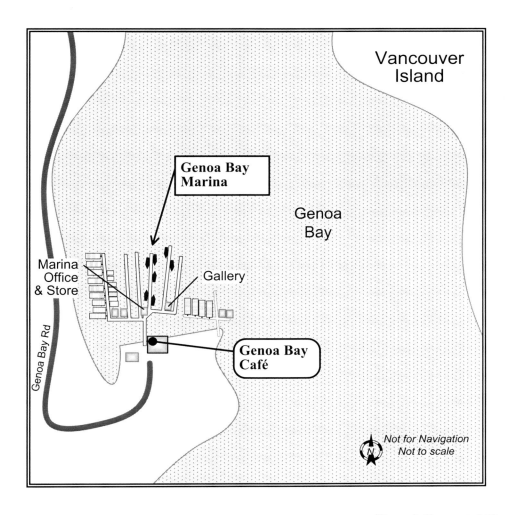

VANCOUVER ISLAND
Genoa Bay

GENOA BAY CAFE

A casual venue with fine dining best describes the Genoa Bay Café, located just upland from the Marina. The Café serves fresh seafood, produce, meats, and poultry from local Cowichan Valley farms. The cute interior has country-style furnishings with linen napkins and wine goblet set tables. The outdoor deck overlooking the Marina has nice patio furniture shaded with large umbrellas and is a popular stop during the summer months. Start your dining experience with a "Feature Wine" or "Feature Beer" along with Baked Brie or Smoked Salmon & Shrimp Chowder.

Lunch	11:30am – 2:30pm Daily
Dinner	5pm – 9pm Daily Days Vary Off Season
Price	Moderate - Expensive
Outdoor Seating	Yes, Deck, Summer Months
Contact	250-746-7621 or 800-572-6481

Entrée choices include the signature Rack of Lamb with mango chutney glaze; the Smoked Pork Tenderloin, the slow Roasted BBQ Ribs, and the Seared Tuna with a maple, balsamic glaze. The less formal lunch menu includes Soup of the Day, Fresh Halibut, Shrimp & Cheese Omelette, and Chicken Burger Apple BBQ. The Smoke Salmon Bagel Melt is another favorite. Don't miss the award winning Chocolate Pecan Pie or the special Genoa Bay Cheesecake. The Genoa Bay Café is a genuine boater's delight.

Genoa Bay Café

Genoa Bay Café

Genoa Bay Café

VANCOUVER ISLAND
Birds Eye Cove

Birds Eye Cove is located in the southwest corner of Maple Bay and offers boaters short term and overnight stays at three marinas; Birds Eye Cove Marina, and Maple Bay Marina; and for yacht club reciprocal members, The Maple Bay Yacht Club Marina. Chisholm Island located on the south side of Maple Bay Marina was named after William Chisholm, who homesteaded the property in 1860, which remained in the family for a 100 years. The whimsical name "Birds Eye Cove" came from Captain Richards, who surveyed the area earlier in 1858.

You can stop in for lunch or dinner at the Shipyard Pub & Restaurant located at Maple Bay Marina or shop at "The Market" (250-748-2100), where you can purchase groceries and gift items or visit the coffee bar for pastries, ice cream, sandwiches, hot dogs, and pizza. Located next to The Market is The Marine Supply Store (250-748-9199) for all your maintenance needs. An open pavilion picnic area called the "Quarterdeck" is available by reservation for clubs and group events. If you wish to explore the area by car, the Maple Bay Marina can help you arrange for a Budget car or truck rental pick up. Overnight moorage guests can use the Marina's Courtesy Shuttle Van for trips to and from the city of Duncan with prior arrangement.

The beautiful Quamichan Inn (250-746-7028) provides pick-up service for boaters from the marinas in Birds Eye Cove and from the public wharf in Maple Bay. This historic Inn and fine dining venue is definitely worth a visit. Call ahead for reservations and pick-up service.

Birds Eye Cove Marina	250-746-5686	VHF 66A	

Marina with permanent and transient moorage. Services include power, fuel, store, and restrooms (no showers). Transient space is located on the north dock just around from the fuel dock, 190 feet.

Short-Term: 1-2 hr short term stays on north dock as available, rates vary by overall length, check in at the fuel dock.

Overnight: Overnight stays in unoccupied slips and on north dock, call ahead for availability, rates approx. $1/ft. Anchorage in Cove.

Maple Bay Marina	250-746-8482	VHF 66A	
	www.maplebaymarina.com		

A full service marina with power, fuel, restrooms, showers, laundry, store, and restaurant. 50-ton travel lift. Floatplane service to Vancouver.

Short-Term: Short term stays permitted as available; no fee up to 2 hrs, a $5/hr fee for 2-4 hrs after which overnight fees apply. Check in at fuel dock.

Overnight: Moorage available for most size craft on H dock (fuel dock), and 30ft and under south side, 31-50 ft north side; vessels over 50 ft on ends of E, F, G, & I docks. Rates are $1.35/ft summers and .95/ft shoulder season. Anchorage nearby.

Maple Bay Marina

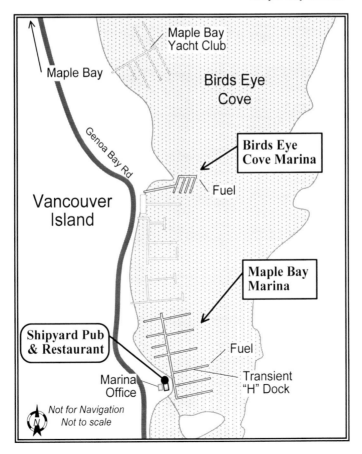

Maple Bay Yacht Club

Birds Eye Cove

Maple Bay

Genoa Bay Rd

Birds Eye Cove Marina

Fuel

Vancouver Island

Maple Bay Marina

Fuel

Shipyard Pub & Restaurant

Marina Office

Transient "H" Dock

Not for Navigation
Not to scale

N

VANCOUVER ISLAND
Birds Eye Cove

SHIPYARD PUB & RESTAURANT 🍽

The Shipyard Pub & Restaurant at Maple Bay Marina is housed in one of the original buildings of a shipyard that stood at this site. Note the old marine engines and other hardware painted and displayed around the building. The Restaurant portion is very inviting with linen set tables and two dining levels overlooking the Marina. The cozy Pub sports warm colours and historic photos and offers cocktails and wine as well as draught, bottled beers, and coolers and ciders. Enjoy an appetizer with your favorite drink like the Tug Boat potato skins stuffed with scallops, shrimp, and dill cream sauce baked with cheddar; or try the Crab Cakes or the Crab-Spinach-Artichoke Dip. Lunch selections include salads, sandwiches, burgers, wraps, and

Lunch	11am – 5pm Daily
Dinner	5pm – 9pm Sun-Thur 5pm – 10pm Fri & Sat
Pub	Open till Late
Price	Moderate
Outdoor Seating	Yes, Patio, Summer Months
Contact	250-746-1026

pasta dishes. The Shipyard Burger with Jack Daniels BBQ sauce is a good choice as is the Shipyard Seafood Fettuccini. The more formal dinner menu includes steak, chicken, and seafood dishes like the Cashew Crusted Halibut topped with sweet chili orange cream, served with seasonal rice and daily vegetables.

Shipyard Pub & Restaurant

QUAMICHAN INN

The Quamichan Inn is located at 1478 Maple Bay Road and offers a fine dining venue with complimentary pick-up service for boaters. The Inn was built in 1911 and is situated on three and a half acres with lovely manicured lawns and gardens. The dining rooms are adorned with period antiques and wallpaper along with old photographs and paintings. Entrees are exquisitely prepared and presented including Duck, Game, Lamb, Beef, and Seafood dishes. Try the Slowly Braised Lamb Shanks, the Classic Indian Curry, or the Panfried Duck Breast served with cranberry, Cointreau Seville relish, and mushroom raviolis finished with rich wine demi

Lunch	11:30am - 2pm Thursdays
Dinner	5:30pm – Close Wed-Sun
Brunch	10am – 2pm Sundays
Price	Expensive
Outdoor Seating	Yes, Patio, Summer Months
Contact	250-746-7028

glace; don't miss the starters like Escargot or the Baked Brie. For a lighter fare, visit the Inn for lunch on Thursdays and enjoy the special soups, salads, or sandwiches and smaller entrees. Sunday Brunch selections include omelettes, French toast, and special Egg Bennies, all served with home-cut hashbrowns and fruit salad.

Quamichan Inn

VANCOUVER ISLAND
Maple Bay

The seaside community (community of homes) at Maple Bay has lovely smooth, pebbled beaches with beautiful views of the Bay and Saltspring Island. It has been noted that the late, famous Jacques Cousteau considered this protected Bay one of his favorite diving spots. Maple Bay attracts swimmers, beach combers, boaters, and kayakers throughout the spring and summer months.

Boaters can dock at the Municipal Wharf at Maple Bay and dine at the classy Grapevine Restaurant or eat at the adjacent Brigantine Inn Pub, which has its own guest dock. Overnight stays are permitted at the Public Wharf with fees as posted.

Brigantine Inn Pub Dock	250-746-5422
	Private Dock

A private 50 foot dock for patrons of Brigantine Pub.
Short-Term: Short term stays permitted while dining at the Pub.
Overnight: No overnight stays.

Maple Bay Public Wharf	250-715-8186 Harbour Manager
	Municipality of North Cowichan

Municipal wharf with 160 feet of available space. Underwater park off end of dock.
Short-Term: Short term stays permitted at no charge up to 4 pm.
Overnight: Overnight stays permitted at .55 per foot after 4pm, use self-registration payment box at head of ramp.

Maple Bay Public Wharf

Brigantine Pub Dock

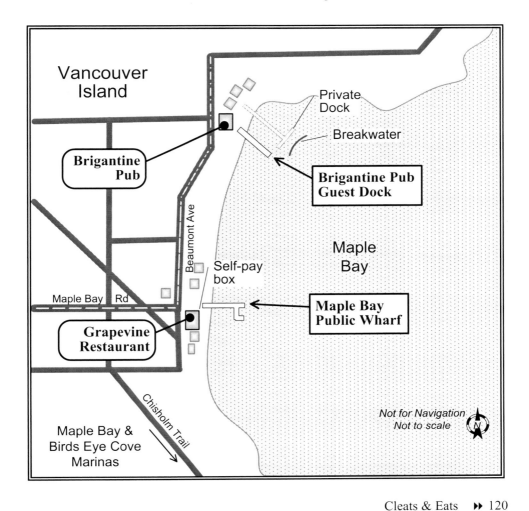

Vancouver Island

Private Dock

Breakwater

Brigantine Pub

Brigantine Pub Guest Dock

Beaumont Ave

Maple Bay

Self-pay box

Maple Bay   Rd

Maple Bay Public Wharf

Grapevine Restaurant

Chisholm Trail

Not for Navigation
Not to scale
N

Maple Bay & Birds Eye Cove Marinas

VANCOUVER ISLAND
Maple Bay

BRIGANTINE INN PUB

Boaters can tie-up at the Brigantine Inn Pub Dock, while dining at the Pub or shopping at the Liquor Store located on the ground level below the Pub. The Pub has great views of the Bay and Saltspring Island from its enclosed deck and from every pub table. Be sure to take note of the bar, which is actually the starboard side of a Brigantine sailing ship, including the mast, boom, and rigging; and note the floor of the Pub, which is like a ship's deck, covered in wide fir planking. Don't miss the historic photos on display, showing the Pub in earlier

Lunch/ Dinner	11am – 9pm Sun-Thu 11am – 10pm Fri & Sat
Price	Moderate
Outdoor Seating	Yes, Enclosed Deck
Contact	250-746-5422 Pub 250-746-5452 Store

times along with the now missing Inn portion of the building. The Brigantine Inn Pub serves soups, salads, burgers, and sandwiches. Evening entrees include pasta dishes, New York steak, and meat pies. For lunch, try the homemade Humus and Hot Crab Dip with pita bread, or try one of the homemade Hot Pot Pies, which are local favorites. On Sunday and Saturday nights starting at 9 pm, "The Brig" presents live entertainment from talented local musicians.

Brigantine Inn Pub

GRAPEVINE ON THE BAY

The Grapevine restaurant is located just upland from the Maple Bay Public Wharf. This classy restaurant has a distinctive décor displaying watercolours of First Nations totems and other art pieces along with native art throw rugs, which complement the orange and olive coloured walls. Natural wood pieces are used in the tables and chairs which fit in nicely with the décor. The meals are excellent, offered with fine wines and beautifully presented. Try the Wild Pacific Salmon, charbroiled and served on top of a vegetable medley finished with herbed white wine veloute; or try the Pork

Lunch	11:30am – 2pm Sun-Fri
Dinner	5:30pm – 8:30pm Sun-Fri
Price	Moderate – Lunch Expensive - Dinner
Outdoor Seating	Yes, Gazebo, Summer Months
Contact	250-746-0797

Tenderloin Oporto, chargrilled and severed on top of a bed of chorizo and infused kale finished with port wine. Be sure to conclude with one of the delicious desserts like the Cassis Mousse with pureed black currants on a layer of vanilla cheesecake drizzled with a cassis mirror glace, or perhaps the Crème Caramel made with an orange caramel sauce and candied orange zest. Lunch at the Grapevine is a treat, as well, and includes special dishes like the Smoked Caesar Salad, Pan Fried Oysters, the Crab & Avocado Salad, and the Panini of the Day. Don't miss this special venue overlooking lovely Maple Bay and Saltspring Island.

Grapevine

VANCOUVER ISLAND
Ladysmith Harbour

Ladysmith, once known as Oyster Harbour, is an active waterway with log booms and fishing fleets as well as pleasure craft. The Timothy Oyster Company is located at Ladysmith and carries on the town's tradition of processing oysters. Ladysmith has much to offer the casual boater with several options for hourly and overnight stays starting with the Maritime Society Docks located near the entrance of the harbor on the west bank. This lovely marina displays colourful flags along the transient moorage spaces and offers a children's fishing hole and picnic area on the docks. Don't miss the interesting historic maritime equipment and refurbished boats at the Maritime Society Museum houseboat. Located further in the Harbour is Fisherman's Wharf, offering transient space during the summer months when the fishing fleet is out. Next in line is Ladysmith Marina, a permanent moorage facility offering overnight transient stays as available. Page Point Marina, located across the Harbour, offers hourly stays while dining at the new Jimmy O's Grill and has some overnight transient slips.

The town of Ladysmith is most easily accessed from the Maritime Society Docks. A path leads from the head of the docks up to a large historic blue coloured warehouse, the home of the Ladysmith Waterfront Art Gallery (250-245-1252). Continue around the left side of the warehouse over the railroad tracks and past the abandoned ghost-like train station, keep left and walk to the lighted crosswalk at Roberts Street.

Ladysmith offers unique cafes, bakeries, and coffee shops, while maintaining its historic past of 100 year-old storefronts. Historic photos and painted pieces of logging and mining equipment are displayed throughout the town in honor of its heritage. Be sure to stop by Salamander Books (250-245-4726) at 535 First Avenue for a selection of history and maritime reference books; and don't miss the Old Town Bakery.

Festivals and events at Ladysmith include the Maritime Festival in late May or early June (www.ladysmithmaritimesociety.ca) celebrating the town's harbour front history; and Ladysmith Days in August hosting music, a parade, entertainment, and eats.

For further exploration in and around Ladysmith, contact the Saltair Taxi, Ladysmith Division (250-268-2114). Sites of interest include the Yellow Point Cranberry Farm (250-245-5283), a family run cranberry farm and home to the Cranberry Cottage Preserves located 10 minutes north of Ladysmith at 4532 Yellow Point Road. Guests can visit the grounds, take a guided tour, and purchase products at the farm store. A special Blossom Festival is held at the farm in late June.

VANCOUVER ISLAND
Ladysmith Harbour

Maritime Society Docks

Page Point Marina

VANCOUVER ISLAND
Ladysmith Harbour

Ladysmith Fisherman's Wharf 250-245-7511   VHF 66A
www.ladysmithfishermanswharf.com

Transient space is available during the summer months (full with fishing fleet Oct-April). Power, water, restrooms, showers, and laundry. Boat launch.

Short-Term: Short term stays are permitted without charge up to 4 hours. Take any open space, rafting encouraged.

Overnight: Moorage available for all size craft at $1.00 per foot plus power. Wharfinger collects fees directly. Anchorage near Bute Island.

Ladysmith Marina   250-245-4521   VHF 66A
www.ladysmithmarina.com

Private marina providing permanent moorage with transient space as available. Power, water, restrooms and showers.

Short-Term: No short term stays.

Overnight: Moorage for all size craft at $1.25 per foot as available in unoccupied slips; call ahead for availability and slip assignment; reservations accepted; security guard on site.

Maritime Society Docks   250-245-1146 or 616-6433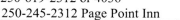
www.ladysmithmaritimesociety.ca

Community marina with guest space as available; power and water.

Short-Term: Short term stays permitted without charge up to 3 pm. Guest space marked yellow and blue.

Overnight: Moorage for all size craft as available marked yellow, $1.00/ft plus power, self-pay station upland at kiosk; wharfinger on site. Anchorage at Bute Is.

Page Point Marina   250-619-2312 or 4036
250-245-2312 Page Point Inn

Private marina with power, showers, laundry, restaurant, and 6 rooms at the Inn. Fuel dock to open spring 2010.

Short-Term: Hourly stays while dining at Jimmy O's Grill; 25 foot space shore side in front of restaurant; larger vessels call for available slip.

Overnight: Overnight stays at $1.50/ft in unoccupied slips, call ahead for assignment; on-site dock manager.

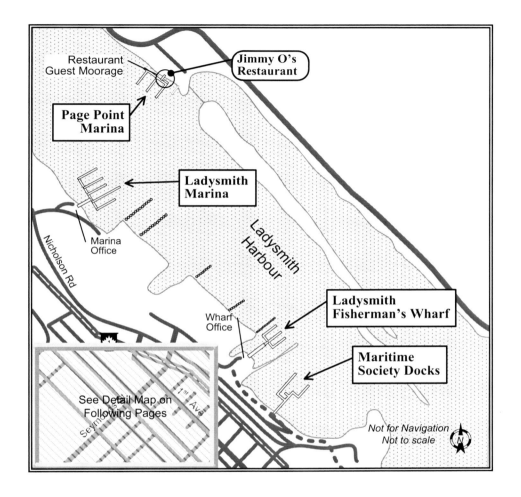

Restaurant
Guest Moorage

**Jimmy O's
Restaurant**

**Page Point
Marina**

**Ladysmith
Marina**

Marina
Office

Nicholson Rd

Ladysmith
Harbour

**Ladysmith
Fisherman's Wharf**

Wharf
Office

**Maritime
Society Docks**

See Detail Map on
Following Pages

1st Ave

Seymour

Not for Navigation
Not to scale

N

LADYSMITH RESTAURANTS			🍽
49th Parallel Grocery	Groceries, Deli, Bakery	10201 First Ave.	250-245-3221 (deliveries)
Appetit	Sandwiches, Tapas, Asian Stir-Fry	534 First Avenue	250-245-1321
Bouma Meats	Custom Cut Meats, Meat Pies	412 First Avenue	250-245-8131
Dragon City Rest.	Chinese Cuisine	316-328 Esplanade	250-245-8689
In The Bean Time	Breakfast, Coffee, Salads, Sandwiches	18 High Street	250-245-2305
George's	Full Menu	510 Esplanada	250-245-2292
Mr. Popper's	Popcorn, Candy	#1 32 High Street	250-245-8696
Northbrook Restaurant III	Steak, Pizza, Pasta, Seafood, Greek	734 Trans Canada Highway	250-245-5000 (deliveries)
Old Town Bakery	Breads, Buns, Pies, Doughnuts	510 First Avenue	250-245-2531
Printingdun Beanery	Coffee, Pastries, Sandwiches	341 First Avenue	250-245-7671
Roberts Street Pizza	Pizza, Pasta, Ribs	20 Roberts Street	250-245-1119 (deliveries)
Royal Dar	Indian Cuisine	120 Roberts Street	250-245-0168
Sporty Grill & Sportsman Pub	Burgers, Pasta, Greek	640 First Avenue	250-245-8857
The Phoenix	Cantonese Cuisine (delivery to docks)	112 High Street	250-245-3263
Transfer Beach Grill	Authentic Mediterranean	422 Esplanade	250-245-1211 (deliveries)
Wigwam	Asian Smorgasbord	438 First Avenue	250-245-3433

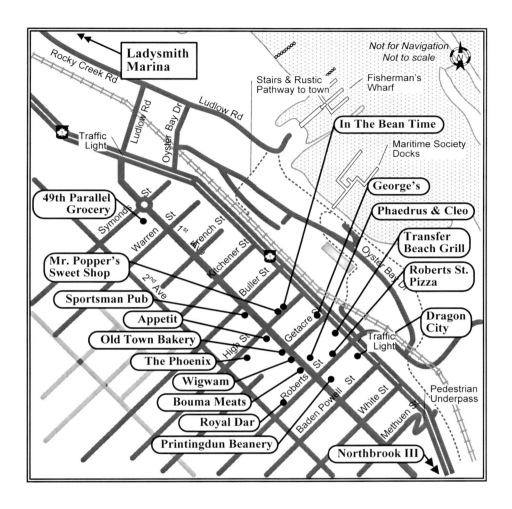

Ladysmith Marina

Rocky Creek Rd

Ludlow Rd

Ludlow Rd

Oyster Bay Dr

Not for Navigation
Not to scale

Stairs & Rustic
Pathway to town

Fisherman's
Wharf

In The Bean Time

Maritime Society
Docks

Traffic
Light

George's

Phaedrus & Cleo

49th Parallel
Grocery

Symonds St

Warren St

1st St

French St

Kitchener St

Buller St

Getacre St

Oyster Bay Dr

Transfer
Beach Grill

Roberts St.
Pizza

Mr. Popper's
Sweet Shop

2nd Ave

Dragon
City

Sportsman Pub

Appetit

Old Town Bakery

The Phoenix

High St

Roberts St

Traffic
Light

Wigwam

Bouma Meats

Royal Dar

Printingdun Beanery

Baden Powell St

White St

Methuen St

Pedestrian
Underpass

Northbrook III

Town of Ladysmith

VANCOUVER ISLAND
Ladysmith Harbour

PRINTINGDUN BEANERY

The Printingdun Beanery is located in town at 341 First Avenue and serves breakfast items all day as well as deli-sandwiches, soups, wraps, and specials like meat lasagna, quiche, and a variety of enchiladas. For lunch, try the Egg Salad Sandwich or the Roast Beef with a Pasta Salad or the Broccoli Salad. Don't miss the baked goods, including muffins, carrot cake, date squares, caramel bars, and a variety of tarts; and of course, the espresso drinks. During the summer months, you can sit outside on the large patio and enjoy a cool cider, beer, or glass of wine. The inside is adorable with country-style furnishings and shelving in front of a red brick wall displaying tea pots, coffee mugs, and other gift items for sale.

Breakfast Lunch	8am – 5pm Mon-Sat Closed Sundays
Price	Moderate
Outdoor Seating	Yes, Patio, Summer Months
Contact	250-245-7671

ROYAL DAR RESTAURANT

The Royal Dar Restaurant is located in town at 120 Roberts Street in an attractive home with a lovely garden entrance. The formal living rooms are utilized as the dining spaces with linen set tables, tile floors, pretty furnishings, and a nice living room fireplace. The Dar serves an extensive selection of quality Mediterranean and Indian cuisine, including salads, appetizers, lamb, chicken, and seafood dishes. Start with a Greek Salad or the Humus & Tzatziki with Pita bread followed by one of the special entrees like the Tandoori Chicken Breast marinated in yogurt and Tandoori spices; or try the

Lunch	11:30am – 2:30pm Tue – Sat
Dinner	5pm – Close Tue-Sun
Price	Moderate
Outdoor Seating	Yes, Patio, Summer Months
Contact	250-245-0168

Braised Lamb Shank roasted in a special curry sauce served with potatoes and carrots. Deli take-out is available from 11:30am till closing and includes whole Tandoori chickens, Salmon Filos, Spinach Pies, and the Famous Spicy Carrots.

TRANSFER BEACH GRILL

The Transfer Beach Grill is conveniently located at 422 Esplanade near the corner of Rogers Street. This cozy, intimate café offers several indoor tables and outdoor seating on the tree-shaded patio. The café walls are adorned with photographs from the home country of owner/chef George Liaros of Elafonissos Island in Greece. George enjoys greeting and conversing with each patron, while creating fresh West Coast seafood dishes, Mediterranean dishes, and authentic Greek and Moroccan foods from local produce. Start with the

Lunch	11am – 2pm Mon-Fri
Dinner	5pm – Close Mon-Sat
Price	Moderate
Outdoor Seating	Yes, Patio, Summer Months
Contact	250-245-1211

Moroccan-styled sizzling prawns with honey yogurt sauce, followed by the Roasted Leg of Lamb served with Greek salad, lemon roasted potatoes, and homemade tzatziki with warm pita wedges. For lunch, try one of the specialty wraps, sandwiches, or soups like the Roasted Veggie Pesto or the Mediterranean Tuna. You won't want to miss the Transfer Beach Grill, one of Ladysmith's newest local favorites.

Transfer Beach Grill

VANCOUVER ISLAND
Ladysmith Harbour

JIMMY O'S GRILL

Jimmy O's is located in the lovely Page Point Inn on the east side of Ladysmith Harbour. The dining room offers casual lodge ambiance with beautiful views of the Harbour and evening sunsets. Casual seating can be found at the fireside bar or on the outdoor deck overlooking Page Point Marina. You can choose from a selection of tasty appetizers for an afternoon lunch or lite dinner, including the Antipasto Platter, the Phyllo Crusted Brie with apple, and a helping of Crab Cakes and Punch Drunk Mussels. The Daily Soup with

Lunch/ Dinner	Noon – 9pm Daily Hours Vary Off Season
Price	Moderate
Outdoor Seating	Yes, Deck, Summer Months
Contact	250-245-2312

Halibut 'n Chips is also a nice choice for lunch. Dinner entrees include the Prime Rib, the Seafood Pot, Shepherd's Pie, and the Daily Pasta. Jimmy O's Grill is Ladysmith's only waterfront restaurant and is a real treat.

Jimmy O's Grill

Jimmy O's Deck

Page Point Dock and Inn

VANCOUVER ISLAND
Nanaimo Harbour

Nanaimo is known as the "Harbour City," which is fitting taken the large harbour basin with numerous marinas and ferry landings. Nanaimo was once the location of five separate native villages. Its name derives from a Coast Salish word Sney-ny-mo, the "meeting place," which continues to be true today. Nanaimo is within easy reach of the Gulf Islands and is both a starting point and a destination among Island cruisers.

Nanaimo Harbour is sheltered by Duke Point, Protection Island, and Newcastle Island. The channel or passage between Newcastle Island and Vancouver Island is referred to as Newcastle Island Passage and can be accessed from either the north end through Departure Bay or through the south end at Nanaimo Harbour. There are numerous marinas along this Passage, which are mostly for permanent moorage and repairs with the exception of Stones Marina located mid-way along the Passage offering hourly and overnight moorage; several pubs and eateries are within easy walking distance of Stones Marina.

Port Nanaimo located behind Protection Island in Nanaimo Harbour is the main guest moorage facility in the area. The Waterfront offers lovely parks and a walkway with shopping and dining within steps of the docks. Located upland from the Waterfront, the Downtown Arts District has numerous galleries, bookstores, and cafes. The Old City Quarter, southwest of the Waterfront and Downtown Districts, can be accessed via the Bastion/Fitzwilliam Street Bridge and is definitely worth a visit for its good restaurants and clothing boutiques.

Across the Harbour on Protection Island is the popular and well known Dinghy Dock Pub, Canada's only floating pub. Boaters can dock at the floats around the Pub or take the Protection Connection Ferry (250-753-8244) for a small fee from the Port Nanaimo Waterfront.

Don't miss visiting the Newcastle Island Marine Park, one of the most memorable places to experience Nanaimo's beauty and history. The docks at Newcastle Island have approximately 1500 feet of space for visiting boaters, or you can anchor in Mark Bay, or take the Nanaimo Harbour Ferry (250-729-8526) for a small fee from Maffeo Sutton Park (April–mid Oct). The Visitor Centre Pavilion on Newcastle Island offers food concessions (cash only). A trail map of the Island is posted at the Pavilion and points out many interesting sites. Interpretive signs along the trails recount the Island's history where you can find actual remnants of the past, including early Native villages, an 1850's coal mine at Shaft Point, an early 1900's Japanese herring saltery, and sandstone and pulp stone quarries. Call 250-754-7893 for additional information regarding Newcastle Island.

Newcastle Marine Park Docks   250-754-7893

Public Wharf of the British Columbia Park System with restrooms and showers, no power. Approximately 1500 feet of space. Camping and summer concessions.

Short-Term: Short term stays permitted at docks until 6 pm without charge.

Overnight: Overnight stays available at $2 per meter, cash only, attendant will come around to collect at 6 pm. Anchorage nearby.

Departure Bay
Ferry Landing

Brechin Public Boat Ramp

Newcastle Island

See Detail Map Following Pages

Stones Marina

Anchorage Marina
Newcastle Marina
Nanaimo Harbour City Marina

Newcastle Marine Park Docks

Moby Dick Marina
Townsite Marina

Protection Island

Nanaimo Yacht Club

Dinghy Dock Pub

Nanaimo

Nanaimo Harbour

Nanaimo Boat Basin

Not for Navigation
Not to scale

See Detail Maps Following Pages

VANCOUVER ISLAND
Nanaimo - Brechin Point

To access Brechin Point from the north, pass through Departure Bay and head southward past the Departure Bay Ferry Terminal and Pimbury Point into Newcastle Island Passage. This passage is also accessible from the south via the Nanaimo Waterfront District. Stones Marina is located about half way along Newcastle Island Passage on the west bank and offers transient overnight moorage as available. A guest dock for vessels under 35 feet is provided without charge while visiting the Marina's Muddy Waters Pub, a nice option and interesting outing for dinghies and runabouts coming from Nanaimo's main waterfront. The guest dock may be used for other restaurants in the area with prior permission, including the neighboring Beefeaters Restaurant and Millers Pub. Additional restaurants are located about ½ km (1/3 mile) south of Stones Marina on Stewart Avenue, including Nauticals Seafood Bar & Grill, a cute nautical theme restaurant; and the Iron Wok (250-754-8861) offering authentic Chinese cuisine and barbeque for eat-in or take-out.

Departure Bay is the terminus of the famous Nanaimo Bathtub Races held annually in late July. Spectators gather at the Departure Bay Beach for the exciting finish and folks celebrate afterwards at Millers Pub, the Beefeaters, and at the Muddy Waters Pub to honor everyone's successful finish. The Bathtub Races start from the Maffeo Sutton Park northwest of the Port Nanaimo docks. "Tubbers" make their way from Nanaimo Harbour, circle Entrance Island and Winchelsea Island before heading into Departure Bay, a grueling 58 km (36 mile) competition. For more information call 250-753- 7223 or visit www.bathtubbing.com.

Stones Marina	250-753-4232 www.stonesmarina.com	

Full service marina with power, repairs, haul out, restrooms, showers, and laundry; Pubs and restaurants nearby. Overnight and short-term transient moorage. Shallow area, check tide tables.

Short-Term:	Short term stays permitted on a 130 ft dock (for boats under 35 feet) in front of Muddy Waters Pub without charge while dining at the Pub; other pubs and restaurants by permission. Marina office located upland.
Overnight:	Moorage in slips for most size vessels at $1.00 per foot, call for reservations. Registration and payment instructions located at the head of the ramp.

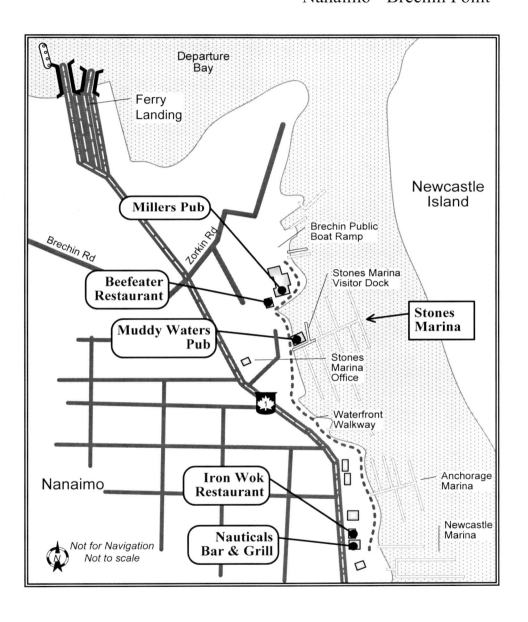

Departure Bay

Ferry Landing

Newcastle Island

Millers Pub

Brechin Rd

Zorkin Rd

Brechin Public Boat Ramp

Stones Marina Visitor Dock

Beefeater Restaurant

Stones Marina

Muddy Waters Pub

Stones Marina Office

Waterfront Walkway

Nanaimo

Iron Wok Restaurant

Anchorage Marina

Nauticals Bar & Grill

Newcastle Marina

Not for Navigation
Not to scale

BEEFEATERS CHOPHOUSE & GRILL

Located on Newcastle Passage, "Beefeaters" is one of Nanaimo's hidden gems featuring Prime Rib and AAA Alberta Beef; or you can enjoy seafood dishes like the Seafood Newburg with snapper, salmon, and prawns in a cream, garlic and fresh herb sauce. Other "Signatures" include the Marinated Lamb Chops, the Mediterranean Beef Souvlaki, and the Filet Mignon. For lunch, try the Prime Rib Sandwich with sautéed onions or perhaps the Greek Salad and Spinach Pie along with a selection from the extensive wine list. Take-out service is available from noon to closing, a nice option for boaters. The restaurant's interior is a pleasant surprise in comparison to the more

Lunch	10am – 4pm Daily
Dinner	4pm – 11pm Daily
Brunch	11am – 4pm Sundays
Price	Moderate
Outdoor Seating	Yes, Patio, Summer Months
Contact	250-753-2333

rustic exterior. The dining room has a formal yet casual appeal with burgundy and cream coloured linen tablecloths and floral print upholstered booths. Flower arrangements and large wine barrels add a finishing touch. Large picture windows provide a nice view of Stones Marina and Newcastle Passage.

Beefeaters ChopHouse & Grill

NAUTICALS SEAFOOD BAR & GRILL 🍽

Located about 1/2 km (1/3 mile) from Stones Marina, at 1340 Stewart Avenue, is the adorable Nauticals Seafood Bar & Grill; and as the name implies, this restaurant is full of nautical appeal with a large deck overlooking Newcastle Island Passage and Newcastle Marina. The Bar area has a glass top through which you can see seashells in a bed of sand and one of the interior walls showcases a collage of shells with fishing nets and other eye-catching décor throughout the restaurant. Nauticals serves fresh seafood,

Lunch/ Dinner	11:30am – 10pm Sun-Thur 11:30am – 11pm Fri & Sat Hours Vary Off Season
Price	Moderate
Outdoor Seating	Yes, Deck, Summer Months
Contact	250-754-8881

including lobster, crab, clams, oysters, beer battered fish 'n chips, Pirates Stew, and Cedar Plank Whiskey Salmon. You can order Steamed Seafood Platters for two like the "Seashells by the Seashore" or the "BC Bounty," which come with mini Corn on the Cob, steamed potatoes, and Andouille Sausage. Nauticals is a fun seafood eatery sure to please.

MUDDY WATERS PUB 🍽

The Muddy Waters Pub is located at Stones Marina on Newcastle Island Passage just south of Brechin Point and Offers a guest dock directly in front of the Pub for patrons arriving by boat. This rustic pub has ample indoor seating and a large outdoor deck overlooking the Marina and boating activity of Newcastle Passage. Folks come here to watch sporting events, play keno, participate in karaoke nights, and to enjoy live entertainment and visit with friends. The Pub serves burgers, salads, sandwiches, and wraps along with main dishes like the Newcastle Sirloin, a flame broiled center

Lunch/ Dinner	11am – 10pm Sun-Thur 11am – 11pm Fri & Sat Pub open till Late
Price	Moderate
Outdoor Seating	Yes, Deck, Summer Months
Contact.	250-754-4220

cut, topped with shrimp, crab, and Hollandaise sauce served with baked potato and fresh vegetables; or try the Italian Chicken poached with wine, sundried and diced tomatoes, pine nuts, and basil & garlic served on a bed of rice with vegetables. Fish 'n Chips is always a Pub favorite to be enjoyed with a select glass of wine, cooler, cider, or beer. Muddy's Liquor Store is located next door to the Pub and is open daily.

VANCOUVER ISLAND
Nanaimo - Port

The Port of Nanaimo is in the heart of the Nanaimo Waterfront and is the main facility for guest moorage. The LightHouse Bistro & Pub is one of the distinctive buildings along the Waterfront which is lined with gift shops, cafes, and a coffee shops. Two floating eateries are located at the docks where you can also purchase fresh fish from commercial fishermen.

Another distinctive building on the Waterfront is the 1853 octagonal Hudson's Bay Company Bastian (250-753-1821) built as the centre of a settlement dedicated to coal mining. The Bastion is now used as a hands-on museum with exhibits on all three floors depicting early life in Nanaimo. The cannons on the second floor are fired daily at noon in the summer months. A Farmer's Market is held on Fridays from 10am to 2pm mid-April through October in front of the Bastion on Pioneer Waterfront Plaza.

A walkway along the Waterfront extends north from the docks to the Maffeo Sutton Park, which is the beginning point for the famous Bathtub Races in late July and the Dragon Boat Festival in early July. Free outdoor concerts are held in the Park every Sunday throughout July and August and children love to play in the nautical themed playground.

The Downtown Art District, located upland from the Port of Nanaimo docks has numerous shops, galleries, and restaurants. The beautiful Port Theatre (250-754-8550 or 4555) is located at 125 Front Street and presents music, dance, comedy, and theatre programs. History buffs will enjoy the Nanaimo Museum (250-753-1821) located in the new Vancouver Island Conference Centre (100 Museum Way and Commercial St.), which features community history, coal mining, and First Nations history. Don't miss visiting the "Old City Quarter" where the old 1886 Railway Station is located and the 1887 Occidental Hotel. The area has great restaurants, clothing boutiques, and day spas. To access this area of town, walk up Bastion Street, pass over the bridge, and continue along Fitzwilliam to Wesley Street, a .6 km (1/3 mile) walk.

Transportation options to explore Greater Nanaimo include: the Budget Rent-A-Car at 33 S. Terminal Ave. (250-754-7368); AC Taxi (250-753-1231); and Swiftsure Taxi (250-753-8911). A nearby point of interest is the Petroglyph Provincial Park located at the south end of town off Highway 1 between Haliburton Street and Highview Terrace. Mythological creatures and other symbolic designs are outlined into the sandstone surface of the rock by Native people of an earlier time.

Dinghy Dock Pub	250-753-2373	
	www.dinghydockpub.com	

Private docks belonging to the Dinghy Dock Pub; eight fingers 40 feet each. The north side slips are reserved. "Protection Connection Ferry" docks on south side.

Short-Term: Short term stays permitted while dining at the Dinghy Dock Pub.

Overnight: No overnight stays. Anchorage in nearby Mark Bay.

Nanaimo Port	250-754-5053	VHF 67	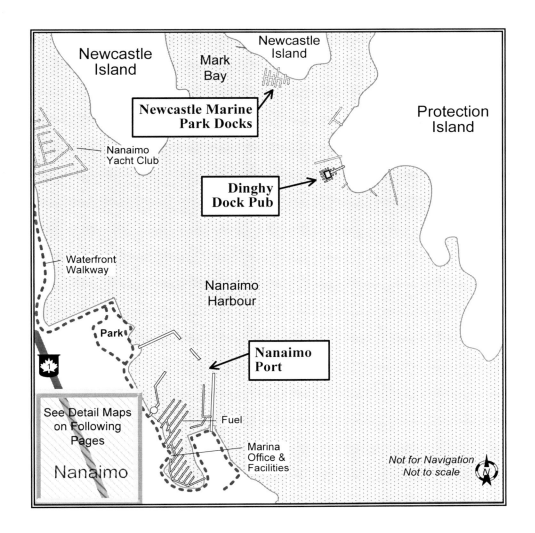
	www.npa.ca		

Full service marina including power, pumpout, fuel, restrooms, showers, and laundry. Small vessels docks c, d, and e; large vessels use south breakwater pier.

Short-Term: Short term stays are without charge up to 3 hours. Stays of 3-6 hours are charged a half-day rate. Check in at office upland.

Overnight: Stays over 6 hours and overnight stays are charged $1.15 per foot plus power, rates vary seasonally. Call ahead to be directed to a slip, reservations a must during the busy summer months.

Newcastle Island

Newcastle Island

Mark Bay

Newcastle Island

Protection Island

Newcastle Marine Park Docks

Nanaimo Yacht Club

Dinghy Dock Pub

Waterfront Walkway

Nanaimo Harbour

Park

Nanaimo Port

See Detail Maps on Following Pages

Nanaimo

Fuel

Marina Office & Facilities

Not for Navigation
Not to scale

VANCOUVER ISLAND
Nanaimo - Port

NANAIMO DOWNTOWN RESTAURANTS 🍽			
Acme Food Company	Full Menu	14 Commercial St	250-753-0042
Bubble Tea Stars	Teas	123 Commercial St	250-591-6979
DeepBlue	Seafood, Duck, Lamb, Chicken	70 Church Street Best Western	250-739-5060
Gabriel's Café	Soups, Sandwiches	183 Commercial St	250-714-0271
Gina's Café	Mexican Cuisine	47 Skinner Street	250-753-5411
Green Olive Bar	Wraps, Pasta, Pizza	150 Skinner Street	250-716-0030
JavaWocky	Coffee, Pastries	90 Front Street #8	250-753-1688
Le Café Francais	Crepes, Salads	153 Commercial	250-716-7866
LightHouse Bistro & Pub	Seafood, Steak, Pasta, Burgers	50 Anchor Way	250-754-3212
Manzavino	Pasta, Pizza	77 Skinner Street	250-754-7745
Minnoz (fine dining)	Seafood, Lamb, Chicken, Beef	11 Bastion Street Bastion Hotel	250-753-2977 Ext 2205
Modern Café	Seafood, Meats	221 Commercial	250-754-5022
Mon Petite Choux	Sandwiches, Soups	101-2 Commercial	250-753-6002
Mrs. Riches	Burgers, Pasta	199 Fraser Street	250-753-8311
Old City Station Pub	Wraps, Burgers	150 Skinner Street	250-716-0030
Penny's Palapa	Mexican Cuisine	Port - H Dock	250-751-3870
Perkins Coffee Co.	Espresso, Pastries	234 Commercial St	250-753-2582
Sake House	Japanese Cuisine	650 Terminal Mall	250-741-8833
Red Martini Grill	Tapas, Wraps	75 Front Street #1	250-753-5181
Serious Coffee	Espresso, Pastries	60 Commercial St	New
Sukkho Thai	Thai Cuisine	123 Commercial St	250-591-8424
Sushi To Go	Japanese Cuisine	90 Front Street #2	No Phone
Tea on the Quay	Sandwiches, Sweets	90 Front Street #4	250-753-2264
Troller's	Fish, Soups, Salads	Port Docks	250-741-1609
Waterfront Confections	Candy, Ice Cream, Popcorn	90 Front St. #6	250-591-5559

NANAIMO ISLAND RESTAURANTS 🍽️

Dinghy Dock Pub	Seafood, Burgers, Wraps, Pasta	Protection Island	250-753-2373
Newcastle Concessions	Burgers, Wraps, Sandwiches	Newcastle Island	250-754-7893

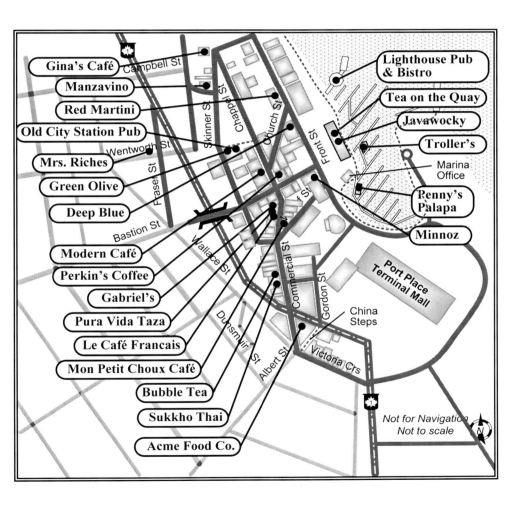

Gina's Café
Manzavino
Red Martini
Old City Station Pub
Mrs. Riches
Green Olive
Deep Blue
Modern Café
Perkin's Coffee
Gabriel's
Pura Vida Taza
Le Café Francais
Mon Petit Choux Café
Bubble Tea
Sukkho Thai
Acme Food Co.

Lighthouse Pub & Bistro
Tea on the Quay
Javawocky
Troller's
Marina Office
Penny's Palapa
Minnoz

Campbell St
Skinner St
Chappel
Church St
Front St
Wentworth St
Fraser St
Bastion St
Wallace St
Dunsmuir St
Commercial St
Gordon St
Albert St
Victoria Crs
Port Place Terminal Mall
China Steps

Not for Navigation
Not to scale
N

NANAIMO OLD QUARTER RESTAURANTS 🍽			
Amazing Thai	Thai Cuisine	221 West 2nd Ave.	250-752-0468
Asteras Greek Taverna	Greek Cuisine	347 Wesley Street	250-716-0451
Bistro Taiyo	Seafood, Sushi	321 Wesley St. #2	250-716-8861
Bocca Café	Coffee, Salads, Sandwiches	427D Fitzwilliam	250-753-1797
Delicado's	Southwestern Food	358 Wesley Street	250-753-6524
Grapevine Trattoria	Italian Cuisine	335 Wesley St #10	250-754-5505
Jakeob's	Ice Cream, Gelato	306 Fitzwilliam St.	250-754-0111
McLean's	Specialty Foods, Deli	426 Fitzwilliam	250-754-0100
New York Style	Pizza, Pasta, Ribs	299 Wallace Street	250-754-0111
Pho A Dong	Vietnamese	428 Fitzwilliam St.	250-741-8699
The Keg	Steaks, Prime Rib, Seafood	350 Robson Street	250-741-1111
Wesley Street Café	Seafood, Venison, Duck, Lamb, Beef	321 Wesley St. #1	250-753-6057

Asteras Greek Taverna

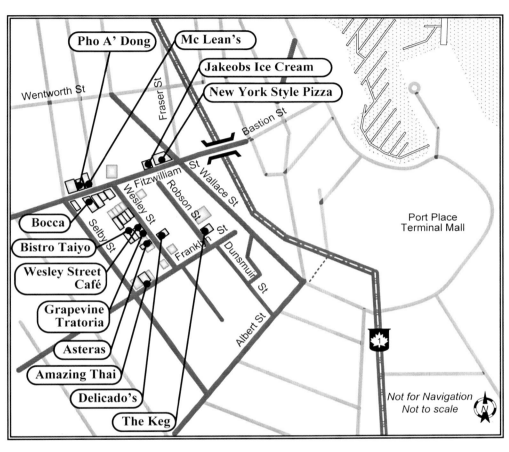

Pho A' Dong

Mc Lean's

Jakeobs Ice Cream

New York Style Pizza

Wentworth St

Fraser St

Bastion St

Fitzwilliam St

Wallace St

Robson St

Wesley St

Selby St

Franklin St

Dunsmuir St

Albert St

Port Place
Terminal Mall

Bocca

Bistro Taiyo

Wesley Street
Café

Grapevine
Tratoria

Asteras

Amazing Thai

Delicado's

The Keg

Not for Navigation
Not to scale

Old Quarter

DINGHY DOCK PUB

The Dinghy Dock Pub on Protection Island is known among boaters all over North America as a must do nautical destination. The Pub has great views of Nanaimo across the Harbour. The docks or floats around the Pub are intended for dinghies but you will see all size boats here up to 35 feet or more. The Pub is filled with fun nautical décor and you can participate in the old tradition of leaving currency (with your name on it) on one of the posts in the Pub to use next time you visit. This tradition was started by miners who left money behind so they would be

Lunch / Dinner	11:30am – 11pm Sun-Thur 11:30am – 12am Fri & Sat
Brunch	10:30am – 2:30pm Sundays
Price	Moderate
Outdoor Seating	Yes, Floating Dock, Summer Months
Contact	250-753-2373

able to buy a drink if they came back broke. Although not built until 1989, the Dinghy Dock Pub carries on this fun tradition. The "little tots" will love fishing through the fishing hole next to the family restaurant area of the Pub, fishing poles are provided. The Pub serves appetizers, pizza, burgers, wraps, pasta, and seafood, all of which is very tasty. A combination of appetizers creates a nice lunch, including the Seafood Stuffed Mushroom Caps, the Mediterranean Clams, and the Crab Cakes with sweet pepper relish. For a dinner main, try the King Crab Legs or perhaps the Cracked Pepper Seared Salmon with wilted spinach and a citrus cream sauce.You will find all your favorite drinks, too, at the Dinghy Dock Pub including Brews on Tap; Bottles of Domestic, Import, and Premium beer; Coolers; Ciders; Cocktails; Coffee drinks; and non-alcoholic drinks like Smoothies, Sodas, and Hot Chocolate. Everyone has fun at the Dinghy Dock Pub meeting new people, sharing stories, and enjoying the live entertainment through the summer months.

Dinghy Dock Pub

LIGHTHOUSE BISTRO & PUB

The Lighthouse Bistro and Pub is located within steps of the Port of Nanaimo docks in a striking building situated over the water resembling a lighthouse. The upstairs Pub serves appetizers, wraps, sandwiches, burgers, and seafood dishes along with fine wines and beer. Try the Lox Salmon Wrap for lunch or the Pacific Pasta with smoked salmon, clams, and Saltspring Is. Mussels. The more formal Bistro downstairs offers a nice venue for dinner including the Mixed Seafood Grill served with a tropical fruit salsa, or try the Baked Fanny Bay Oysters, or perhaps the New York Strip Loin with a skewer of prawns. Both the Bistro and the Pub have wonderful ocean views, and you can sit outside under the gazebo during the summer months.

Lunch/ Dinner	11am – 10pm Daily Hours Vary Off Season
Pub	11am – 12am Sun-Thur 11am – 1am Fri & Sat
Price	Moderate - Expensive
Outdoor Seating	Yes, Gazebo, Summer Months
Contact	250-754-3212

LightHouse Bistro & Pub

VANCOUVER ISLAND
Nanaimo - Port

MODERN CAFÉ

The Modern Café is a short walk from the Port of Nanaimo Waterfront at 221 Commercial Street. This classy Café has table and booth seating, large colourful paintings, and modern light fixtures with brick interior walls. The food is excellent with great presentation like the BC Wild Salmon grilled and topped with pesto over a warm couscous salad served with seasonal vegetables; or try the Chicken Supreme stuffed with dried tomatoes, almonds, and goat cheese topped with a warm apricot glaze served with vegetables and roasted potatoes. Don't forget about dessert, including the homemade Strawberry Shortcake

Breakfast	9am – 2pm Sat & Sun
Lunch	11am – 5pm Daily
Dinner	5pm – 10pm Daily
Price	Moderate
Outdoor Seating	Yes, Sidewalk, Summer Months
Contact	250-754-5022

topped with strawberry compote and whipped cream, or try the Apple Tarte Tatin or the Cheese Cake of the Day. Tapas are served throughout the afternoon along with wine and cocktails, which can be enjoyed in the bar area. The Modern Café serves breakfast on the weekends and offers some unique dishes like the Homemade Crepes stuffed with fresh vegetables and cheese then oven baked and served over rosti potatoes.

Modern Cafe

WESLEY STREET CAFÉ

The Wesley Street Cafe is located in the "Old City Quarter" at 321 Wesley Street. This intimate venue offers an excellent selection of fine wines and a quality menu, including the Pan Seared Duck Breast and Duck Leg Confit with herbed gnocchi, blackberry balsamic gastric, and rosemary jus; or try the Grilled Beef Striploin and Braised Short Rib with Brie scented potato pave, crispy red onion fritter, and port jus with watercress coulis. Lunches are superb as well like the Duck Liver Pate with assorted pickled vegetables, or try the Wesley Steamer Pot. Don't miss this fine dining venue with linen set tables, warm burgundy colours, and warm friendly service.

Lunch	11:30am – 2:30pm Tue-Fri
Dinner	5:30pm – 9pm Tue-Fri
Price	Moderate – Lunch Expensive - Dinner
Outdoor Seating	Yes, Patio Summer Months
Contact	250-753-6057

The Wesley Street Cafe

VANCOUVER ISLAND
Sidney – Canoe Cove

Canoe Cove has a rich and colourful history. The small inlets of Canoe Cove were used by rumrunners in the 1920's during the U.S. Prohibition from which contraband liquor was shipped to the San Juan Islands and other locations in Puget Sound. A marina was established in Canoe Cove by the end of the 1920's, which gave birth to what is now Canoe Cove Marina. A boat construction operation began at the Marina in the 1930's with the last wooden boat launched in 1964. Moorage and storage facilities at the Marina have expanded over the years and Canoe Cove Marina has grown into one of the largest yacht repair facilities in British Columbia. Canoe Cove is strewn with rocks and requires a careful study of the charts.

For eats, stop by Sofie's Café, located at Canoe Cove Marina, or dine at the historic Stonehouse English-style pub and restaurant just upland from the Marina. Be sure to visit the Morgan Warren Art Gallery (250-655-1081) located at the Marina next door to the Café. Ms Warren's watercolours are well known for their accuracy and meticulous detail of North American birds. Her paintings are included in many private collections, including that of Prince Philip, Duke of Edinburgh and works owned by Her Majesty, Queen Elizabeth II. Next door to the art gallery is a set of stairs, which lead up to the Stonehouse Pub.

The Swartz Bay Ferry Terminal is located northwest of Canoe Cove and receives passengers from Tsawwassen, Victoria, and the Gulf Islands. Adjacent to the Ferry terminal is the Swartz Bay Public Wharf within an easy walk to Canoe Cove Marina via a trail through the Marina's wooded property. The trail is located across the road from the Wharf, enter the left most trailhead.

Canoe Cove Marina	250-656-5566 VHF 66A
	www.canoecovemarina.com

A full service marina with restrooms, showers, laundry, a marine supply store, and fuel dock, lift and repairs. Study charts carefully for this landing.

Short-Term:	Short term stays are permitted at the fuel dock and in unoccupied slips when available, call ahead for availability.
Overnight:	Overnight stays in unoccupied slips as available at $1.25/ft.

Swartz Bay Wharf	250-655-3256
	Wharfinger

A Public Wharf managed by the Southern Gulf Islands Harbour Commission offers short-term and overnight stays on the 85 foot dock located adjacent to the Swartz Bay Ferry Terminal.

Short-Term:	Short term stays up to 4 hours are without charge. Stays of 4-12 hours are permitted with rates as posted. Payment box at dock.
Overnight:	Overnight stays permitted with rates as posted. Use the self-registration payment box at the head of the dock.

Swartz Bay Wharf

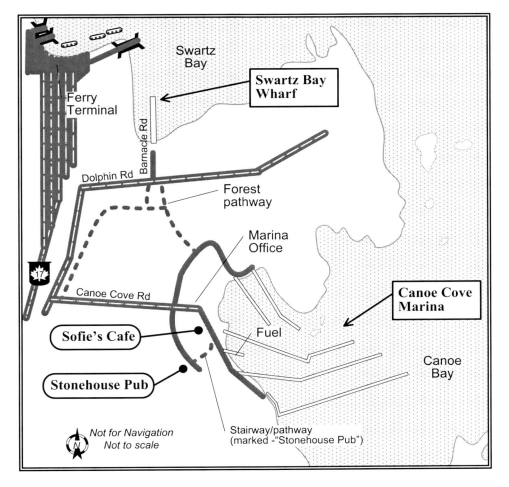

SOFIE'S CAFE

Sofie's Café is a great stop for breakfast in a friendly nautical environment where you can enjoy omelettes, French toast, and Benny's like the Sidney Spit Benny with smoked salmon or baby shrimp. Try a fresh bagel spread with smoked salmon and cream cheese or the bacon, egg and cheese bagel. Breakfast is available all day on Sundays and until noon on Saturdays for late weekend risers. For lunch try the Shrimp Salad Sandwich or the Mandarin Chicken Salad. Burgers are offered along with soups by the cup or bowl including the Pacific Seafood Chowder and the Soup of the Day. Sofie's is open till 7pm on Wednesdays for special wine and beer night.

Breakfast	7:30am – 11am Daily
Lunch	11am – 3pm Daily
Price	Moderate
Outdoor Seating	Yes, Deck Summer Months
Contact	250-656-5557

Sofie's Cafe

STONEHOUSE PUB

Lunch/ Dinner	11am – 11pm Sun-Tue 11am – 12am Wed-Sat
Price	Moderate
Outdoor Seating	Yes, Patio, Summer Months
Contact	778-426-1200

The Stonehouse Pub is just upland from Canoe Cove Marina accessible by a set of stairs located next to the art studio. If you have docked at the Swartz Bay Wharf next to the ferry terminal, take the trail through the Marina's treed property for an easy walk to the Pub. This British-style Stonehouse Pub and Restaurant is literally in a stone house, which was built in 1935 and sports wood and tile floors, leaded-glass windows, and a cozy bar. Patrons appreciate the friendly service and good food, including appetizers, wraps, and "chef favorites" like the Stuffed Yorky, a fluffy Yorkshire pudding stuffed with beef, cheddar, and other goodies; or try the Lemon Basted Halibut; or perhaps the Portobello Mushroom & Yam Wrap with creamy humus dressing. It has been said, that Hugh Rodd, the original owner and builder of the stone house, has been heard walking the halls of his English manor. Hugh also built boats and designed the "Minto," a popular tender in the region. Hugh's stone house became the Stonehouse Pub in 1985 and recently re-opened after a short stint of repairs and upgrades.

Stonehouse Pub

VANCOUVER ISLAND
Sidney – Deep Cove

Deep Cove is located at the head of Saanich Inlet on the northwest side of Saanich Peninsula and should not be mistaken for the community and cove by the same name in Indian Arm. Deep Cove at Saanich is surrounded by suburban homes and rural roads located outside of Sidney, offering a tranquil setting. The Marina situated at the southeast end of the Cove is currently closed and most likely will be placed on the market. Boaters can anchor in the protected Cove and dinghy to the Chalet restaurant's private beach for the purpose of dining at the "Deep Cove Chalet." This historic Chalet was built as a teahouse for the B.C. Electric Rail Line in 1913 and has been a restaurant ever since.

The Muse Winery (250-656-2552) is located across the lane from the Chalet and offers wine tasting, a sales room, and a bistro lunch.

Chalet Beach Access	250-656-3541
	The Chalet

Private waterfront beach belonging to the Chalet restaurant. Guests of the restaurant may arrive by dinghy.

Short-Term: Dinghy left at beach while dining at The Chalet.
Overnight: No overnight craft.

Deep Cove Chalet Beach

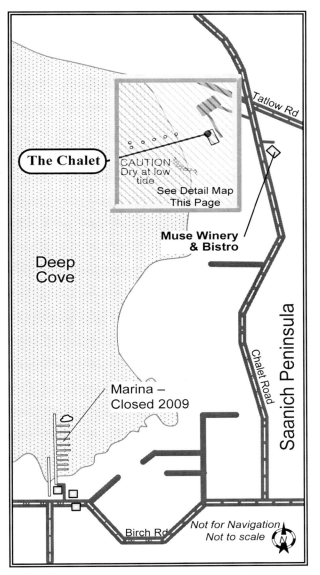

The Chalet

CAUTION
Dry at low tide
See Detail Map
This Page

Tatlow Rd

Muse Winery & Bistro

Deep Cove

Saanich Peninsula

Chalet Road

Marina – Closed 2009

Birch Rd

Not for Navigation
Not to scale
N

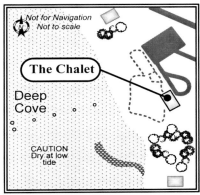

Not for Navigation
Not to scale
N

The Chalet

Deep Cove

CAUTION
Dry at low tide

DEEP COVE CHALET

Deep Cove Chalet is a casual, fine dining country venue with stunning views of Saanich Inlet. The white linen tablecloths and formal table-settings contrast with the rustic wood paneled walls and the brick fireplace. The menu is inspired by local produce and in-house smoked salmon with house made breads and pates accompanied by a world class wine reserve. Creative starters include the Lobster Bisque, Onion Soup, and the Spinach Salad with Swiss cheese and smoked salmon in a warm dressing; or enjoy a helping of Escargots or Oysters on the half shell. Entrees change seasonally and may include theYellow Fin Tuna, Quails Normande, and the

Lunch	Noon – 2pm Wed-Sun
Dinner	5:30pm – Close Daily Hours Vary Off Season Closed January
Price	Expensive – Very Exp.
Outdoor Seating	For Special Occasions (weddings, meetings)
Contact	250-656-3541

Roasted Venison, or perhaps the Breast of Duck or the Nova Scotia Lobster. For a classic French dessert, finish with the Le Fromage, an array of assorted cheeses, or enjoy a light souffle.

Deep Cove Chalet

Deep Cove Chalet

VANCOUVER ISLAND
Sidney - Port

It is no wonder that the beautiful town of Sidney with its lovely waterfront walkways and gorgeous views of Georgia Strait and the Olympic and Cascade Mountain ranges has earned the title of "Sidney-by-the-Sea." The modern Port Sidney Marina and Seaport Place, which contains several restaurants, is located right on the waterfront along with the Seaside Walkway, Park, and Gazebo, where visitors can enjoy concerts during the summer months. The Sidney Pier Hotel (250-655-9445) offers first-class accommodations and houses the Georgia Deli and Haro's Restaurant along with the Haven Spa (250-655-9797). To the south is the Beacon Avenue Wharf used for the passenger ferry from Sidney to nearby Sidney Spit Marine Park and at the south end of town is the terminus for the Washington State Ferry from Anacortes and Friday Harbor.

Adjacent to the Marina and Seaport Place is Beacon Avenue, which runs from the waterfront westward and is Sidney's main street lined with cafes, restaurants, art galleries, boutiques, coffee shops, bakeries, and unique book stores. Be sure to visit The Boater's Exchange shop at 2527 Bevan Avenue (250-655-3101). The shop carries both used and new boating supplies and equipment tucked in every little nook in this interesting store. The Sidney Summer Market is held every Thursday evening from June through August; a portion of Beacon Avenue is closed to vehicle traffic from 5pm to 9pm when folks can enjoy the carnival atmosphere with live entertainment and purchase local crafts, fresh produce, and ethnic foods.

The Summer Sounds Concert Series is held at Beacon Park every Sunday afternoon from July to September, a fun time for the whole family. Families will also enjoy the Ocean Discovery Centre located in the Sidney Pier Hotel open 10am to 6pm daily; staff provides instruction on undersea life with aquaria touch-tanks and microscopes. For a geological family experience, visit the "Mineral World Scratch Patch" (250-655-4367) located near the Marina at 9891 Seaport Place, where you can identify rocks, gemstones, and shells, and pan for gold or dig for fossils. The Sidney Historical Museum (250-655-6355), located at 2423 Beacon Avenue at the corner of 4th Street, is a must for history buffs and for those who want to gain a true appreciation for Sidney and the Saanich Peninsula. The Museum portrays the early pioneers of North Saanich and the town of Sidney through photographs and artifacts. If you love aircraft, don't miss visiting the B.C. Aviation Museum (250-655-3300) located near the Airport just southwest of Beacon Avenue at 1910 Norseman Rd. accessible via the Peninsula Taxi & Limo Service (250-656-1111). To take in a concert or performance, contact the Mary Winspear Centre (250-656-0275) located on the west end of Beacon Avenue for information and tickets.

Port Sidney Marina

250-655-3711   VHF 66A

www.portsidney.com

A full-service marina with power, restrooms, showers, laundry, computer work stations, and snack bar. Customs clearance is located on "F" Dock.

Short-Term: Short term stays are available at $5 per hour until 5pm. Call ahead for dock or slip assignment.

Overnight: Moorage for all size vessels. Rates are $1.35 per foot May-Sept. and .85 per ft Oct. – April plus power. Call ahead for reservations and slip assignment.

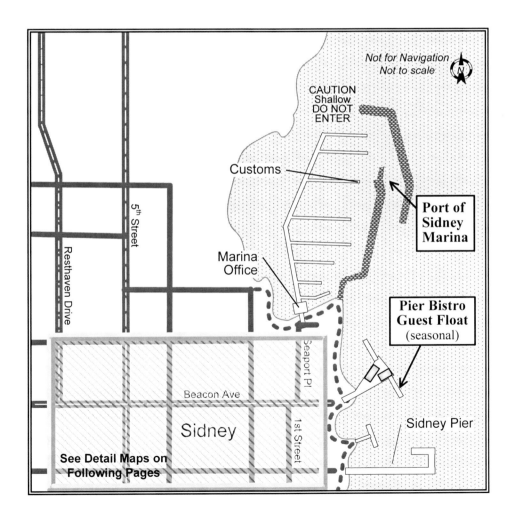

VANCOUVER ISLAND
Sidney - Port

SIDNEY RESTAURANTS			🍽
Alexander's Coffee	Espresso, Sweets	2385 Beacon Ave.	250-656-3234
Beacon Landing Liq	Liquor Store	2537 #106 Beacon	250-655-6531
Beacon Landing Restaurant & Pub	Chicken, Seafood, Lamb, Pasta, Pizza	2537 Beacon Ave.	250-656-6690
Big Moo Diner	Burgers, Soups, Ice Cream, Panini	109 Beacon Ave.	250-656-5775
Bistro Suisse	Duck, Seafood, Pork, Beef, Brunch	2470 Beacon Ave.	250-656-5353
Boondocks	Burgers, Wraps, Fish, Pizza, Pasta	9732 First Street	250-656-4088
Café 3rd Street	All Day Breakfast	2466 Beacon Ave.	250-656-3035
Carlos Cantina & Grill	Southwestern Mexican Cuisine	9816 Fourth Street	250-656-3833
Chef on The Run	Sandwiches, Take-out Meals	9781B Second St.	250-655-3141
Fairway Market	Groceries, Deli	2531 Beacon Ave.	Not Listed
Fish on 5th	Fish, Burgers, Wraps, Sandwiches	9812 Fifth Street	250-656-4022
Fresh Cup Roastery & Café	Espresso, Panini, Pastries, Gelato	2360 Beacon Ave.	250-656-5668
Georgia Café & Deli	Espresso, Sweets, Sandwiches, Salads	9805 Seaport Place Sidney Pier Hotel	250-655-9720
Good Fortune	Chinese Cuisine	9838 Third Street	250-656-5112 (will deliver)
Green Wasabi	Japanese Cuisine	9810 Fourth Street	250-656-0068
Haro's	Seafood, Pork, Lamb, Chicken	9805 Seaport Place Sidney Pier Hotel	250-655-9700
Lunn's Bakery	Chocolates, Cakes, Pastries, Sandwich	2455 Beacon Ave.	250-656-1724

Sidney Promenade

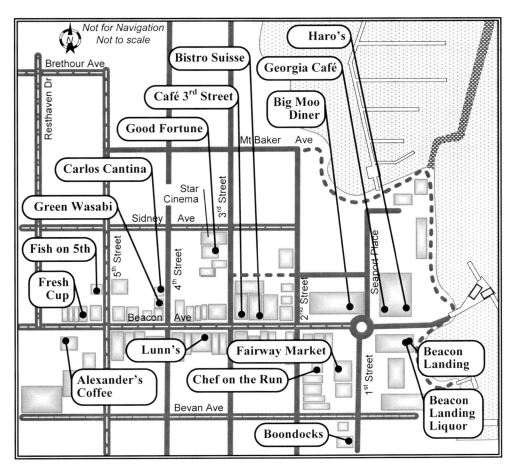

VANCOUVER ISLAND
Sidney - Port

SIDNEY RESTAURANTS			🍽
Margie's Corner Deli	Smoked Meats, Panini	2527 #104 Beacon	250-656-1657
Maria's Souvlaki	Pita Wraps, Salads, Skewers	9812 Second Street	250-656-9944
Odyssia Restaurant	Steak, BBQ, Pizza, Seafood, Greek	9785 Fifth Street	250-656-5596
Pier Bistro	Breakfast, Burgers, Fish, Salads	2550 Beacon Ave. Government Wharf	250-655-4995
Pier 1 Restaurant	Stir Fry, Burgers, Chicken, Veal	2500 Beacon Ave.	250-656-1224
Quiznos	Sub Sandwiches	2360 #101 Beacon	250-655-8934
Red Brick Café	Salads, Soups, Sandwiches	2423 #106 Beacon	250-655-1822
Rogers Chocolates	Fine Chocolates	2423 Beacon Ave.	250-655-0305
Sabhai Thai	Thai Cuisine	2493A Beacon Ave	250-655-4085
Salty's by the Sea	Fish & Chips	2359 Beacon Ave.	250-655-0400
Serious Coffee	Espresso, Muffins, Panini, Soups	2417 #102 Beacon	250-655-7255
Sidney Bakery	Breads, Pastries, Pasties, Sweets	2507 Beacon Ave.	250-656-1012
Starbucks	Espresso, Muffins	2471 Beacon Ave.	250-655-0949
Stonestreet Café	Soups, Salads, Sandwiches, Pizza	2505 Beacon Ave.	250-655-1166
The Rumrunner	Seafood, Chicken, Beef, Burgers	9881 Seaport Place	250-656-5643
Theo's Family Rest.	Pasta, Stir Fry, Greek	9819 Fifth Street	250-656-7666

Pier Bistro Dock

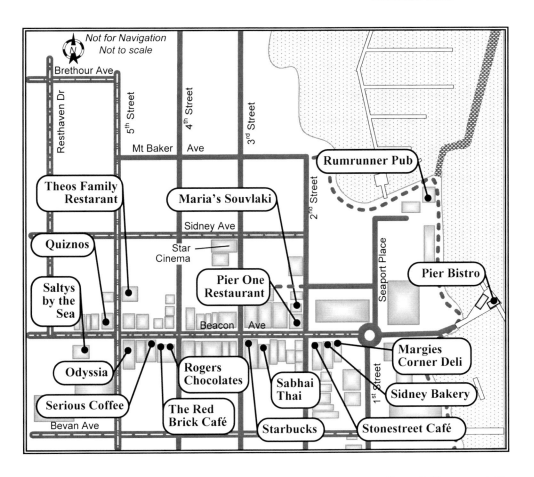

Not for Navigation
Not to scale

Brethour Ave

Resthaven Dr

5th Street

4th Street

3rd Street

2nd Street

Mt Baker   Ave

Rumrunner Pub

Theos Family
Restarant

Maria's Souvlaki

Sidney Ave

Quiznos

Star
Cinema

Pier One
Restaurant

Pier Bistro

Saltys
by the
Sea

Seaport Place

Beacon   Ave

Margies
Corner Deli

Odyssia

Rogers
Chocolates

Sabhai
Thai

1st Street

Sidney Bakery

Serious Coffee

The Red
Brick Café

Starbucks

Stonestreet Café

Bevan Ave

BEACON LANDING RESTAURANT & PUB

The attractive Beacon Landing Restaurant & Pub is located at the foot of Beacon Avenue along the promenade with beautiful views of the ocean, the San Juan Islands, and snow covered Mt. Baker. Ample seating is available in the Pub and at the large bar in addition to the more intimate booths and tables in the restaurant dining area. The outdoor patio with a glass-wall wind break extends along the promenade for summer dining. The Restaurant & Pub has a varied menu with a focus on seafood, including the Cedar Plank Roasted Wild Salmon, and the Beacon Landing

Lunch/ Dinner	11am – 11pm Daily
Price	Moderate - Expensive
Outdoor Seating	Yes, Patio, Summer Months
Contact	250-656-6690

Cioppino; or try the Crusted Halibut topped with a tropical salsa served with seasonal vegetables and potato or fettuccini. For lunch, try one of the fresh made pizzas, or perhaps the Chicken Panini or the Halibut Burger. Don't forget about the delicious appetizers, including the Roasted Veggie Stack, the Tuna Tataki, and the Saltspring Island Mussels. The Blackberry Apple Pie and the Chocolate Coffee Cheesecake are good choices for a finishing touch.

Beacon Landing Restaurant

BISTRO SUISSE

Bistro Suisse, located at 2470 Beacon Avenue, is a small, intimate bistro displaying flags (cantons) of Switzerland and decorated with paintings from local artists. The dining space has soft earth tone colours, hardwood floors, and area rugs. Bistro Suisse offers unique appetizers and unique drinks along with Swiss and German style entrees. Start with some piping hot Onion Soup made with a touch of Brandy or perhaps the Deep Fried Brie with wild blueberry sauce. For lunch, try the "Quiche of the Day" or the Spinach Salad with sautéed mushrooms and silvered almonds or perhaps the

Lunch	11am – 2:30pm Daily
Dinner	5pm – 8pm Daily
Price	Moderate - Expensive
Outdoor Seating	No
Contact	250-656-5353

Avocado and Shrimp with brandy sauce. Another favorite is the Bratwurst with sauerkraut and red cabbage. Dinner choices include roasted pork, lamb, seafood, duck, and beef dishes and a cheese fondue. The Scalloped Veal in a creamy mushroom sauce; and the Beef Tenderloin Tips Stroganoff are just a few of the European style dishes. Don't forget dessert, like the "Blumbleberry Pie" or the Chocolate Mousse finished off with a Kaffee Kirsch.

BOONDOCKS

Boondocks is a casual dining venue off the beaten path located at 9732 First Street. This rustic pub-style restaurant has lots of character sporting a fun nautical décor with numerous items and memorabilia. There is something for everyone on the menu, including soups, sandwiches, wraps, burgers, and pizza along with chicken, steaks, and pasta and seafood dishes. Try the Hot Beef Sandwich or the Spicy Chorizo Pizza or perhaps the Shellfish Fettuccini or the Fisherman's Stew. "Big Plates" include the New York Steak, served with potatoes and vegetables; and the Chicken Cordon Bleu, stuffed with Emmenthaler cheese and ham. Boondocks is a fun, old-fashioned restaurant that has remained on the Sidney radar.

Lunch/ Dinner	11am – 10pm Tue-Thur 11am – 11pm Fri & Sat 11am – 9pm Sun & Mon
Price	Moderate
Outdoor Seating	Yes, Deck in Back and Picnic Tables in Front
Contact	250-656-4088

HARO'S

Haro's fine dining restaurant is located in the Sidney Pier Hotel sporting classy modern furnishings and offering majestic views of Georgia Strait and Mount Baker. The lovely tiled patio, enclosed with a glass windbreak, provides comfortable summer seating. For a special treat, don't miss the lunch & dinner starters like the Prosciutto & Melon Salad with pernod caramel, or try the Steamed Mussels served in a white wine sauce with fire-roasted tomato butter and grilled bread. Dinner mains change with the seasons and may include the Vancouver Island Lamb, Grilled Canadian Rib Eye, and Wild Pacific Salmon served with local seasonal vegetables offered with quality wines and local micro brews.

Lunch	11am – 4pm Daily
Dinner	5pm – 9pm Daily
High Tea	2pm – 4pm Daily
Price	Moderate - Expensive
Outdoor Seating	Yes, Patio, Summer Months
Contact	250-655-9700 866-659-9445

Salads, chowder, and tapas are popular items for lunch; and for a special treat, don't miss Afternoon Tea served with freshly baked scones, Devonshire cream, Wildwood preserves, petite tarts, and sweets.

Haro's Restaurant

PIER BISTRO 🍽️

The Pier Bistro is located on the Government Wharf across from the Fish Market. This small attractive Bistro is literally over the water with fabulous ocean and mountain views, a great spot to watch all of the boating activity. Pretty wood furnishings along with nautical photos and décor set the mood for this casual seaside venue serving sandwiches, burgers, and signature fish 'n chips. The Pier Bistro is best known for its homemade clam chowder and large dinner salads served with pita bread. Choices include the Grilled Salmon Salad, Cob Salad, and Thai Salad to name a few. The Pier's three-course Sunset Special starts with a choice of soup or salad followed by halibut or salmon, and concluded with a homemade dessert. Breakfast items include Omelettes and Eggs Benny.

Breakfast	9am – 11am Daily Until 2pm Sundays
Lunch	11am – 5pm Daily
Dinner	5pm – 4pm Thur-Mon May – Sept Only
Price	Moderate
Outdoor Seating	Yes, Patio, Summer Months
Contact	250-655-4995

The Pier Bistro is open May through September and offers a seasonal guest dock for boats 20 feet and under, a convenient option for boaters coming from nearby Sidney Spit or neighboring marinas.

THE RUMRUNNER 🍽️

The Rumrunner Pub has been an icon in Sidney since June 1990 and takes its name from the colourful local history of liquor smugglers during the U.S. Prohibition. One of the period's most notable smugglers was Johnny Schnarr, who became an early regular of the Rumrunner and never had to pay for his tab. Bill Singer, then owner of the Rumrunner, had planned a 100th Birthday party for Johnny, who unfortunately passed away one year too soon. While visiting the Rumrunner, be sure to note the historic photos of these earlier times.

Lunch/ Dinner	11am – 11pm Sun-Thur 11am – 12am Fri & Sat Kitchen open till 10pm
Price	Moderate
Outdoor Seating	Yes, Patio, Summer Months
Contact	250-656-5643

Children are welcome in the restaurant portion of the Pub, which serves salads, sandwiches, halibut 'n chips, burgers, and pasta. Entrees include the Grilled Sirloin Steak, the Braised Beef Short Ribs, and the Pan Roasted Chicken. Don't miss the special Prime Rib dinner on Thursday, Friday, and Saturday nights. The outdoor patio overlooking the promenade has great views of the San Juan Islands, Mt. Baker, and the area's boating activity and is a popular venue during the summer months.

VANCOUVER ISLAND
Sidney – Tsehum Harbour

Van Isle Marina is located west of Armstrong Point and Thumb Point in Tsehum Harbour. The Marina is owned and operated by the Dickinson family, which began the business in 1955 and is continued today by the third generation. Boaters appreciate the personal touch and friendly service at this large, spacious moorage basin. You will find the Blue Peter Pub, the Dockside Grill, and "The Latch" restaurant just upland from the Marina. The Harbour Road Bakery & Deli (250-655-0005) is within easy walking distance southwest of the Marina.

The town of Sidney is within easy reach via bus, taxi, or car. Transportation options include: the Yellow Cab (250-381-2222); Peninsula Taxi (250-656-1111); Budget Car Rental (250-953-5300); and Discount Car Rentals (250-657-2277). Special rates are given to customers of Van Isle Marina at Discount Car Rentals.

If you wish to relax aboard your vessel, you will find all the necessary amenities at Van Isle Marina. For grocery delivery to your boat, contact Thrifty Foods (250-656-0946), or walk west on Harbour Road (past the Deli) to the corner of Resthaven Drive, where you will find the Resthaven Grocery Store (250-656-1140). On your walk along Harbour Road, you will pass several marine supply stores: South Island Marine, the Waypoint Marine, and the All Bay Marine.

Blue Peter Dock	250-656-4551 Blue Peter Pub & Restaurant	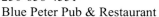

The 20 foot guest float at the Blue Peter Dock is suitable for dinghies and runabouts and is located on the east side of the restaurant.

Short-Term: Short term stays are permitted while dining at the Blue Peter Pub or Restaurant.

Overnight: No overnight stays.

Van Isle Marina	250-656-1138 VHF 66A www.VanIsleMarina.com	

A full service marina with power, restrooms, showers, laundry, marine store, and fuel dock with customs clearance.

Short-Term: Short term stays are $5 per hour; check in at the fuel dock for slip assignment.

Overnight: Moorage for all size vessels. Rates are $1.35 per foot April – Oct. and $1.15 per foot Nov. – March plus power. Call for reservations and slip assignment.

Blue Peter Dock

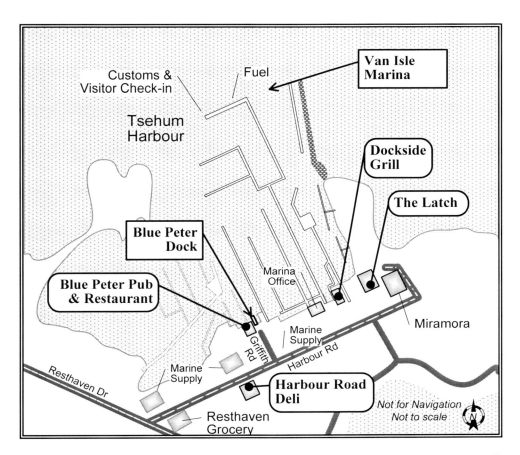

Van Isle Marina

Customs & Visitor Check-in

Fuel

Tsehum Harbour

Dockside Grill

The Latch

Blue Peter Dock

Blue Peter Pub & Restaurant

Marina Office

Miramora

Griffith Rd

Marine Supply

Harbour Rd

Marine Supply

Harbour Road Deli

Resthaven Dr

Resthaven Grocery

Not for Navigation
Not to scale

N

VANCOUVER ISLAND
Sidney – Tsehum Harbour

BLUE PETER PUB & RESTAURANT

The Blue Peter Pub & Restaurant is located at 2270 Harbour Road, just west and adjacent to Van Isle Marina. Blue Peter has its own float on the east side of the Restaurant for one runabout size boat or you can tie-up at the adjacent Marina. This waterfront pub and restaurant has nice views of Tsehum Harbour and the Marina with an out-door deck for summer enjoyment. The casual Pub serves burgers, soups, sandwiches, ribs, and pasta dishes along with good beers and mixed drinks. Be sure to ask about Pub specials like the "all you can eat" Roast Beef Buffet. The more formal Restaurant with its cozy fireplace and linen set tables, offers fine dishes like Pan Seared Halibut, Chargrilled Sirloin, and Baked Salmon glazed with a lemongrass reduction. Prawn Linguini, Seafood Stuffed Crepes, and Stuffed Breast of Chicken are offered at lunch among other selections.

Pub Lunch/ Dinner	11am – 11pm Kitchen open till 9pm
Restaurant Lunch	11am – 2:30pm Daily
Restaurant Dinner	5pm – 9pm Daily
Price	Moderate
Outdoor Seating	Yes, Deck, Summer Months
Contact	250-656-4551

Blue Peter Restaurant

DOCKSIDE GRILL ⦿

The Dockside Grill is located on the east side of Van Isle Marina and is the latest addition to the Tsehum Harbour waterfront. Boaters enjoy this convenient venue sporting light hardwood floors and furnishings, French doors, and a side patio for summer dining. The Grill, owned by Fish on Fifth in Sidney, offers appetizers, wraps, salads, and seafood dishes like the Baked Wild Sockeye with sundried tomato, asparagus, and pea risotto; or try the Lobster Ravioli, or Braised Red Snapper.

Lunch/ Dinner	11am – 9pm Fri & Sat 11am – 8pm Sun-Thur
Price	Moderate
Outdoor Seating	Yes, Patio, Summer Months
Contact	250-656-0828

For Lunch enjoy a Bourbon Glazed Salmon Wrap or the Grilled Lamb Wrap and don't miss the special ciders and brews among other quality "Patio Drinks."

Dockside Grill

THE LATCH

The Latch Restaurant is located east of the Van Isle Marina at 2328 Harbour Rd. in a historic home built in 1926 as the summer residence for Walter Nichol, who was Lieutenant Governor of British Columbia from 1920-1926. The home incorporates B.C. woods with fir slabs, on which the bark has been left, for the home's exterior; and tree-trunks of various sizes were used for the porches and balconies. Be sure to take note of the decorative interior panels in the Drawing Room and the Dining Room as well as the wood carvings at the head and foot of the stairs.

Breakfast	7:30am – 9:30am Tue-Sun Inn Guests Only
Dinner	5pm – 9:30pm Tue-Sun
Price	Expensive
Outdoor Seating	No
Contact	250-656-4015

The Latch offers a continental cuisine with an Italian focus, including veal, pasta, chicken, and seafood, along with duck, lamb, and other meat dishes. Try the Cannelloni Crepe stuffed with veal, chicken, and pork; or try the Penne Ala Rustica with tender veal, wild mushrooms, and asparagus in a parmesan cream sauce. The Salmon Renaissance with scallop mousse and fresh spinach wrapped in a Filo pastry is also a good choice as is the pan roasted Duck Supreme with blueberry demi-glaze. Reservations are recommended.

The Latch Dining Room

The Latch

The Latch

Blakely Island **175**
Blakely Island Marina...175

Lopez Island **177**
Fisherman Bay 177

Orcas Island... **187**
Deer Harbor 187
Doe Bay 191
East Sound 195
Olga 203
Orcas Landing...207
Rosario..213
West Beach 217
West Sound...221

San Juan Island **225**
Friday Harbor 225
Roche Harbor..239

Shaw Island... **247**
Blind Bay..247

San Juan Islands

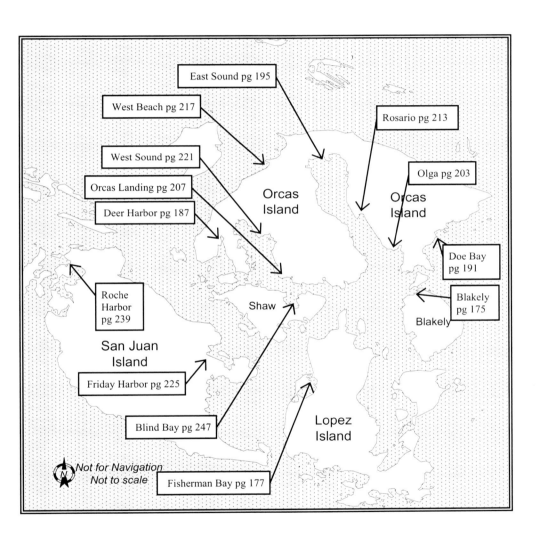

East Sound pg 195

West Beach pg 217

Rosario pg 213

West Sound pg 221

Olga pg 203

Orcas Landing pg 207

Orcas
Island

Orcas
Island

Deer Harbor pg 187

Doe Bay
pg 191

Roche
Harbor
pg 239

Shaw

Blakely
pg 175

Blakely

San Juan
Island

Friday Harbor pg 225

Blind Bay pg 247

Lopez
Island

Not for Navigation
Not to scale

Fisherman Bay pg 177

BLAKELY ISLAND
Blakely Island Marina

Lovely Blakely Island Marina offers short-term stays on the inside of the fuel dock and overnight stays at the Marina, which is tucked behind the Blakely Island Store in a protected inlet. The views and lovely setting provide an ideal spot to stretch your legs and enjoy a respite at the quaint Island Store for espresso, soup, ice cream and other treats.

The airstrip adjacent to the Marina is strictly for private use as are the roads. Eighty percent of the property on Blakely Island is held in trust by the Seattle Pacific University as an environmental research center. The first European settlers arrived on Blakely Island in the late 1800's, including Theodor Spencer whose family lived here for three generations. A sawmill once stood at Thatcher Bay, which cleared most of the trees on the Island by the 1950's. The cleared land was sold to individuals and in 1976 Mr. Crowley donated 967 acres to the Seattle Pacific University. The Island is once again covered with trees and most of the houses serve as vacation homes.

BLAKELY ISLAND STORE & FOUNTAIN 🍽

This adorable store includes an old-fashioned snack and soda bar serving donuts, espresso, and homemade soups, including chili and clam chowder. Don't forget to order a classic soda or ice cream to follow that juicy hotdog while enjoying the views of Peavine Pass. The Store stocks groceries, clothing, books, and gift items. Seating is available at the Fountain Bar and at tables along the view windows of the store, or you can enjoy the lovely outdoor patio with great views of Obstruction Island. Pilots enjoy	Snack/ Lunch	7am – 6pm mid May – mid Sept
	Price	Moderate
	Outdoor Seating	Yes, Patio, Summer Months
	Contact	360-375-6121

watching light aircraft arrive and depart from the adjacent private airstrip. Blakely Island and its roads are private; however, the Marina is open to the public for everyone's enjoyment.

Blakely Island Marina, Store, & Soda Fountain

Blakely Island Marina   360-375-6121   VHF 66A

Full service marina with a fuel dock, restrooms, showers, laundry, and store open Memorial Day through Labor Day. Covered picnic area.

Short-Term: Short-term stays located on the inside portion of the fuel dock is without charge up to 1 hour. Rates for stays over one hour are posted on the door of the store with a payment envelope drop box.

Overnight: Guest moorage in 16 slips and unoccupied slips as available for most all size vessels, call ahead for space. Rates are $1.20/ft including water and power. Use the envelop drop box at the door after hours.

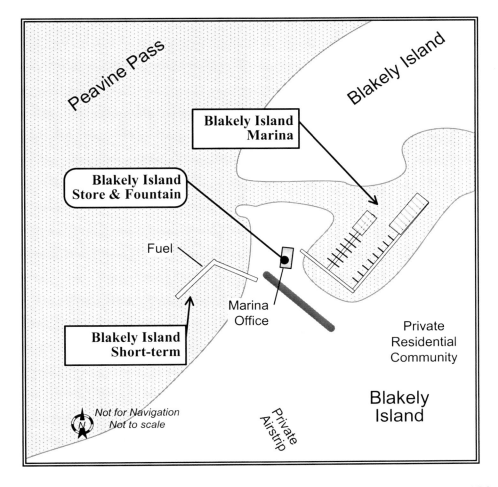

LOPEZ ISLAND
Fisherman Bay

Fisherman Bay and Lopez Village is known as a friendly and welcoming community and is home to many artists, musicians, farmers, and fisherman. Fisherman Bay has two marinas for short-term and overnight moorage as well as private docks located in the Bay. The Galley Dock, located south of Lopez Islander Marina, has guest space and buoys for boaters dining at The Galley Restaurant.

The Village of Lopez is within a ½ mile (.8 km) walk north from Fisherman Bay or you can rent bicycles (available May – Sept) from the Lopez Bicycle Works (360-468-2847), located on Fisherman Bay Road, directly across the street from the Island Marine Center Docks. Boaters can also reach Lopez Village by dinghy. The public beach with dinghy access is located in front of the Bay Café. Stairs lead up from the beach to old Post Road, which puts you right in the Village. Be sure to take along your backpack for shopping purposes.

Lopez Village has several good restaurants, coffee shops, and a bakery along with interesting art galleries and gift shops. To sooth the acing muscles, contact The Wellspring Massage & Bodyworks (360-468-4842). A seasonal Farmers Market is held in the village on Saturdays from mid May through September offering unique local art, hand-crafted jewelry, soaps, and locally grown vegetables, fruit and meats. Be sure to visit the Lopez Historical Museum (360-468-2049), located at the corner of Washburn Place and Weeks Road, open noon to 4pm (May – September) to read about local history, including detailed diaries by early settlers.

A point of interest is the Lopez Island Vineyards (360-468-3644) located 1 ½ miles (2.4 km) north of the village at 724 Fisherman Bay Road and can be reached by bicycle on a scenic 3 mile (4.8 km) round-trip ride. This family run vineyard hosts a tasting room (open seasonally) noon to 5pm Wednesday through Saturday, offering wines made from grapes grown on site and family vineyards in Yakima, Washington. Guests are invited to bring a picnic and enjoy the gardens and outdoor tables.

Lopez Island, Fisherman Bay, and Lopez Village is truly a place to relax and enjoy island life in a friendly environment.

Lopez Bicycle Works

Public Dinghy Beach Access

Public Dinghy Beach Access

LOPEZ ISLAND
Fisherman Bay

Island Marine Center Docks
360-468-3377 VHF 69

www.islandsmarinecenter.com

Full service marina with power, restrooms, and showers; 1,000 ft of dock space. Pumpout, haulout, repairs. Bicycle and kayak rentals nearby.

Short-Term: Contact marina for short-term tie-up. Fees for short-term tie-up vary according to boat length between $5 and $20 for 2 hours.

Overnight: Guest moorage is available for all size craft; rates vary based on length of vessel.

Lopez Islander Marina Resort
360-468-2233 VHF 78A

www.islander.com

Full service marina with fuel, power, restrooms, showers, and laundry along with lodging, a restaurant and swimming pool. Bicycle and kayak rentals nearby.

Short-Term: Contact marina for short-term tie-up. No charge for Islander Restaurant guests - $20 for up to 2 hours for guests not dining at the Islander Restaurant.

Overnight: Guest moorage is available for all size craft; rates vary based on length of vessel. Reservations accepted.

Lopez Village Public Beach

Located just north of the entrance to Fisherman Bay, the public beach provides dinghy access to Lopez Village. A set of stairs leads from the beach up to Old Post Road in the heart of Lopez Village.

Dingy Access: This is a public beach available for dinghy beach access.

The Galley Dock & Buoys
360-468-2713

www.galleylopez.com

This private dock and its buoys, located immediately across Fisherman Bay Road from the Galley Restaurant, are available to guests dining at The Galley.

Short-Term: Two (2) buoys and a dinghy dock offer no charge tie-up facilities for guests while dining at the Galley. Two white ball shaped buoys are immediately north and west of the dock and are marked with fading blue paint as "The Galley." Dinghy space is at the head of the dock near the ramp.

Overnight: Overnight moorage by prior arrangement only.

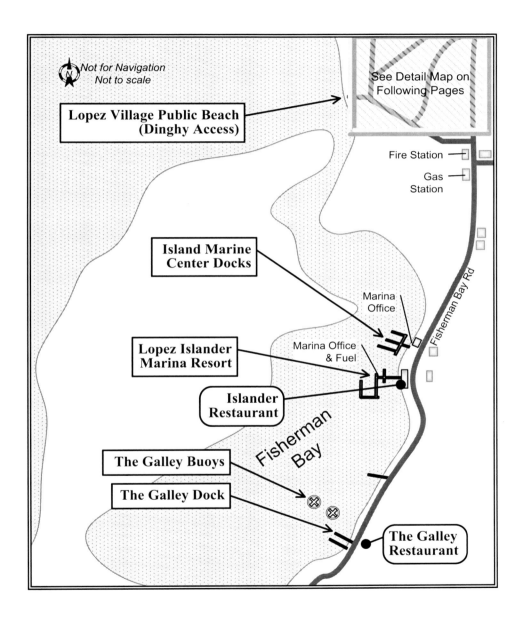

LOPEZ ISLAND
Fisherman Bay

Not for Navigation
Not to scale

Lopez Village Public Beach
(Dinghy Access)

See Detail Map on
Following Pages

Fire Station

Gas
Station

Island Marine
Center Docks

Marina
Office

Fisherman Bay Rd

Lopez Islander
Marina Resort

Marina Office
& Fuel

Islander
Restaurant

Fisherman Bay

The Galley Buoys

The Galley Dock

The Galley
Restaurant

LOPEZ ISLAND
Fisherman Bay

LOPEZ VILLAGE RESTAURANTS			
Bay Café	Seafood, Beef, Chicken, Pork	9 Old Post Road	360-468-3700
Blossom Grocery	Organic Foods	135-B Lopez Road	360-468-2204
Bucky's (April – Sept)	Burgers, Tacos, Sandwiches, Fish	Lopez Plaza	360-468-2595
Caffe La Boheme	Espresso, Teas, Soda	Lopez Plaza	360-468-3533
Holly B's Bakery	Fresh Baked Breads & Pastries, Sweets	Lopez Plaza	360-468-2133
Isabel's Espresso	Espresso, Teas, Milkshakes	Lopez Road North	360-468-4114
Just Heavenly Fudge	Fudge, Ice Cream	9 Old Post Road	360-468-2439
Lopez Island Liquor Store	State Liquor Store	37 Washburn Pl Road #D	360-468-2407
Lopez Village Market	Groceries	214 Lopez Road	360-468-2266
Love Dog Café	Seafood, Steak, Pasta	#1 Village Ctr.	360-468-2150
Vita's Wildly Delicious	Deli Sandwiches, Gourmet Food, Wine	Village Road	360-468-4268
Vortex	Wraps, Salads, Quesadillas, Tortillas	Lopez Road South	360-468-4740

Love Dog Cafe

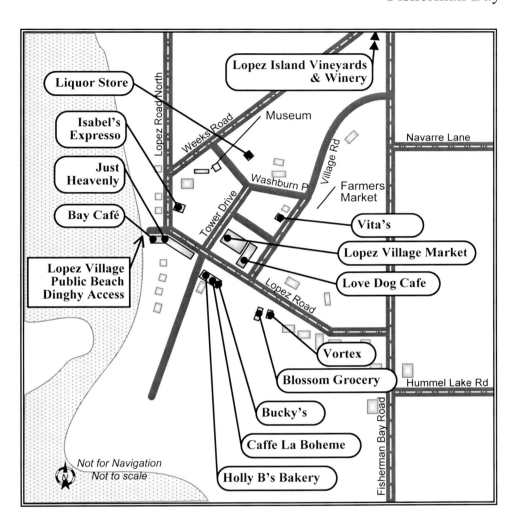

Lopez Island Vineyards & Winery

Liquor Store

Isabel's Expresso

Just Heavenly

Bay Café

Museum

Navarre Lane

Lopez Road North

Weeks Road

Washburn P

Village Rd

Farmers Market

Tower Drive

Vita's

Lopez Village Market

Love Dog Cafe

Lopez Village Public Beach Dinghy Access

Lopez Road

Vortex

Blossom Grocery

Hummel Lake Rd

Bucky's

Caffe La Boheme

Fisherman Bay Road

Holly B's Bakery

Not for Navigation
Not to scale
N

FISHERMAN BAY RESTAURANTS			
Islander Restaurant	Breakfast, Seafood, Beef, Chicken	Fisherman Bay Road	360-468-2233
The Galley	Breakfast, Seafood, Beef, Mexican	3365 Fisherman Bay Road	360-468-2874

LOPEZ ISLAND
Fisherman Bay

BAY CAFÉ

The Bay Café is located along the shore on Old Post Road with beautiful views of San Juan Channel and the entrance to Fisherman Bay. The Café is about a 1 mile (1.6 km) walk from the marinas or you can arrive by bicycle or dinghy. The Café is an islander's favorite for fine dining, offering seafood, beef, pork, chicken, shell fish, and pasta dishes along with nightly seafood specials. All entrees are served with homemade soup, house salad, and fresh baked bread. The menu changes seasonally to take advantage of local produce, fish, and meat like the

Dinner	5:30pm – Close Daily Hours Vary Off Season
Price	Moderate - Expensive
Outdoor Seating	Yes, Deck, Summer Months
Contact.	360-468-3700

Alaskan King Salmon stuffed with organic arugula and basil pesto served with sweet corn and swisschard potato cake; or try the Rack of Lamb with roasted sweet and red potato hash. Desserts also vary and may include the Coffee Crème Caramel and the Blueberry Lime Curd Tart. It's hard not to linger over dessert and coffee in this cozy café with its warm colors, attractive art pieces, or leave the lovely deck during a warm summer evening.

Bay Cafe

ISLANDER RESTAURANT

The Islander Restaurant is within steps of the Lopez Islander Marina docks with great views of Fisherman Bay. This Tiki-style restaurant has attractive woven bamboo-mat ceilings, large knotty-pine pillars and ceiling beams, and two large stone fireplaces. The summer deck runs the length of the restaurant with comfortable white patio furniture and umbrellas for shade. Lovely hanging flower baskets adorn the deck and exterior of the restaurant. The Islander serves seafood dishes, steak, chicken, sandwiches, and burgers. Slow roasted Prime Rib, the Islander specialty, is served with sour cream, horseradish au jus, and baked potato.

Breakfast	8:30am – 11am Daily
Lunch/ Dinner	11:30am – 10pm Daily Hours Vary Off Season
Price	Moderate
Outdoor Seating	Yes, Deck, Summer Months
Contact.	360-468-2233

Other favorites include the Grilled Alaska Salmon, the Islander Coconut Prawns, and Pan Fried Pacific Oysters. For lunch try the homemade Islander Clam Chowder or the Grilled Fish Tacos. Beer, wine, and cocktails are available in the Tiki Bar along with appetizers or full menu.

Islander Restaurant Deck

LOPEZ ISLAND
Fisherman Bay

LOVE DOG CAFÉ ᴛ⦿ᴧ

The Love Dog Café is a friendly family restaurant with lots of country charm. The Café's porch overlooking a grass field and Fisherman Bay, is used for outdoor seating during the summer months. The changing menu is based largely on organic, locally produced products like the Ribeye Dinner with a portobello-cabernet reduction served with rosemary roasted red potatoes and fresh green beans; or try the Salmon Stuffed Manicotti served with a green salad. The Love Dog Paella is a summertime favorite, a one pot extravaganza of fish and shell fish with saffron rice. For lunch, enjoy a Crab Benny or a Coconut Prawns 'n Salad. Children will appreciate the kid's menu or you can ask for a reduced portion on most menu items.

Lunch	11:30am – 3pm Daily Except Wed
Dinner	5pm – 8pm Daily Except Wed Hours Vary Seasonally
Price	Moderate - Expensive
Outdoor Seating	Yes, Porch, Summer Months
Contact	360-468-2150

THE GALLEY ᴛ⦿ᴧ

The Galley is located just across the street from The Galley Guest Dock. This casual restaurant has been nicely decorated with colorful ethnic-style art work and décor created by the owner's daughter. The white-washed brick walls, wood-plank ceiling, and fireplace complement the decor. The more rustic pub is adjacent to the dining room and serves drinks and appetizers. The Galley Restaurant offers an extensive selection of dishes created from local produce, Lopez Island beef, and fresh seafood, including nightly specials like the Encrusted Halibut, the Angus Prime Rib, or the Top Sirloin with

Breakfast	8am – 11am Daily
Lunch/ Dinner	11am – 9pm Daily Hours Vary Off Season
Price	Moderate
Outdoor Seating	Picnic Table
Contact	360-468-2874

mushroom caps and cracked black pepper in a brandy reduction. Lunch items include sandwiches, burgers, and ethnic dishes like the Chimichanga, Fajita Wrap, and the Asian Chicken Salad. Boaters may also want to come by dinghy to The Galley for breakfast or simply stop to enjoy appetizers and rub elbows with the local farmers and fishermen.

VITA'S WILDLY DELICIOUS

Vita's is located in a historic home on Village Rd. North and is the locals best kept secret. Like the name implies, you will find delicious gourmet food such as deli salads, shrimp cakes, chicken satay, and other delights. Items will be heated upon request and you can dine at the deli bar along with a glass of fine wine or a cup of espresso. The grilled Panini and deli sandwiches are good items to-go, like the Rockin Ruben with smoked pastrami, sauerkraut, Swiss cheese, and a tangy deli dressing; or try the Grilled Eggplant & Sweet Red Peppers with a feta-pesto spread. For meals to take back to the boat, choices include the Crusted Chicken Breast, Meat Loaf, Pork Loin, and Pesto Lasagna. For an added treat, visit the Art Gallery located upstairs or the Colin Goode Gallery located next door.

Lunch	10am – 5pm Mon - Fri
	10am – 3pm Saturday
	Closed Dec. – Feb.
Price	Moderate
Outdoor Seating	Yes, Picnic Tables, Summer Months
Contact	360-468-4268

Vita's Wildly Delicious

ORCAS ISLAND
Deer Harbor

Deer Harbor is a popular overnight destination for boaters seeking a fun family vacation or intimate stay for two. The BellPort Deer Harbor Marina offers both hourly and overnight transient moorage. Registration is located in the floating office and gift shop on the north side of the pier. Children enjoy playing on the sandy beaches at Deer Harbor and can purchase beach toys at the Marina gift shop. The Deer Harbor Store & Grill located at the head of the docks carries basic grocery items and serves up orders for house-made sandwiches and breakfast items to be enjoyed aboard your boat or at the picnic tables on the pier. You won't want to miss dinner at the historic Deer Harbor Inn (360-376-4110) open to the general public in addition to guests of the Inn. The Historic Cayou Cove B&B (360-376-3199) is also located nearby and is within walking distance of the Marina. Overnight guests of the Marina have access to the swimming pool located across the road, which is owned by a timeshare company; check in at the pool. For the explorers at heart, you can walk the country roads or rent bicycles through the Marina's gift shop, which also rents kayaks. For Island transportation, contact the Orcas Island Shuttle Bus (360-376-7433), which makes stops at major points on the Island.

American and British settlers arrived in Deer Harbor in 1852 and the Harbor took its name from the numerous deer hunts and winter's meat supply of the Hudson Bay Company of which Louis Cayou, the B&B's name sake, was a member. Today, Deer Harbor continues to be a gathering place where boaters love to relax, visit, and share their stories.

Deer Harbor Marina and Store

Deer Harbor Marina	360-376-3037 VHF 78A	
	www.deerharbormarina.com	

A full service marina owned by BellPort Group: fuel, pumpout, restrooms, showers, laundry, and store. Slips up to 50 ft and side-ties up to 120 ft. plus two (2) buoys located at southwest corner of docks. Pool access and bicycle rentals.

Short-Term: Short term stays marked yellow on east side of dock in front of store and in unoccupied slips for 2 hours at no charge, call ahead.

Overnight: Guest moorage is available for all size craft at $1.45/ft per day. Reservations a must during the busy summer months.

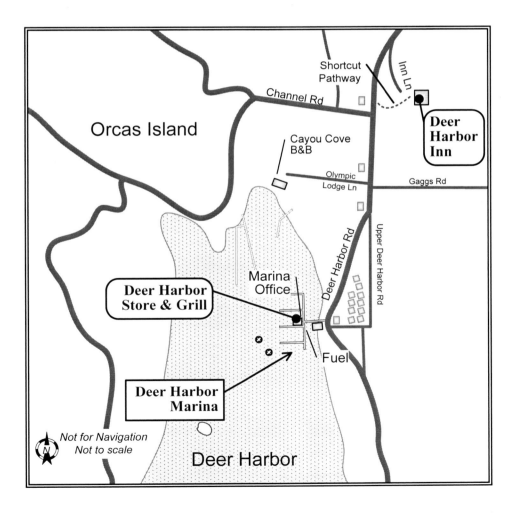

ORCAS ISLAND
Deer Harbor

DEER HARBOR INN

The Deer Harbor Inn is located about a ½ mile (.8 km) walk north of the Marina. A sign along the road points to a short-cut through the trees to the Inn's backyard, or you can call the Inn for their complimentary pick up service, look for their blue vintage cadillac. The Inn and Restaurant is the site of Deer Harbor's first commercial orchard where you can still see 100 year old apple, pear, and plum trees. Around 1910, the Nortons acquired the orchard property and began boarding school teachers from Seattle, which led to establishing the Island's first resort. The Nortons became known for their chicken buffet dinners and homemade desserts. Today the Carpenter family carries on the tradition of excellent home cooked

Dinner	4pm – 9pm Daily mid-April – October Days and Hours Vary Off Season
Price	Moderate - Expensive
Outdoor Seating	Yes, Deck, Summer Months
Contact	360-376-1040 360-376-4110 Inn

meals. The beautiful family rooms welcome you with warm white and maroon colors, lovely wall prints, lace curtains, and linen-set tables. The outdoor deck has a beautiful island view of Deer Harbor. Dinners begin with homemade rolls and a large pot of homemade soup and a generous salad portioned out by an attentive host. Mains include steak, chicken, and Seafood dishes like the Fresh Halibut served in a light orange sauce with creamy mashed potatoes topped with grilled asparagus and broccoli, or try the New York Steak & King Crab Combo. Special after dinner drinks are available in addition to select wines and brews. Don't forget the homemade blackberry cobbler or the fresh homemade ice cream for dessert.

Deer Harbor Inn Deck

DEER HARBOR STORE & GRILL

The Deer Harbor Store & Grill is located on the pier at the Marina and stocks grocery items, ice cream, and beverages. You can purchase your fix'ns from the store and rent one of their barbeques, which may be used on the docks, or you can purchase cooked dogs and hamburgers directly from the store's grill. Deli sandwiches and espresso drinks are also available. You can even order breakfast items all day, including eggs, sausage, hashbrowns, biscuits & gravy, and toasted bagels with creamcheese. Don't miss the Marina's gift shop next door, which carries sportswear, fishing gear, gifts, and toys for the kids. Bicycles can be rented through the Marina for touring the Island..

Store Grill	7am – 7pm Daily 8am – 4pm Off Season
Store Hrs.	7am – 9pm Daily, Summers 8am – 6pm Daily Off Season
Price	Moderate
Outdoor Seating	Yes, Pier
Contact	360-376-3037

Deer Harbor Marina Store & Grill

ORCAS ISLAND
Doe Bay

The Resort at Doe Bay has beautiful ocean views and has been in operation for over 25 years, offering dinghy beach access, several rustic cabins, and waterfront camping and yurts. The on-site grocery store carries a nice selection of gifts and food items. This 1908 building was once a post office and part of a complete village port used for freight and passengers in earlier times. Visitors can enjoy the "clothing optional" soaking tubs and sauna for fifteen dollars per person. The number of day-use guests is limited, so call ahead for availability during office hours, 9am – 6pm daily in the summers. Doe Bay Café is located on the back side of the store with nice water views. The Café is open to the general public for breakfast, lunch, and dinner; it is best to call ahead as Doe Bay Resort is frequently booked by family groups and weddings during the summer months. The Annual Doe Bay Fest is held mid-August hosting popular entertainers and bands from Seattle along with food venders. Tickets can be pre-purchased or purchased on site.

Located in Doe Bay is tiny (6 acre) Doe Island, a Marine State Park with five camp sites (no water) and a 30 foot Guest Dock. Doe Island is within easy reach of Doe Bay Resort via dinghy.

Doe Bay Resort
360-376-2291
www.doebay.com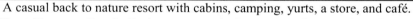

A casual back to nature resort with cabins, camping, yurts, a store, and café.

Short-Term: Beach dinghy access at the Resort. Anchor 100 feet off shore to keep clear of eelgrass.

Overnight: No dock at the Resort for overnight stays. Doe Island Marine State Park nearby.

Doe Island Marine State Park
360-376-2073
WA State Marine Parks

Doe Island is a Marine State Park with rustic camp sites and a seasonal 30 foot guest dock.

Short-Term: Short term stays on park dock at no charge until 1pm. Doe Bay Resort is within easy reach via dinghy.

Overnight: Stays after 1pm and overnight stays are permitted at the dock during the summer months at 50 cents per foot. A self-registration payment box is located at the bulletin board on shore. The dock is removed Oct 15 – April 1.

Doe Bay Resort and Beach Access

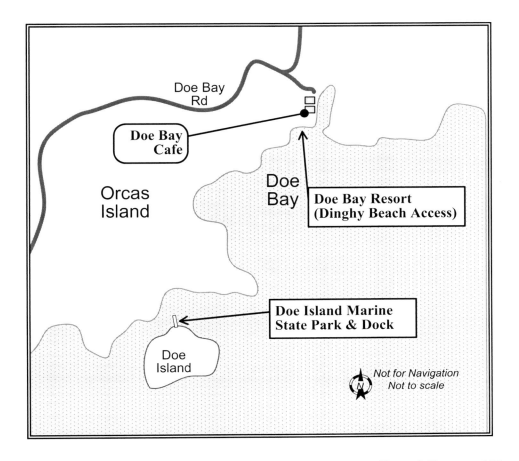

DOE BAY CAFÉ

The rustic Doe Bay Resort has welcomed visitors for over 25 years and is worth a visit for its historic store and café and for its beautiful setting on the southeast side of Orcas Island overlooking Doe Bay. The Café makes use of organic produce from the Resort's on-site garden. The dinner menu changes weekly to reflect produce in season, including fish selections like the Roasted Alaskan King Salmon served with potato-black truffle hash and sauteed greens in a pesto vinaigrette with roasted corn, basil, and grape tomato relish; or try the Seared Alaskan Halibut in a smokey vegetable paella with steamed clams and wilted chard in a saffron broth. Don't miss the starters like the Buck Bay Littleneck Clams or the Cheese Plate with aged Humbolt Fog Goat Cheese, roasted almonds, and lavender honey crostini with rosemary fig compote. Pizza Night is held on Thursdays and music is presented on most weekends during the summer months.

Breakfast/ Lunch	8am – 2pm Daily May – September
	8am – 2pm Mon-Fri October - April
Dinner	6pm – 10pm Daily May - September
	5pm – Close Thur-Sun October - April
Price	Moderate - Expensive
Outdoor Seating	Yes, Deck, Summer Months
Contact	360-376-8059

Doe Bay Cafe

Doe Bay Resort Store

Doe Bay Resort Beach Access

ORCAS ISLAND
East Sound

The town of Eastsound is the commercial center on Orcas Island. Although Eastsound is the largest town on the Island, it maintains a very charming village appeal, offering a variety of attractive shops, including clothing boutiques, galleries, book stores, coffee shops, and good restaurants. The Orcas Farmers' Market is held on Saturdays in the Eastsound Village Green, May through mid-October and includes arts, crafts, and eats. Summer music concerts are also scheduled in the Village Green. Be sure to visit the Orcas Island Historical Museum (360-376-4849) on 181 North Beach Rd. The Museum is made up of several old log cabins (the oldest built in 1880) depicting the life of early settlers and is open Tuesday through Sunday during the summer months; call ahead for the latest hours of operation. For further exploration, bicycle rentals are available through Wildlife Cycles (360-376-4708) at 350 North Beach Rd. Children will appreciate the short ride to The Funhouse (360-376-7177) for ages 7-18 years located at 30 Pea Patch Lane (just off Enchanted Forest Road) for hands-on science exhibits, arts & crafts, and other fun activities. For all your pet's needs, visit Pawki's Pet Shop (360-376-3648) on Main Street.

Eastsound Public Beach	360-376-2273 Chamber	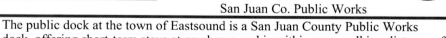
	360-378-8420 Parks	

Two short strips of sandy/rocky beach (one across the street from the Outlook Inn, and one next to Christina's Café) providing public access by dinghy. Bring dinghy well up shore.

Short-Term: Dinghy access via Eastsound Public Beach. Steps near Outlook Inn lead up to the village.

Overnight: Anchorage is available in the bay seaward (south) of the public dock. Do not anchor further in, keep clear of eelgrass.

Eastsound Public Dock	360-370-0501	
	San Juan Co. Public Works	

The public dock at the town of Eastsound is a San Juan County Public Works dock, offering short-term stays at no charge and is within easy walking distance of the village. The dock is normally available April through October.

Short-Term: Short term tie up is available without charge on the 40 foot dock at Eastsound with rafting encouraged on the outside portion of the dock. The Dock is removed during the off season.

Overnight: No overnight stays permitted at the dock but anchorage is available in the bay with beach dinghy access at Eastsound.

East Sound Dock

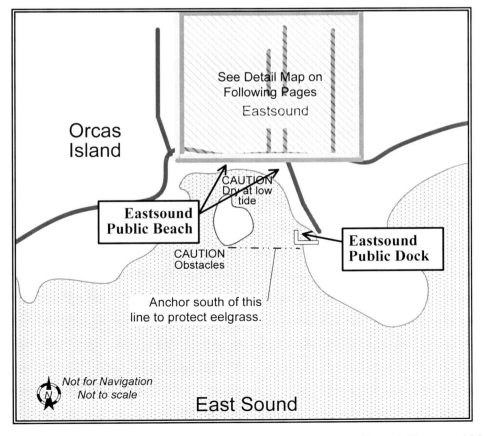

See Detail Map on
Following Pages
Eastsound

Orcas
Island

CAUTION
Dry at low
tide

**Eastsound
Public Beach**

**Eastsound
Public Dock**

CAUTION
Obstacles

Anchor south of this
line to protect eelgrass.

Not for Navigation
Not to scale

East Sound

ORCAS ISLAND
East Sound

EASTSOUND RESTAURANTS			🍽
Bilbo's Festivo	Mexican and Southwest Cuisine	310 A Street	360-376-4728
Chimayo	Southwest Cuisine	123 N Beach Rd	360-376-6394
Christina's	Seafood, Lamb, Meat	310 Main Street	360-376-4904
Darvill's	Espresso Bar and Bookstore	296 Main Street	360-376-2135
Eastsound Wine & Spirits	Wine, Beer Shop	Rose Street & Prune Alley	360-376-2616
Ecotopian	Seafood, Duck, Lamb	365 Beach Road	360-376-9212
Enzo's Caffe	Espresso, Gelato, Panini, Soups	365 N Beach Rd	360-376-3732
Erb's Vegetarian	Organic	188 A Street	360-376-7834
Home Grown Market Natural Foods	Deli Foods and Groceries	8B N Beach Rd	360-376-2009
Island Market	Deli Bar, Groceries	469 Market St.	360-376-6000
Kathryn Taylor Chocolates	Fine Crafted Chocolates	109 N Beach Rd	360-376-1030
Lower Tavern	Burgers & Pub Food	2 Prune Alley	360-376-4848
LuLu's	Pasta, Pizza, Salads	A St & Prune	360-376-2335
New Leaf Café Outlook Inn	Breakfast, Duck, Ribs, Seafood	171 Main Street	360-376-2200
Portofino Pizzeria	Pizza, Salads, Sandwiches	274 A Street	360-376-2085
Rose's Café	Sandwiches, Salads, Baked Goods, Deli	382 Prune Alley Old Fire Station	360-376-4292
Sunflower Café	Breakfast, Quiche, Sandwiches, Soups	29 N Beach Rd	360-376-5435
Teezer's	Cookies, Espresso	A St & N Beach	360-376-2913
Thai Sisters Café	Thai Cuisine	18 Urner Street	360-376-3993
The Kitchen	Wraps, Rice, and Noodle Bowls	249 Prune Alley	360-376-6958

EASTSOUND RESTAURANTS CONTINUED 🍽️			
Vern's Bayside	Breakfast, Seafood, Burgers, Steak	246 Main Street	360-376-2231

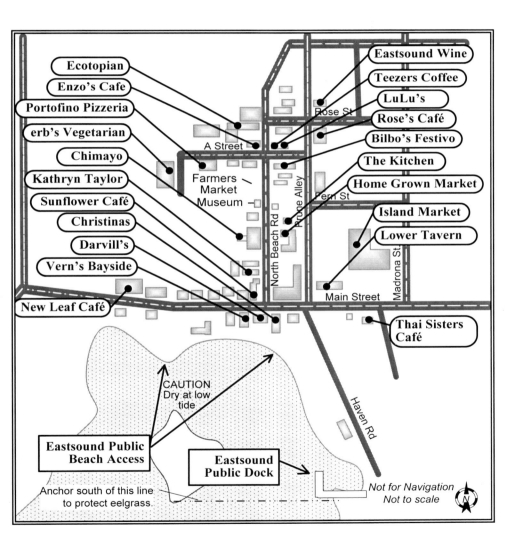

ORCAS ISLAND
East Sound

CHRISTINA'S

Christina's is located on the second floor of the Porter Building on Main Street and has fabulous views of East Sound from the formal dining space and from the lovely deck overlooking the sea. This classy restaurant with its warm woods, area rugs, and attractive table settings specializes in Northwest cuisine featuring local produce and seafood like the Morningstar Farm Mixed Greens with honey-lavender vinaigrette, or start with the Baked Buck Bay Oysters with pernod cream sauce, bacon, and spinach. The menu varies periodically and may include the Curried Seafood Stew, or perhaps the Pan Roasted Chicken with

Dinner Bar Menu	5pm – 9pm Daily 4pm – 11pm Fri & Sat Hours Vary Off Season
Price	Expensive
Outdoor Seating	Yes, Deck, Summer Months
Contact	360-376-4904

chorizo bread pudding; or you might try the Pan Seared Ling Cod served with Italian farro, snap pea saute, and salsa verde. Reservations are recommended for this very special venue in Eastsound. Be sure to take note of the featured art work and photography displayed at Christina's.

Christina's Deck

ECOTOPIAN

The Ecotopian is a classy new dining venue with dark warm woods and a theater décor sporting a stage with red drapery. On-stage music entertainment and solo artists are scheduled from time to time with possible other programs in the future as this new venue evolves. The elegant looking restaurant serves a nice selection of appetizers and quality Mains, including seafood, duck, lamb, and other meats with selections changing frequently. Start with the Chili Lime Soup, an aromatic broth with Buck Bay clams, prawns, and smoked salmon served with grilled baguette;

Dinner	5pm – 10pm Tue-Thur 5pm – 12am Fri & Sat
Price	Moderate - Expensive
Outdoor Seating	No
Contact	360-376-9212

Or perhaps the Tossed Local Greens followed by the Crispy Peking Duck, oven roasted breast and leg confit in a balsamic reduction served with local strawberries, fresh basil, and wild rice. Another excellent choice is the Roasted Chicken served with local fingerling potatoes, orange-glazed baby carrots, and fresh thyme orange jus. The Ecotopian has a separate lounge with bar-style tables to enjoy evening cocktails, wine, and brews along with a special bar menu.

Ecotopian

NEW LEAF CAFÉ

The New Leaf Café is located in the charming Outlook Inn directly across from the public beach stair access, a perfect spot for an early morning breakfast or dinner via dinghy. Breakfast choices include Omelets, Eggs Benedict, Brioche French Toast, and Lox, Bagels, & Cream Cheese. The Inn sports a lovely new lounge where you can enjoy "Small Eats" like the Judd Cove Oysters, pan fried and served with a caper tarter sauce; and "Signature Cocktails" like the Lavender Sidecar, a lavender and vanilla infused vodka with brandy, cointreau, muddled with orange and lime served up with a lavender sugar rim. For an evening meal, enjoy one of the specialty entrees like the Shellfish Gratin of Crab, Lobster, & Prawns; or try the Ribeye Steak, herb crusted and pan roasted, served with pan jus.

Breakfast	8:30am – 10:30am Mon-Fri 8:30am – Noon Sat & Sun July – August Days Vary Seasonally
Dinner	5:30pm – 8:30pm Daily July – August Days Vary Seasonally
Lounge	4pm – 11pm Daily
Price	Moderate
Outdoor Seating	Yes, Patio, Summer Months
Contact	360-376-2200

New Leaf Café

ROSE'S CAFÉ

Rose's Café & Deli is equal to any deli you might find in Europe. Rose's, located off the beaten path at 382 Prune Alley, is housed in a stucco building having the appearance of a home with a lovely front porch perfect for summer dining. The deli offers fine cheeses, meats, bread, and wine to create your own picnic lunch; or you can enjoy lunch in the Café serving delicious soups, salads, and sandwiches using quality deli ingredients. Start your lunch with the Tomato Soup with feta and roasted red peppers, or the Black Bean Soup with ham and smoked chiles. Sandwiches include the Provolone Roasted Red Bell Pepper with tapenade on baguette, or try the Bright Meadow Farm

Café	10am – 4pm Mon-Sat
Deli	10am – 6pm Mon-Fri 10am – 5pm Saturdays
Price	Moderate
Outdoor Seating	Yes, Porch, Summer Months
Contact	360-376-4292 Café 360-376-5805 Deli

Ham & Gruyere on a baguette with sweet cream butter. The salads are equally tasty and don't forget the House Made Ice Cream for dessert or the Farm Rhubarb Pie.

Rose's Cafe

ORCAS ISLAND
Olga

The enchanting tiny village of Olga is an ideal island setting with beautiful views, country homes, a quaint Post Office, and two eateries, both of which are located in historic structures. Be sure to visit the Orcas Island Artworks, located on the corner of Olga Road and Point Lawrence Rd. The James Hardman Gallery (360-376-4588) is located upstairs above the Artworks and is worth a visit. On your ¼ mile (.4 km) walk to the Orcas Island Artworks & Café, be sure to stop by the Jerry Weatherman Potter (360-376-4648) at 3rd Street and Olga Road.

To learn about the interesting history of Olga, sign up for the Olga History Tour, (360-376-5974) held on Wednesdays starting at 2:30pm, July through August; meet at the Orcas Island Artworks. A five dollar donation is suggested for the Guide. Families will enjoy visiting the Buck Bay Shellfish Farm (360-376-5280), a third generation family-run operation. A variety of live shellfish for purchase are kept in containers with saltwater pumped from the bay nearby. The Farm supplies shellfish to several restaurants on the Island and is open to the public Memorial Day to Labor Day. An attendant can help with your purchase, or use the self-service honor system. The Farm is located ½ mile (.8 km) walk east of the Café on Point Lawrence Road just off the intersection with Obstruction Pass Road on Buck Bay. Further up the road from Buck Bay at 716 Pt. Lawrence Road is the Buck Bay Lavender Farm (360-376-2908); the lavender fields are open to the public from 10am to 6pm June through September and are in bloom beginning mid July. You may want to bring your fold-up bicycles or walking shoes to visit these interesting sites near Olga.

Olga Public Dock

Olga Public Dock

Maintained by Community

An enchanting stop with a historic country store, post office, art shops, and two eateries within easy walking distance of the 100 foot public dock.

Short-Term: Short term stays up to 2 hours is without charge. Stays over two hours are to be paid as posted. Float is removed in off season.

Overnight: Payment for overnight moorage should be made at the self-registration box attached to the dock ramp, 3 night maximum.

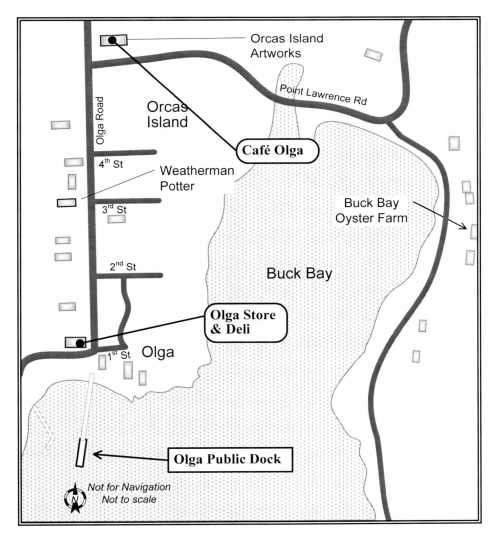

CAFÉ OLGA

Café Olga is located ¼ mile (.4 km) north from the guest dock at the corner of Olga Rd. and Point Lawrence Road. The Café is housed in The Orcas Island Artworks cooperative with quality pottery, sculptures, jewelry, and fine art. This building was once a strawberry barreling plant, which was built in 1937. A Japanese farmer devised the technique of packing strawberries in special wood barrels and placing them in cooled containers for shipment to various locations. Take note of the gabled dormers and casement windows. The original loading dock serves as an outdoor dining space for the Café. Café Olga serves tasty dishes like the Alaska Halibut, pan seared with lemon lime butter, or try the Grass Fed Beef Tenderloin or the Stuffed Chicken Breast with fresh basil, goat cheese, and roasted red peppers. For lunch try the Roasted Chicken & Cashew

Breakfast	9am – all day
Lunch	until 4pm Daily
Dinner	5pm – 8pm Sun-Wed 5pm – 6pm Thur-Sat Hours Vary Off Season
Price	Moderate - Expensive
Outdoor Seating	Yes, Deck, Summer Months
Contact	360-376-4408

Salad or the Melted Fontina Sandwich with marinated red peppers on focaccia with lettuce, tomato, and onions. Don't miss the Blackberry Pie, a nice finish for any meal.

Café Olga

OLGA STORE & DELI

The Olga Store & Deli, just upland from the Olga Public Dock, was built in 1860 and was established at its present location in 1911. The Deli offers daily homemade soups and freshly made sandwiches like the Olga Store Vegie, or try the Turkey on a ciabatta roll with roasted red pepper mayo and Asiago cheese; or perhaps the Roast Beef with Dijon mayo, Havarti cheese, lettuce and tomato. You can sit around the old fashioned wood stove, the outdoor patio, or the dining bar overlooking the entrance to East Sound.

Deli Foods	10am – 5pm Tue-Sun Hours may Vary
Price	Moderate
Outdoor Seating	Yes, Patio, Summer Months
Contact	360-376-5195

Don't miss the baked goodies like the cream berry scone, cinnamon buns, and the blackberry pie with Lopez Island Creamery ice cream.

Olga Store & Deli

ORCAS ISLAND
Orcas Landing

Orcas Landing is an attractive, fun location offering gift shops, boutiques, and three dinning venues plus an espresso shop and a village grocery store that carries deli items and serves up espresso drinks. The dock, located next to the Ferry Terminal at Orcas Landing is owned by San Juan Co. and provides 4-hour stays at no charge. At the end of the pier is the Orcas Island Eclipse Charters (360-376-6566), offering whale watching tours, historic tours, and a Water Taxi Service (360-376-3711) as well as the Sea Shanty Gift Shop. Other gift shops include the Monkey Puzzle next to the Village Store, and the Orcas Mopeds & Gifts (360-376-5266) just west of the Orcas Hotel. The neighboring Cottage Gift shop sells ice cream and souvenirs.

You won't want to miss dining at the Historic Orcas Hotel, offering a casual café and the Octavia's dining room with lovely views of Blind Bay. Breakfast and casual eats can be enjoyed at the adjacent Mamie's Restaurant & Boardwalk Cottages overlooking Harney Channel and Blind Bay.

Orcas Landing Dock

Orcas Landing Dock

Orcas Landing	360-370-0500	
	San Juan County	

Orcas Landing next to the Orcas Island ferry terminal offers 4-hour stays on a 160 foot plus dock; portion of dock leased to Eclipse Charters.

Short-Term: Maximum stay of 4 hours at no charge.

Overnight: No overnight stays. Anchorage in nearby Blind Bay and approx. four park buoys for $10/night, registration box on Blind Island.

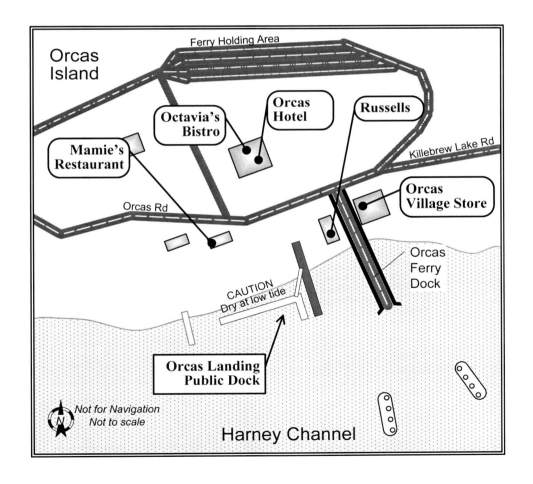

ORCAS ISLAND
Orcas Landing

RUSSELLS

The adorable Russels Home Décor shop hosts an espresso bar, popular with passengers waiting for the ferry and conveniently located just upland from the public transient dock. The shop carries fine jewelry, apparel, and home décor along with a selection of fine wines. Visitors enjoy the lovely patio with umbrella shaded tables and the great views of Harney Channel.

Hours	8:30am – 6pm Daily Summers 9am – 6pm Daily Off Season
Price	Moderate
Outdoor Seating	Yes, Patio Deck, Summer Months
Contact	360-376-4389

Russels

MAMIE'S RESTAURANT

Mamie's Restaurant, adjacent to The Boardwalk Cottages, is perched on a ridge overlooking Orcas Landing. The Café, with its glass-wall enclosed deck, takes in the beautiful views of Harney Channel with a bird's-eye view of all the pleasure craft and ferry boat traffic. To start the day, try the Crab Omelete, the French Toast, or perhaps "The Boardwalk" with two eggs, hashbrowns, and an English muffin. If you are looking for quick eats before or after your day's cruise, you can order chicken & fish baskets or burgers for take-out or dining in like the Grilled Salmon and Jim's Chicken Burger, or try the Pulled Pork Sandwich or Lauren's Kielbasa Dog.

Breakfast	7am – 11am Daily
Lunch/ Dinner	11am – 6:30pm Hours Vary Off Season
Price	Moderate
Outdoor Seating	Enclosed Deck, Year-round
Contact	360-376-2971

Mamie's Restaurant

ORCAS ISLAND
Orcas Landing

OCTAVIA'S

Octavia's Bistro and the Orcas Cafe are located in the historic Orcas Hotel within easy reach of the Orcas Landing Dock. This beautifully restored Victorian Hotel was built in 1904 by Joseph van Bogaert, who was commissioned by landowner William Sutherland. Bogaert's daughter, Octavia along with her husband, managed the Hotel, which became popular for the garden fresh fruits and vegetables and Octavia's fried chicken and fruit pies. Current owners, Doug and Laura Tidwell, have re-created the fine dining experience and gracious Hotel accommodations. The beautiful dining room has antique furnishings, wainscoting, lace curtains, and linen set tables. Great views of Harney Channel can be seen from the dining room as well as from the lovely

Café Lunch/ Dinner	6am – 11am Daily 11am - 8pm Daily Hours Vary Off Season
Octavia's Bistro	5pm – 10pm Summers (seat by 8:30pm) Hours Vary Off Season
Price	Moderate
Outdoor Seating	Yes, Porch, Summer Months
Contact	360-376-4300

wrap-around porch. Music is usually held on Friday nights. The meals are excellent with selections that change frequently. The Steak and Mango Entrée Salad is delicious with marinated flank steak strips, mango slices, avocado, and tomato served on seasonal greens tossed in citrus vinaigrette; or start with the Mixed greens with fresh pears, dried cranberries, goat cheese, and candied Hazelnuts followed by a main like the Pan Seared Natural Beef Tenderloin, or perhaps the Flame Grilled Salmon with mango salsa, rice, and fresh vegetables. The Orcas Hotel Café on the west side of the building offers espresso and breakfast items and lunch service including salads, burgers, and sandwiches.

Orcas Hotel

ORCAS VILLAGE STORE

In addition to being a well-stocked grocery, the Orcas Village Store has a wonderful deli case with meats and cheeses, including duck and chicken pate', pastrami, pancetta, cappacola, and Italian roast beef among other meat selections. You can create your own meat & cheese tray by adding several of the many cheeses available such as provolone, gruyere, chimay, German, Swiss, and Triple Blue, among others. If you prefer sandwiches, fill out the order form for a custom made sandwich; or you can purchase ready-made sandwiches, roasted chicken, baked lasagna, and whole quiches along with desserts in the deli section. The Orcas Village Store is a fun place to shop for groceries and eats or stop by for a cup of espresso.

Deli Foods	6am – 9pm Daily Summers 6am – 8pm Daily Off Season
Price	Market Prices
Outdoor Seating	No
Contact	360-376-8860

Orcas Village Store

ORCAS ISLAND
Rosario

A casual bygone elegance best describes Rosario Resort. The historic Moran Mansion is a highlight and a must see. The property was recently purchased with the intention of refurbishing the resort and expanding the docks to provide for additional slips; construction has not yet begun at present. Currently, reservations for overnight moorage is required May through September; March and April is first-come, first-serve. Hourly stays are located on the docks next to the Harbor Master/Marina Office, call ahead for available space. The Moran Mansion is open Monday through Saturday 10am to 6pm for public viewing during the summer months (June to mid-Sept) with nightly organ concerts beginning at 5pm; admission is five dollars. The Mansion is open on Saturdays only during the off-season. Casual dining is offered at the Cascade Grill near the Marina docks and swimming pool; both are open during the summer months. The formal dining room in the Moran Mansion is closed until further notice.

Moran Mansion (360-376-2222) was built in 1906 by former Seattle mayor and ship builder, Robert Moran. After building the USS Nebraska and other notable ships, Moran decided to retire at age 49 and began acquiring parcels of land on Orcas Island. In his later years, Robert Moran donated 5,000 acres to the State of Washington, which became Moran State Park. During the Great Depression, Moran had difficulty finding a buyer for his Mansion, which eventually sold several times and was opened in 1960 to the public as Rosario Resort.

Be sure to visit beautiful Moran State Park, which has several fresh water lakes and numerous hiking trails. Mt. Constitution and its stone observation tower is located in the Park and is a must do for the stupendous views. Once you witness the captivating views of islands, ocean, and mountains as far as the eye can see, this island paradise will be set in your heart forever. For transportation to Moran State Park and other points of interest on Orcas Island, call the seasonal Orcas Island Shuttle (360-376-7433); or call the Orcas Island Taxi (360-376-TAXI). The Orcas Island Shuttle Co. also rents cars and can deliver and retrieve your car anywhere on the Island for free with a 24-hour advanced notice.

Rosario Resort Marina

Rosario Resort Marina	360-376-2222 VHF 78A
	www.rosarioresort.com

Rosario Resort Marina is a full service marina, including showers, restrooms, fuel, store, restaurant, and swimming pool; 38 slips with plans for additional slips.

Short-Term: Short term stays for 2 hours dockside next to Harbor Marina Office and on buoys for 6 hours at no charge at Harbor Master's discretion, call ahead for space. Landing fee of $25 if use showers, pool etc. For extended hours, make payment at the Marina Office. Rates are posted.

Overnight: Slips for vessels in 25-50 ft slips as assigned; yachts up to 45 ft on buoys. Larger vessels anchor out (dinghy dock located at end of channel next to Cascade Grill). Guests may use all of the Resort's amenities.

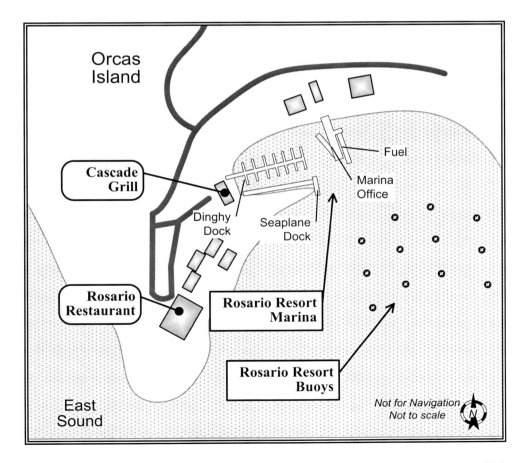

CASCADE BAY GRILL

Roasario's Cascade Bay Grill & Store is located just upland from the Marina, adjacent to the Marina Swimming Pool. The Store stocks groceries and gift items and offers indoor window-side seating for the Grill; or you can sit outside at the umbrella shaded tables. The Cascade Grill serves up fish 'n chips, pizza, and burgers for lunch, including their signature CBG Burger with a house secret sauce; or try the Alaskan Amber beer battered Cod Chips. Scrambles, bacon, and hash browns are offered for breakfast, including the Meat Lovers bacon, ham, and sausage scramble with onion, tomato, and cheddar cheese. Non-meat eaters will appreciate the Ultimate Vegetarian Scramble. A variety of donuts and pastries are also available along with coffee and espresso.

Breakfast	8am – 11am Daily mid-May to mid-Sept
Lunch/ Dinner	11am – 8pm Daily mid-May to mid-Sept
Price	Moderate
Outdoor Seating	Yes, Deck & Lawn, Summer Months
Contact	360-376-2222 Ext 720

Cascade Bay Grill

Cascade Bay Grill

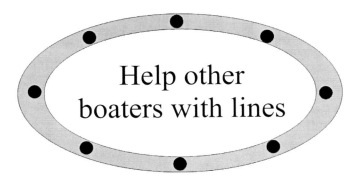

Help other
boaters with lines

ORCAS ISLAND
West Beach

West Beach is a fun family resort with cute cottages along the beach with camp sites and RV sites situated upland. The West Beach Store has cozy seating and a wood stove to enjoy while reading the local news, playing board games, or relaxing with an espresso or ice cream creation. Internet access is available at the Store so guests can check email or take care of other business. Boaters should beware of the abundant eelgrass when approaching the docks at West Beach.

Don't miss visiting The Right Place Pottery (360-376-4023), located directly across the road from the Resort at 2915 Enchanted Forest Rd. The pottery shop specializes in personalized plates, mugs, bowls, tea sets, and other items. During the summer months, folks of all ages can try their hand at the potter's wheel for a small fee. Items are also available to paint, a fun project for the whole family.

If you want to stretch your legs, you can rent bicycles at the Store and ride the Enchanted Forest Road into the village of Eastsound. Be sure to stop by the Orcas Island Pottery (360-376-2813), located a short distance south of West Beach at 338 Old Pottery Road. This excellent pottery shop is set among beautiful gardens, picnic tables, and fountains overlooking President's Channel.

A point of interest at the West Beach Resort is the 1930's smokehouse, where overnight guests of the Resort can smoke fish with alder or apple wood, ask for the salmon brine recipe.

West Beach Resort Dock

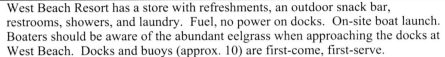

West Beach Resort

360-376-2240
www.westbeachresort.com

West Beach Resort has a store with refreshments, an outdoor snack bar, restrooms, showers, and laundry. Fuel, no power on docks. On-site boat launch. Boaters should be aware of the abundant eelgrass when approaching the docks at West Beach. Docks and buoys (approx. 10) are first-come, first-serve.

Short-Term: Short-term stays up to 2 hours without charge. Report to the Marina Store upon arrival and for payment over 2 hours.

Overnight: Overnight stays are as available on buoys and in boat slips for vessels up to 29 feet. Report to the Marina Store for payment and registration. Buoys $18/day and slips $25/day for vessels up to 25ft and .60/ft for vessels over 25 feet.

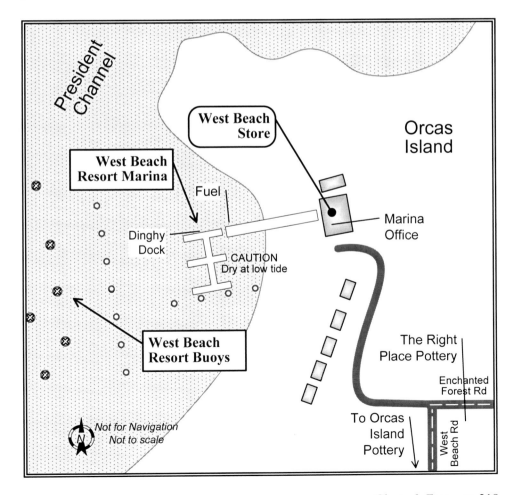

WEST BEACH STORE

Although not considered a restaurant, the West Beach Store is a great place to stop for banana splits, milkshakes, hot-fudge Sundaes, and root beer floats or pick up a cup of espresso, a glass of lemonade or soda drinks. Great views of President Channel can be enjoyed from the outdoor eating bar and picnic table. The Store carries groceries, fishing supplies, gifts, and toys. West Beach is a fun, friendly stop where you can satisfy your ice cream hankerings.

Ice Cream	8am – 9pm Daily Summer Months Days Vary Seasonally
Price	Moderate
Outdoor Seating	Yes, Deck, Summer Months
Contact	360-376-2240

West Beach Resort

West Beach Resort

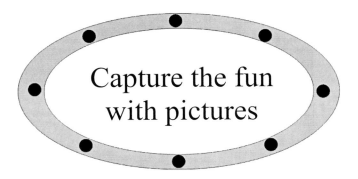

Capture the fun
with pictures

ORCAS ISLAND
West Sound

The Boddington Public Dock at the tiny community of Westsound provides a sense of peace in a tranquil country setting. The Westsound Café, located in the historic Kingfish Inn, is within easy walking distance of the Public Dock and is open to the general public for dinner and weekend lunches. The Inn is 100 years old and once served as a grocery store and a post office. The Community Hall, located near the Dock at 884 Deer Harbor Road, was built by volunteers in 1902 and is available to the public for special events. To book the hall, call 360-376-2314. The property was deeded to Westsound in 1900 by Alexander Chalmers, an early pioneer and sea captain, who moved to Orcas Island in 1893 from England. George Adkins, another early pioneer and owner of the Westsound Store, provided the building materials for the Community Hall.

If you are planning to dine at the Westsound Café, you might want to make overnight reservations at West Sound Marina or anchor out as overnight stays are not permitted at the Boddington Public Dock. The West Sound Marina is located a short distance east of the Public Dock in West Sound Harbor.

Boddington Public Dock

West Sound Marina   360-376-2314   VHF 16

Casual full service marina with repairs, power, fuel, restrooms, and showers. The 300 foot guest dock is the southernmost float and is marked "guest dock." Pumpout and haulout. Chandlery and Marina Office located upland, offering charts, books, marine supplies, inflatable's.

Short-Term: Short term stays at no charge while shopping at the Chandlery.

Overnight: Overnight stays are $1.00/ft. 24-hour reservation requested. Anchorage in West Sound.

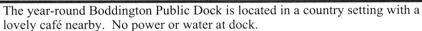

Boddington Public Dock	360-370-0500	
	San Juan Co. Public Works	

The year-round Boddington Public Dock is located in a country setting with a lovely café nearby. No power or water at dock.

Short-Term: Two connected 40 ft docks available for short-term stays without charge.

Overnight: No overnight stays permitted at the dock. West Sound Marina nearby. Anchorage in West Sound.

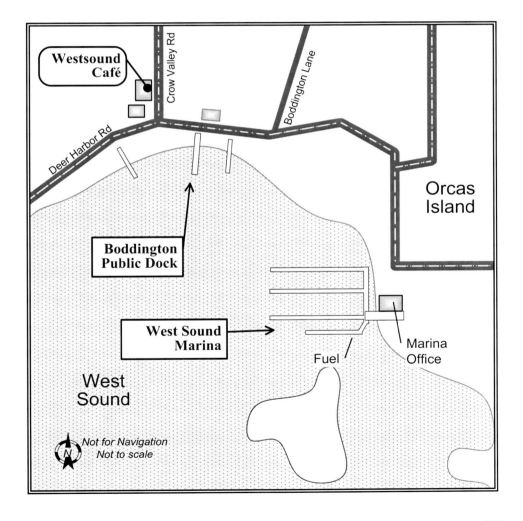

WESTSOUND CAFE

The West Sound Café is one-quarter mile (.4 km) west of the Boddington Public Dock at the corner of Deer Harbor Rd. and Crow Valley Road in the historic Kingfish Inn within sight of the public dock. Views of West Sound can be enjoyed from inside the Café and from the lovely outdoor deck. The menu varies seasonally and features local seafood and produce along with Northwest wines and locally brewed beers. Starters include Fried Oysters, Calamari, and Mixed Greens, or begin with the Seafood Bisque consisting of halibut, clams, and cod in a creamy white wine saffron broth served with bread. Mains include entrée salads, burgers, fish tacos, and seafood dishes like the Thai Curry

Breakfast	Guests of the Inn Only
Lunch	11:30am – 3pm Fri & Sat
Dinner	5pm – 8pm Tue – Sat Closed Nov. – Dec.
Price	Moderate
Outdoor Seating	Yes, Deck, Summer Months
Contact	360-376-4440

Halibut Fillet in a spicy green curry sauce over Jasmine rice served with local organic greens. Other seasonal choices may include Grilled Salmon topped with a ginger, coconut, and tomato peanut sauce served with Asian slaw.

West Sound Cafe

Kingfish Inn B&B

West Sound Cafe

SAN JUAN ISLAND
Friday Harbor

Friday Harbor has much to offer visitors and is the largest town in the San Juan Islands. The town is filled with locals and tourists alike during the summer months. The town of Friday Harbor offers great views, great restaurants, boutiques, book stores, art galleries, and several museums, all within easy walking distance of the guest docks at the Port of Friday Harbor. Ladies may want to check out the Lavendera Spa (360-378-3637) or the Focused Bodywork (360-378-5166) spa services. Guys and gals alike love Kings Marine Chandlery (360-378-4593) for boating supplies, clothing, and accessories located upstairs above the King's Market at the corner of Spring & First.

Allow several days to take in all that Friday Harbor and the surrounding area has to offer. After breakfast or lunch, visit The Whale Museum (360-378-4710) at 62nd First Street N. to enjoy exhibits and educational programs. After an evening of fine dining, you may want to take in a seasonal performance at the Island Stage Left (360-378-5649) or at the San Juan Community Theatre (360-378-3210).

Points of interest beyond the town of Friday Harbor include the San Juan Vineyards, the Pelindaba Lavender Farm, and the American Camp National Historical Park. The San Juan Vineyards (360-378-9463) are located three miles (4.8 km) from Friday Harbor on Roche Harbor Road. The tasting room and gift shop are in an old schoolhouse built in 1896. Visitors may bring a picnic lunch, purchase a bottle of wine and enjoy views of the vineyards from the deck. Be sure to sample the Madeline Angevine and Siegerrebe wines produced from these on-site varieties. The Pelindaba Lavender Farm (866-819-1911) located at 33 Hawthorne Lane offers lavender products from their fragrant blooming fields, or you can enjoy an icy glass of lavender lemonade on the Farm's shady front porch; Store hours are 9:30am to 5:30pm May through September.

Visitors have several options for transportation in Friday Harbor: the M&W Auto car rentals (360-378-2886), located at 725 Spring Street; Susie's Moped Rentals (360-378-5244), located one block from the Ferry Terminal on Nichol's Street; and the Island Bicycles (360-378-4941) at 380 Argyle Avenue. These rental services are happy to provide maps and driving directions. For taxi service, call Bob's Taxi (360-378-6777), Classic Cab (360-378-7519), or San Juan Taxi (360-378-8294). The San Juan Transit bus (360-378-8887) runs from 9am to 5pm approximately every hour with scheduled stops around San Juan Island.

Don't miss visiting the American Camp National Historic Park (360-378-2902), located about 6 miles (9.6 km) south of Friday Harbor on Cattle Point Road. The Park commemorates the boundary dispute between Great Britain and the U.S. over the Oregon Territory, which ignited in June of 1859 when an American shot a British owned pig. American soldiers and the British Royal Marines remained on the island for 12 years, until Kaiser Wilhelm I of Germany, as arbitrator, awarded the San Juan Islands to the United States. Two historic buildings survive, along with the remains of an earthen gun emplacement. Other building sites are identified, including the locations of the Hudson's Bay Co. Farm, the old town of San Juan, and the American Camp Cemetery.

Friday Harbor Port Marina

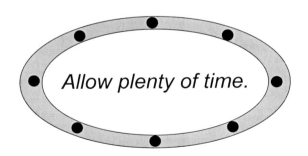

Allow plenty of time.

SAN JUAN ISLAND
Friday Harbor

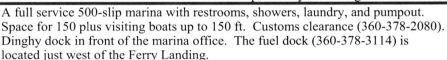

Friday Harbor Port Marina   360-378-2688   VHF 66A
www.portfridayharbor.org

A full service 500-slip marina with restrooms, showers, laundry, and pumpout. Space for 150 plus visiting boats up to 150 ft. Customs clearance (360-378-2080). Dinghy dock in front of the marina office. The fuel dock (360-378-3114) is located just west of the Ferry Landing.

Short-Term: Short-term stays up to 4 hours are without charge, call the office for space assignment. Short-term stays are located on both sides of Breakwater A and on the inside of Breakwater B. Yachts normally use the breakwater, and vessels up to 44 feet are normally assigned slips. Vessels 35 feet and under can tie on the inside of "H" Dock.

Overnight: Stays over 4 hours and overnight stays are charged based on vessel length and vary seasonally ranging from .75/ft to $1.75/ft; six dollar reservation fee. Reservations are a must during the busy summer months. Anchorage is an option north of the marina.

Cannery House with Marina views

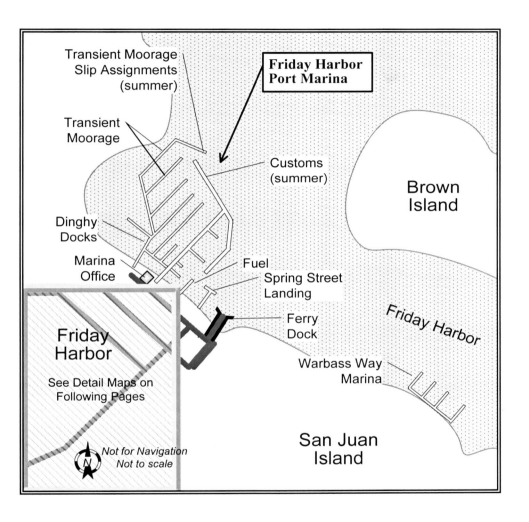

Transient Moorage
Slip Assignments
(summer)

**Friday Harbor
Port Marina**

Transient
Moorage

Customs
(summer)

Brown
Island

Dinghy
Docks

Marina
Office

Fuel

Spring Street
Landing

Friday
Harbor

See Detail Maps on
Following Pages

Ferry
Dock

Friday Harbor

Warbass Way
Marina

Not for Navigation
Not to scale

San Juan
Island

N

FRIDAY HARBOR RESTAURANTS			🍽
Backdoor Kitchen	Seafood, Lamb, Chicken, Steak	400 A Street	360-378-9540
Bakery Café Demeter	Coffee, Baked Goods	80 Nichols Street	360-370-5443
Blue Water Bar & Grill	Breakfast, Baskets, Sandwiches, Burgers	7 Spring Street	360-378-2245
Bistro Garden	Pizza, Sandwiches	180 Web Street	360-378-1174
Blue Dolphin	Breakfast, Burgers, Sandwiches	185 First Street	360-378-6116
Bluff Restaurant in Friday Harbor House	Seafood, Pork, Lamb	130 West Street	360-378-8455
Cannery House	Sandwiches, Soups	174 N First St.	360-378-6505
China Pearl	Seafood, Noodles	51 Spring Street	360-378-5254
Church Hill Coffeehouse	Breakfast, Espresso, Sandwiches	1 Harrison Street	360-378-2772
Coho Restaurant	Seafood, Beef	120 Nichols St.	360-378-6330
Dos Diablos	Mexican Cuisine	40 Spring Street	360-378-8226
Downriggers	Breakfast, Seafood, Chicken, Pasta, Steak	10 Front Street	360-378-2700
F. H. Ice Cream	Ice Cream, Espresso	Memorial Park	No Phone
F. H. Seafood	Seafood Market	Main Dock	360-378-5779
Friday's Crabhouse	Seafood, Burgers	65 Front Street	360-378-8801
Front Street Ale House	Seafood, Sandwiches, Pizza, Steak	1 Front Street	360-378-Beer
Garden Path Café	Burgers, Sandwiches, Soups, Salads, Fish	135 Second St.	360-378-6255
Golden Triangle	Seafood, Noodles	140 First Street	360-378-1917
Haley's Bait Shop & Grill	Burgers, Steaks, Salads, Fish 'n Chips	175 Spring Street	360-378-4434
Herbs Tavern	Burgers, Fish	80 First Street	360-378-7076
Jimmy's Paradise Café (bowling lanes)	Burgers, Sandwiches, Chicken, Steak	365 Spring Street	360-378-3131

SAN JUAN ISLAND
Friday Harbor

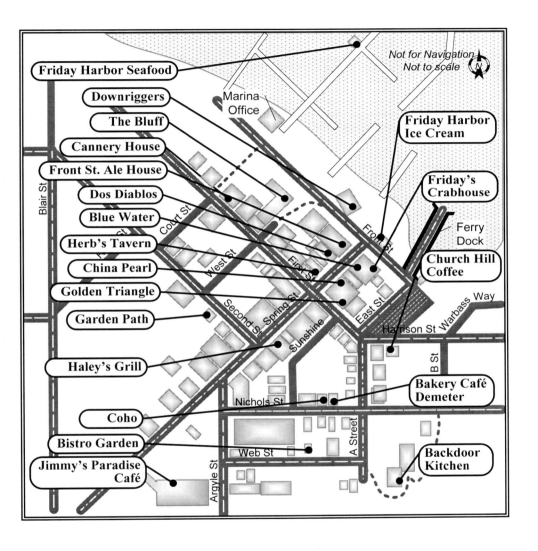

Not for Navigation
Not to scale

Friday Harbor Seafood

Downriggers

The Bluff

Cannery House

Front St. Ale House

Dos Diablos

Blue Water

Herb's Tavern

China Pearl

Golden Triangle

Garden Path

Haley's Grill

Coho

Bistro Garden

Jimmy's Paradise Café

Marina Office

Friday Harbor Ice Cream

Friday's Crabhouse

Ferry Dock

Church Hill Coffee

Bakery Café Demeter

Backdoor Kitchen

Blair St

Court St

West St

First St

East St

Second St

Spring St

Sunshine

Harrison St

Warbass Way

B St

Nichols St

A Street

Web St

Argyle St

Front St

SAN JUAN ISLAND
Friday Harbor

FRIDAY HARBOR RESTAURANTS			🍽
Latte Shop (world's skinniest)	Espresso, Pastries	127 Spring Street	No phone
Maloula's	Mediterranean, Greek (mid April – Sept)	1 Front Street (take elevator)	360-378-8485
Market Chef	Deli Sandwiches, Soups, Salads	225 A Street	360-378-4546
Mi Casita	Mexican Cuisine	95 Nichols Street	360-378-6103
Pazzo Vivo Bistro	Pizza, Burgers, Fish, Sandwiches, Pasta	175 First Street	360-378-4118
Peppermill	Seafood, Chicken, Steak, Pasta	680 Spring Street (Best Western)	360-378-7060
Rocky Bay Café	Breakfast, Burgers, Sandwiches, Chicken	209 Spring Street	360-378-5051
San Juan Florist & Sweet Shop	Ice Cream, Flowers, Chocolates	160 First Street	360-378-2477
SJ Coffee Roasters	Espresso, Ice Cream, Candy	18 Cannery Landing	360-378-4443
Steps Wine Bar & Café	Seafood, Chicken, Lamb, Beef	140A First Street	360-370-5959
Sweet Retreat	Coffee, Shakes, Dogs	264 Spring Street	360-378-1957
The Doctor's Office	Espresso, Ice Cream, Sandwiches, Soups	85 Front Street	360-378-8865
The Hungry Clam	Baskets, Burgers, Sandwiches	A & First Street	360-378-3474
The Naked Bean	Espresso, Pastries	150 First Street	360-378-2600
The Place Bar Grill	Seafood, Lamb, Pasta	#1 Spring Street	360-378-8707
Vinny's Ristorante	Seafood, Pasta, Steak	165 West Street	360-378-1934

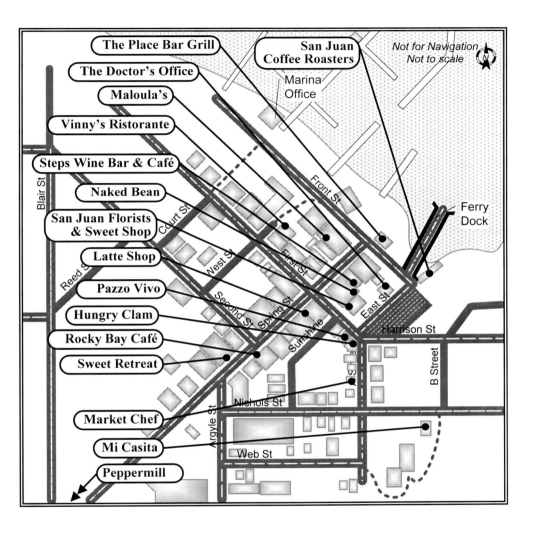

Not for Navigation
Not to scale

The Place Bar Grill

San Juan
Coffee Roasters

The Doctor's Office

Maloula's

Vinny's Ristorante

Steps Wine Bar & Café

Naked Bean

San Juan Florists
& Sweet Shop

Latte Shop

Pazzo Vivo

Hungry Clam

Rocky Bay Café

Sweet Retreat

Market Chef

Mi Casita

Peppermill

Marina
Office

Ferry
Dock

Blair St

Front St

Court St

West St

First St

East St

Reed St

Second St

Spring St

Sunshine

Harrison St

B Street

Argyle St

Nichols St

Web St

SAN JUAN ISLAND
Friday Harbor

BACKDOOR KITCHEN

The Backdoor Kitchen is a hidden gem, both literally and figuratively speaking. To find the Backdoor from the Ferry Terminal, walk up East Street, then to the end of "A" Street, where you will see the "Green Man Landscape & Design" business, walk around the backside of this building through the lovely landscaping, you will pass fountains, sculptures, bamboo, and rare plants before reaching the Backdoor. This intimate restaurant sports dark warm woods, colorful artwork, attractive light fixtures, and formal table settings. Menu selections

Dinner	5pm – Close Wed-Mon
Lounge	5pm – Close Wed-Sat
Price	Expensive
Outdoor Seating	Yes, Patio, Summer Months
Contact	360-378-9540

include seafood, beef, lamb, and duck with the use of seasonal local farm produce, such as the Seared Sea Scallops topped with ginger beurre blanc, served with sesame scallion rice cakes and local organic vegetables; or try the Marinated Lamb Sirloin served with mashed potatoes, seasonal vegetables, and gremolata.

Backdoor Kitchen

COHO RESTAURANT

The Coho Restaurant is located in the lovely, historic Craftsman House on Nichols Street. This attractive restaurant incorporates fresh seafood, local produce, and local meats in their delicious and artful dishes. Start with Coho's creative Green Salad tossed with a blood-orange curry vinaigrette and topped with roasted beets, candied pecans, and Quail Croft Farms goat cheese. Mains include the Lopez Island Grass Fed Tenderloin and Coho's Signature Alaskan Salmon, or try the Organic Chicken Breast wrapped in grape leaves served with

Dinner	5pm – 9pm Mon-Sat June – September Hours Vary Off Season
Price	Expensive
Outdoor Seating	No
Contact	360-378-6330

Basmati rice-stuffed Spanikopita, green garlic tomato chutney and a Sorrell yogurt sauce. For a sweet conclusion, try the Crème Brulee or the Italian Cannoli, or perhaps an after dinner drink. The Coho owns two nearby accommodations in three historic buildings, the Harrison House Suites and the Tucker House Inn where guests can enjoy a fabulous four-course breakfast.

MARKET CHEF

The Market Chef is part deli, part market, and specialty cook shop and is a local's favorite eatery. The deli case is filled with entrees, side dishes, vegetables, and deli salads to be enjoyed as take-out or eaten in the café. For lunch, order one of the specialty sandwiches along with fresh homemade soup and a garden salad. Salads are made with Waldron Island's "Nootka Rose Farm" organic salad greens and sandwiches are prepared with Baked organic breads. Sandwich choices include the Applewood Smoked Ham with sharp cheddar and

Dinner	10am – 5pm Mon-Fri Till 4pm Off Season
Price	Moderate
Outdoor Seating	Yes, Patio, Summer Months
Contact	360-378-4546

Major Grey's chutney, or try the Curried Egg Salad Sandwich with roasted peanuts, crunchy sprouts, and a touch of chutney. A selection of small-producer wines and a fine selection of micro-brewed beers are available at The Market Chef. Patrons can dine indoors or enjoy the backyard or front patio at this 1940's style home located on 'A' Street.

SAN JUAN ISLAND
Friday Harbor

BLUFF RESTAURANT

The Bluff Restaurant is located in the Friday Harbor House Inn perched on the crest of a hill overlooking the Harbor. Outdoor garden seating is available during the summer months on the lovely patio. The dining room space has recently been remodeled reflecting a new-age casual appeal, including a separate classy bar. In addition to the new mainstay menu, seasonal nightly specials are offered like the local caught King Salmon, Lopez Island Rack of Lamb, and the Carlton Farms Tenderloin. Lunch items are served all day and include sandwiches, fish tacos, oysters, and crab cakes; or enjoy one of the pasta dishes and salads.

Lunch	11am – all day
Dinner	5pm – 10pm Daily Hours Vary Off Season
Price	Moderate - Expensive
Outdoor Seating	Yes, Patio, Summer Months
Contact	360-378-8455

Bluff Restaurant

STEPS WINE BAR & CAFÉ

This somewhat hidden Café located down a lovely alley just off First Street, offers over 50 wines, friendly service, and great food. Steps works with local farmers to obtain fresh produce, meat, fish, and other ingredients for their creative dishes. The dining spaces are small and cozy, while the food is robust like the Roasted Duck Breast with soft polenta and local arugula-zucchini sweet onion relish; or try the Eggplant & Goat Cheese Cannelloni served with Chickpeas-Cucumber Pepper Salad. Don't forget the Brown Butter Carrot Cake for dessert or the Mexican Chocolate Decadence.

Dinner	5pm – 9pm Mon – Sat
Happy Hr	5pm – 6pm Mon-Thur
Price	Moderate - Expensive
Outdoor Seating	No
Contact	360-370-5959

Steps Wine Bar & Cafe

THE PLACE BAR & GRILL

This Bar & Grill is The Place for close-up views of the water, pleasure boats, and ferry arrivals and departures, a true enchanting island venue. The Place sits directly over the water housed in the oldest building in Friday Harbor. This family owned and operated fine-dining restaurant serves seafood, lamb, chicken, beef, and vegetable dishes using local, seasonal products. Start with the Mushroom Saute' Appetizer, a sauté of shiitake and button mushrooms with artichoke hearts, sun-dried tomatoes, garlic, and fresh basil served with toast rounds and warm goat cheese. For an entrée, try the Alaskan King Salmon grilled with blackening spices served over Asian slaw; or try the Painted Hills Filet Mignon with a Whidbey's Port demi glace. The ambiance is satisfying, too, with formal set tables and lace curtains. "The Place" has brought it all together with location, décor, and cuisine.

Dinner	4:30pm – 9pm Daily Summer Months Hours Vary Off Season
Price	Expensive
Outdoor Seating	No
Contact	360-378-8707

The Place Bar & Grill

VINNY'S RISTORANTE

If you love Italian food and romantic settings, you will love Vinny's. It is set on the crest of a hill next to the Friday Harbor House. The white linen-set tables, soft overhead lighting, warm colors, and Italian art pieces, all help set the stage for a special evening. For starters, try the Caprese Salad made with tomatoes, basil, and mozzarella cheese tossed in olive oil and balsamic vinegar along with the Westcott Bay Mussels steamed with Vermouth, garlic, onion, tomato, and basil. Mains include veal, lamb, chicken, beef, and fish, including the Veal Marsala and the Cioppino Stew, or try one of the varied pasta dishes like the Four Cheese Rigatoni or the Fettuccini Romano.

Dinner	4pm – 9pm Daily
Price	Moderate - Expensive
Outdoor Seating	No
Contact	360-378-1934

Vinny's

SAN JUAN ISLAND
Roche Harbor

Roche Harbor Resort is the place to see and be seen. You will see boats of every kind and boaters of every ilk, but it's the "big boys" who stand out here. The staff at Roche Harbor walks a fine line between formal and casual to meet the needs of every boater.

The historic village of Roche Harbor is very picturesque with its famous 1886 Hotel de Haro (visited by President Theodore Roosevelt), "Our Lady of Good Voyage Chapel," and the former home of John S. McMillin, founder of the Roche Harbor Lime & Cement Co., which was known as the largest lime works west of the Mississippi. McMillin built his hotel near the original Hudson's Bay Post and by 1890 a company town had grown, complete with the lime factory, a barrel works, warehouse docks, offices, a company store, church, school, and homes. Today, the historic Hotel de Haro (360-378-2155), the Company Town Cottages, the McMillin Home, the Chapel (Summer Sunday Mass), and the Roche Harbor Market (360-378-5562) still stand. The new Quarryman Hall Suites provide additional lodging at the Resort and include the Afterglow Spa (360-378-9888). Lovely town homes, fitting in character, are just upland overlooking the Harbor.

Be sure to visit the lime kilns across the road from the Roche Harbor Market and don't miss seeing the Mausoleum, a family memorial built by McMillin during the Great Depression. The broken column on the seven-pillar Mausoleum represents the broken column of life. In the center of the structure stands a round table made of limestone and cement surrounded by six stone and cement chairs, which contain the family ashes. The trail head to the Mausoleum (about a ½ mile or .8 km walk) starts behind the cottages at the end of the air strip. Another must see is the Sculpture Park, located behind the cottages on the south side of the air strip. The Park displays nearly 100 pieces of art set along a trail and open spaces through the woods. To obtain trail maps of the lime kilns and other points of interest, stop by the front desk in the Hotel to obtain a copy at a minimal cost.

History buff's will want to visit English Camp (360-378-2902) located off of West Valley Road at Garrison Bay, accessible via Susie's Mopeds (360-378-6262) or by Bob's Taxi (360-378-6777). Boaters may wish to anchor in Garrison Bay and dinghy over to English Camp and use the National Park's guest dock, which accommodates runabouts and dinghies. In 1846, the British and Americans agreed upon the 49th parallel as the boundary between the two nations, but the San Juan Islands were still in dispute. Joint occupation of San Juan Island was agreed upon until the dispute could be resolved. Four historic buildings and a small formal garden have been restored at English Camp. An audio-visual program about the Pig War, which led to the buildup of troops on both sides of the dispute, is held in the barracks.

For another unique outing, visit the Westcott Bay Orchards (360-378-3880), which produces and bottles ciders from a variety of apples. The Orchard is located on the northwest side of Westcott Bay at 43 Anderson Lane, a half-mile (.8 km) walk or ride from Roche Harbor. Visits and tours are by appointment.

Be sure to allow plenty of time at Roche Harbor to take in all the sights and activities conveniently located at this landing. Roche Harbor offers both casual and fine dining venues and a few shops, including the Sportswear Boutique (360-370-7735), and the Roche Harbor Gift Shop (360-370-7730), and Dominique's House Furnishings (360-378-2605). The Cannon Salute and "Colors Ceremony" at sunset is a long-standing tradition at the Resort and can be viewed while dining at McMillin's. Another excellent dining option is to take a taxi to the Duck Soup Inn, located a few miles inland on Roche Harbor Road. This first class fine dining venue has received rave reviews in Bon Appetit and other notable magazines.

English Camp

English Camp and Park Dock

SAN JUAN ISLAND
Roche Harbor

Roche Harbor Marina	360-378-2155 Ext 450 VHF 78A
	800-586-3590

A quality full service marina with restrooms, showers, laundry, fuel, pumpout, restaurants, grocery, and shops. Moorage for vessels up to 150 feet. Customs clearance dock (360-378-2080). Swimming pool and tennis courts.

Short-Term: Short-term stays are permitted without charge on both sides of the breakwater but stay clear of the customs area. A maximum of 2 hours during the busy summer months.

Overnight: Day and overnight moorage at the most easterly dock(s) for $1.55/ft and .80/ft off-season. Reservations a must during the busy season.

San Juan Co. Dock - Roche	360-370-0500
	San Juan Co. Public Works

The southwest slips/docks located near the shore in Roche Harbor are leased from the Marina by the County for dinghy access (marked yellow). A pre-purchased permit is required

Short-Term: Permits are required for usage; a decal is issued after payment of $15 per dinghy, maximum 6 hours. Contact San Juan Public Works, who can email the application.

Overnight: No overnight stays.

Mausoleum

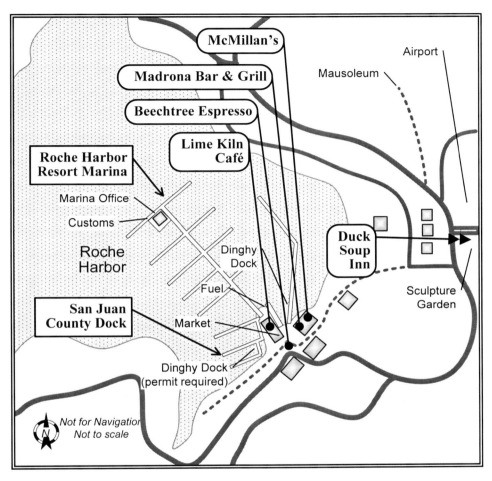

McMillan's

Madrona Bar & Grill

Beechtree Espresso

Lime Kiln Café

Airport

Mausoleum

Roche Harbor Resort Marina

Marina Office

Customs

Roche Harbor

Dinghy Dock

Duck Soup Inn

Fuel

San Juan County Dock

Market

Sculpture Garden

Dinghy Dock (permit required)

Not for Navigation
Not to scale

N

Roche Harbor

BEECHTREE ESPRESSO BAR

The Beechtree Espresso Bar is located under the green and white striped tents near the Roche Harbor Market and offers espresso drinks, snacks, ice cream cones, and milkshakes. You can stroll the beautiful grounds, walkways, and gardens at Roche Harbor Resort, while enjoying your favorite ice cream flavor or espresso.

Espresso/ Ice Cream	7am – 4pm May-June 7am – 8pm June-Aug 7am – 2pm September
Price	Moderate
Outdoor Seating	Yes, Benches
Contact	360-378-2155 (Resort)

LIME KILN CAFE

The Lime Kiln Café is the breakfast venue for Roche Harbor Resort, serving smoked ham, hashbrowns, scrambles, pancakes, and delicious Dungeness Crab Eggs Benedict. The Café has continued its tradition of making fresh donuts throughout the summer months, an enjoyable treat anytime of day. Marine baskets, burgers, and sandwiches are offered at lunch like the Grilled Portabella Mushroom Burger; or try the Griddle Dilla filled with sliced avocado, lettuce, and tomato with your choice of crab or chicken finished with chipotle mayonnaise and salsa. Tables are available on the pier for summer outdoor dining.

Breakfast	7am – 11am Daily Summers Winter Hours Vary
Lunch/ Dinner	11am – 8pm Daily July - August Hours Vary Off Season
Price	Moderate
Outdoor Seating	Yes, Pier, Summer Months
Contact	360-378-2155 Ext 420

McMillin Home and Restaurants

MADRONA BAR & GRILL

The Madrona Grill is located downstairs in the historic McMillin home at Roche Harbor Resort. The long expansive deck overlooking the Harbor and all the activities of the Marina is a popular summer venue. Additional seating is available in the gazebo and in the cozy sport bar. The Grill serves sandwiches, burgers, small plates, and kiln-fired pizzas. Thin crust pizzas include the Huckleberry BBQ Chicken made with smoked Gouda cheese, red onion slices, fresh cilantro, and breast of chicken covered in a huckleberry barbeque sauce. Small Plates include the Dungeness Crab & Artichoke Quesadilla, or try the Westcott Bay Manila Clams & Mussels, or perhaps the Grilled Korean Beef Kabobs. The Madrona Bar & Grill is definitely a "fun-time" place.

Lunch/ Dinner	11am – 10pm Daily mid May – Sept
	Closed Off Season
Price	Moderate
Outdoor Seating	Yes, Deck, Summer Months
Contact	360-378-2155 Ext 400

Madrona Bar & Grill Deck

MCMILLIN'S

McMillin's is the formal dining venue for Roche Harbor Resort and is located on the upper floor in the former home of John S. McMillin, founder of the Roche Harbor Lime & Cement Company. Period paintings, warm woods, and white linen set tables help create the mood for an intimate fare. The views of Roche Harbor are splendid, the perfect place to witness the lowering of the flags honored with national anthems and a cannon salute each evening at sunset during the summer months. McMillin's serves fresh seafood, quality beef, and San Juan Island lamb. Try the Wild Spot Prawn & Dungeness Ravioli, or the Wild Salmon with dill crème fraiche, or perhaps the Morel Crusted Tenderloin Beef, Yakima's Double R Ranch signature beef. McMillin's is the finishing touch for a complete Roche Harbor experience.

Dinner	5pm – 10pm Daily Summers Closed Tue and Wed Nov - March
Price	Expensive
Outdoor Seating	No
Contact	360-378-5757

McMillin's Restaurant

DUCK SOUP INN 🍽

The Duck Soup Inn is located about 5 miles (8 km) from Roche Harbor at 3090 Roche Harbor Road and can be reached by taxi (360-378-6777). Situated on a beautiful country estate, the Inn uses herbs, edible flowers, vegetables, and fruit from the estate's garden. The restaurant has won recognition from Gourmet Magazine, Bon Appetit, and other notable publications. The appetizers, entrees, and desserts are beautifully presented and the extensive wine list provides the perfect pairing for each meal. Duck, lamb, rabbit, steak, and seafood are

Dinner	5pm – 10pm Tue-Sun Hrs Vary Seasonally Closed Nov - March
Price	Expensive
Outdoor Seating	No
Contact	360-378-4878

among the entrees, which are served with sourdough bread, soup, and a seasonal salad. Start with one of the appetizers like the Westcott Bay Applewood Smoked Oysters or the Calamari Caprese Salad. Entrees vary seasonally and may include the Grilled Duck Breast, the Grilled Rack of Lamb, and the Moroccan Spiced Prawns served with creamy polenta with a feta crema. The Vegetarian dish may include the Curried Roasted Vegetables or perhaps the Twice Baked Corn Souffle with goat cheese and green chile lime crema. The Raspberry Cobbler with Muscat custard sauce and the Pelindaba Lavender Panna Cotta with peaches and blueberries provide the finishing touch. The Duck Soup Inn is a real treat not to be missed.

Duck Soup Inn

SHAW ISLAND
Blind Bay

Shaw Island is the smallest of the San Juan Islands that are serviced by ferries and is mainly undeveloped; the approximate 200 residents that live on the Island wish to maintain this peaceful setting. The only commercial property on the Island is the adorable country General Store adjacent to the Ferry Landing and a manufacturing company located inland, which makes fish tags. School bus service is not available on the Island so children walk to the "one-room school house," which is listed on the Register of Historic Places. Bicyclists are often seen enjoying a ride along country roads with split rail fences, flocks of sheep, and abundant deer, heron, and eagles.

From 1976 until June of 2004, the Franciscan nuns (dressed in their long brown habits) operated Shaw Island's General Store and worked as Ferry Agents, attending to loading and off-loading cars and passengers for the ferries each day. A new opportunity arose for the aging nuns, and they have moved on to the Franciscan Center in Bridal Veil, Oregon. Visitors to Shaw Island still look for the nuns at the Ferry Dock and inquire as to their whereabouts. Nuns on the Island from the Benedictine Order, who are dressed in black and white habits, are often mistaken for the Franciscan nuns. The Benedictine nuns attend to organic gardens on the Island and care for cattle, sheep, and llamas.

The Shaw General Store with its enduring charm and character is a special treasure in the San Juan Islands.

Shaw General Store and Dock

Shaw General Store Dock   360-468-2288

Docks belonging to the Shaw General Store are located next to the Ferry Landing and are suitable for runabouts and small cruisers. Check in at the Store to insure appropriate tie space, don't block permanently moored boats.

Short-Term: Short term stays are permitted while eating or shopping at the Shaw General Store at no charge.

Overnight: Overnight stays are not permitted at the Shaw General Store docks; however, anchorage is available in Blind Bay, which is within easy reach by dinghy.

Harney Channel

Shaw General Store Dock

Ferry Dock

Shaw General Store

Picnic Area

Blind Bay Rd

Restrooms

Shaw Island

Blind Bay

Not for Navigation
Not to scale

N

SHAW ISLAND
Blind Bay

SHAW GENERAL STORE

The Shaw General Store is definitely worth a visit if you love nostalgic country stores. The Store was built in 1924 and has wood-plank walls and flooring and a few antiques. The Store has a nice selection of groceries, including organic and local products along with clothing and gift items. Tables and antique chairs are located in the back of the Store where you can relax and enjoy a cup of espresso and hard ice cream. Flower pots and hanging baskets adorn the front porch set with country-style benches or you can enjoy the new picnic area overlooking Blind Bay.

Hours	9am – 7pm Mon-Sat 10am – 5pm Sunday Hours Vary Off Season
Price	Moderate
Outdoor Seating	Yes, Picnic Area
Contact	360-468-2288

Shaw General Store

Shaw General Store

Shaw Picnic Area

Index

4

49th Parallel Grocery, 95, 127

A

Acme Food Company, 141
Alexander's Coffee, 159
Amazing Thai, 143
American Camp, 225
Amineh's, 95
Anglers Anchorage Marina, 87
Appetit, 127
Arigado Sushi, 61
ArtSpring, 57
Asteras Greek Taverna, 143
Atrevida Bakery Boat, 14
Auntie Pesto's, 61, 65
Aurora Restaurant, 47

B

B.C. Aviation Museum, 157
Backdoor Kitchen, 229, 233
Bakery Café Demeter, 229
Barb's Buns, 61
Barnacle Barney's, 95
Bay Café, 181, 183
Beacon Landing, 159
Beacon Landing Restaurant & Pub, 159, 163
Bedwell Harbour, 45
Beechtree Espresso Bar, 243
Beefeaters ChopHouse & Grill, 137
Bennett Bay, 21
Big Moo Diner, 159
Bilbo's Festivo, 197
Billy's Delight Parlor, 95
Birds Eye Cove, 115

Birds Eye Cove Marina, 115
Birds Eye Cove Market, 115
Bistro Garden, 229
Bistro Suisse, 159, 164
Bistro Taiyo, 143
Blakely Island, 175
Blakely Island Marina, 176
Blakely Island Store & Fountain, 175
Blossom Grocery, 181
Blue Dolphin, 229
Blue Peter Dock, 167
Blue Peter Pub & Restaurant, 169
Blue Water Bar & Grill, 229
Blue's Bayou Cafe, 89
Bluenose Marina, 101
Bluff Restaurant, 229, 235
Bo's Boat Store, 105
Boathouse Café, 105
Bocados Bistro, 61, 65
Bocca Café, 143
Boddington Public Dock, 222
Bonnie Martin Restaurant, 95
Book Nook Café, 95
Boondocks, 159, 164
Bouma Meats, 127
Breakwater Public Dock, 59
Breezy Bay Dock, 75
Brentwood Bay, 85
Brentwood Bay Lodge Marina, 87
Brentwood Lodge & Spa, 85
Brentwood Public Dock, 87
Brickworks on the Bay, 23
Brigantine Inn Pub, 121
Brigantine Inn Pub Dock, 119
Bruce's Kitchen, 61
Bubble Tea Stars, 141

Buck Bay Lavender Farm, 203
Buck Bay Shellfish Farm, 203
Bucky's, 181
Burgees Café, 83, 84
Butchart Gardens, 85
Butchart Gardens Dinghy Dock, 86

C

Café 3rd Street, 159
Café Olga, 205
Café Talia, 61
Caffe La Boheme, 181
Calvin's Bistro, 61
Cannery House, 229
Canoe Cove, 149
Canoe Cove Marina, 149
Capernwray Centre, 81, 83
Cara Vaggio Café, 95
Carlos Cantina & Grill, 159
Cascade Bay Grill, 215
Cayou Cove B&B, 187
Chalet Beach Access, 153
Cheese Farm Shop, 53
Chef on The Run, 159
Chemainus, 93
Chemainus Bakery, 95
Chemainus Foods, 95
Chemainus Municipal Dock, 94
Chemainus Sushi, 95
Chemainus Theatre, 93
Chemainus Valley Museum, 93
Cherry Point Vineyards, 101, 105
Cherry Point Vineyards Bistro, 108
Chimayo, 197
China Pearl, 229
Christina's, 197, 199
Church Hill Coffeehouse, 229
Coho Restaurant, 229, 234
Cowichan Bay, 101

Index

Cowichan Bay Seafood Market, 105

D

Dancing Bean Café, 95, 97
Darvill's, 197
Deep Cove Chalet, 155
DeepBlue, 141
Deer Harbor Inn, 189
Deer Harbor Marina, 188
Deer Harbor Store & Grill, 190
Delicado's, 143
Ding Ho Chemainus, 95
Dinghy Dock Pub, 139, 142, 145
Dockside Grill, 170
Doe Bay, 191
Doe Bay Café, 193
Doe Bay Resort, 191
Doe Island Marine State Park, 191
Dos Diablos, 229
Downriggers, 229
Dragon City Restaurant, 127
Duck Soup Inn, 246
Dungeness Marina, 102

E

Eastsound, 195
Eastsound Public Beach, 195
Eastsound Public Dock, 195
Eastsound Wine & Spirits, 197
Eat Restaurant, 18, 19
Ecotopian, 197, 200
Embe Bakery, 61
Enzo's Caffe, 197
Erb's Vegetarian, 197

F

Fairway Market, 159
Fairway Restaurant, 35
Fans Sports Grill, 95

Fernwood Point, 49
Fernwood Public Wharf, 50
Fish on 5th, 159
Fisherman Bay, 177
Fisherman's Wharf, 125
Fishermen's Wharf, 102
Fresh Cup, 159
Friday Harbor, 225
Friday Harbor Ice Cream, 229
Friday Harbor Port Marina, 227
Friday Harbor Seafood, 229
Friday's Crabhouse, 229
Front Street Ale House, 229
Fulford Harbour, 53
Fulford Harbour Public Wharf, 54
Fulford Inn Pub, 55
Fulford Outer Public Wharf, 53

G

Gabriel's Café, 141
Gabriola Museum, 3
Galiano Inn & Spa, 15
Galiano Inn Dock, 17
Gallery Tour, 77
Ganges, 57
Ganges Centennial Wharf, 59
Ganges Marina, 59
Garage Grocery, 18
Garden Path Café, 229
Garrison Bay, 239
Genoa Bay, 111
Genoa Bay Cafe, 113
Genoa Bay Marina, 112
George's, 127
Georgia Café, 159
Gina's Café, 141
Glads Ice Cream, 61
Glenterra Vineyards, 101
Golden Triangle, 229
Good Fortune, 159
Grand Central Emporium, 18, 20

Grapevine On The Bay, 122
Grapevine Trattoria, 143
Green Olive Bar, 141
Green Wasabi, 159

H

Haley's Bait Shop & Grill, 229
Harbour Grill, 11
Harbour House Inn, 61
Harbour Road Deli, 167
Harbourside Café, 95
Harlan's Chocolates, 61
Haro's, 159, 165
Hastings House, 61, 66
Hastings House Spa, 66
Herbs Tavern, 229
Hilary's Cheese, 105
Holly B's Bakery, 181
Home Grown Market, 197
Hope Bay, 31
Hope Bay Cafe, 33
Hope Bay Wharf, 32
House Piccolo, 61, 67
Howling Wolf Farm, 83
Hummingbird Pub, 11

I

In The Bean Time, 127
Iron Wok, 135
Isabel's Espresso, 181
Island Marine Center Docks, 179
Island Market, 197
Islander Restaurant, 182, 184

J

Jakeob's, 143
JavaWocky, 141
Jimmy O's Grill, 131
Jimmy's Paradise Café, 229
Just Heavenly Fudge, 181

Index

K

Kanaka Public Dock, 59
Kathryn Taylor
   Chocolates, 197
King's Market, 225
Kingfish Inn, 223
Kudo's, 95, 98

L

La Berengerie, 13
Ladysmith Marina, 125
Latte Shop, 231
Lavendera Spa, 225
Le Café Francais, 141
LightHouse Bistro & Pub,
   141, 146
Lighthouse Pub, 79
Lime Kiln Cafe, 243
Liquid Café, 105
Local Bar & Bistro, 61
Lopez Historical
   Museum, 177
Lopez Island, 177
Lopez Island Vineyards,
   177
Lopez Islander Marina
   Resort, 179
Lopez Village Market,
   181
Lopez Village Public
   Beach, 179
Love Dog Café, 181, 185
Lower Tavern, 197
LuLu's, 197
Lunn's Bakery, 159
Lyall Harbour, 77
Lyall Harbour Public
   Wharf, 77

M

Madrona Bar & Grill, 244
Maloula's, 231
Mamie's Restaurant, 210
Manzavino, 141
Maple Bay, 119
Maple Bay Marina, 115
Maple Bay Public Wharf,
   119

Margie's Corner Deli, 161
Maria's Souvlaki, 161
Maritime Museum, 101
Maritime Society Docks,
   125
Maritime Society
   Museum, 123
Market Chef, 231, 234
Market Place Café, 63
Masthead Restaurant, 105,
   107
Max & Moritz, 18
Mayne Inn Dock, 22
Mayne Island, 21
McLean's, 143
McMillin's, 245
Meadowvale Farm, 95
Mexico Café, 63
Mi Casita, 231
Millers Pub, 135
Mineral World Scratch
   Patch, 157
Miners Bay, 25
Miners Bay Dock, 26
Miners Bay Museum, 25
Miners Bay Trading Post,
   27
Minnoz, 141
Moby's Pub, 63, 68
Modern Café, 141, 147
Mon Petite Choux, 141
Montague Harbour, 7
Montague Harbour
   Marina, 9
Montague Harbour
   Wharf, 9
Montague Provincial
   Park, 9
Moorings Café, 48
Moran Mansion, 213
Moran State Park, 213
Morning Bay Vineyards
   & Winery, 39, 45
Morningside Bakery, 56
Mouats, 57
Mr. Popper's, 127
Mrs. Riches, 141
Muddy Waters Pub, 138
Muse Winery, 153

N

Nanaimo, 133
Nanaimo Museum, 139
Nanaimo Port, 139, 140
Nauticals Seafood Bar &
   Grill, 138
New Leaf Café, 197, 201
New York Style Pizza,
   143
Newcastle Concessions,
   142
Newcastle Marine Park
   Docks, 134
North Island Coffee Co.,
   52
Northbrook Restaurant
   III, 127

O

Ocean Discovery Centre,
   157
Oceanfront Grand Resort
   Dock, 103
Octavia's, 211
Odyssia Restaurant, 161
Old City Station Pub, 141
Old Town Bakery, 127
Olga, 203
Olga History Tour, 203
Olga Public Dock, 204
Olga Store & Deli, 206
Orcas Island, 195
Orcas Island Historical
   Museum, 195
Orcas Island Shuttle Bus,
   187
Orcas Island Shuttle Co.,
   213
Orcas Island Taxi, 213
Orcas Landing, 208
Orcas Mopeds, 207
Orcas Village Store, 212
Otter Bay, 35
Otter Bay Bistro, 37
Otter Bay Marina, 36
Outlook Inn, 197
Oystercatcher Bar & Grill,
   63

Index

P

Page Point Marina, 125
Page's Resort Marina, 4
Pasta Fresca, 63
Patterson's Market, 53
Pazzo Vivo Bistro, 231
Pelindaba Lavender Farm, 225
Pender Is. Golf & Country Club, 35
Pender Island Bakery, 43
Pender Island Cab, 31
Pender Island Museum, 35
Penny's Palapa, 141
Peppermill, 231
Perkins Coffee Co., 141
Pho A Dong, 143
Pier 1 Restaurant, 161
Pier 66 Marina, 103
Pier Bistro, 161, 166
Playbill Dining Room, 95
Poets Cove Marina, 46
Pomodoro Pizza, 63
Port Browning, 39
Port Browning Café & Pub, 41
Port Browning Marina, 40
Port Browning Public Wharf, 40
Port Side Marina, 87
Port Sidney Marina, 158
Portofino Pizzeria, 197
Pot of Gold Coffee, 83
Preedy Harbour, 81
Printingdun Beanery, 127, 129

Q

Quamichan Inn, 118
Quarryman Hall Suites, 239
Quiznos, 161

R

Raven Market Cafe, 51
Red Brick Café, 161
Red Martini Grill, 141
Rendezvous, 63
Resthaven Grocery Store, 167
Roberts Street Pizza, 127
Roche Harbor, 239
Roche Harbor Marina, 241
Roche Harbor Market, 239
Rock Cod Café, 105, 108
Rock Salt, 56
Rocky Bay Café, 231
Rogers Chocolates, 161
Rosario Resort, 213
Rosario Resort Marina, 214
Rose's Café, 197, 202
Rotary Dinghy Dock & Park, 60
Royal Dar Restaurant, 127, 129
Russells, 209

S

Saanich Inlet, 85
Sabhai Thai, 161
Sake House, 141
Salt Spring Adventures Co., 57
Salt Spring Island, 49
Salt Spring Marina, 60
Salt Spring Noodle Bar, 63
SaltSpring Inn, 63, 69
Saltspring Roasting, 63
Salty's by the Sea, 161
San Juan County Dock, 241
San Juan Island, 225
San Juan Sweet Shop, 231
San Juan Transit, 225
San Juan Vineyards, 225
Saturna Cafe, 80
Saturna General Store, 80
Saturna Island, 75
Saturna Island Winery, 75
Saturna Point Store, 77
Schooners, 105, 110
Scoops Ice Cream, 18
Seagrille, 90
Seahorses Cafe, 91
Seahorses Café Dock, 87
Seaside Restaurant, 73
Seaside Restaurant Dock, 72
Serious Coffee, 141, 161
Sharkie's Pizza, 33
Shaw General Store, 249
Shaw General Store Dock, 248
Shaw Island, 247
Shipyard Pub & Restaurant, 117
Sidney, 157
Sidney Bakery, 161
Sidney Historical Museum, 157
Sidney Pier Hotel, 157
Silva Bay, 3
Silva Bay Bar & Grill, 6
Silva Bay Inn Dock, 5
Silva Bay Marina, 5
Silver Shadow Taxi, 53
SJ Coffee Roasters, 231
Small Tall Treats, 95
Sofie's Cafe, 151
South Pender Island, 45
Sporty Grill & Sportsman Pub, 127
Springwater Lodge, 27, 28
Starbucks, 161
Steps Wine Bar & Café, 231, 236
Stonehouse Pub, 152
Stones Marina, 135
Stonestreet Café, 161
Sturdies Bay, 15
Sturdies Bay Bakery, 18
Sturdies Bay Public Dock, 17
Sukkho Thai, 141
Sunflower Café, 197
Sunny Mayne Bakery, 29
Sunny Mayne Bakery Café, 27
Sushi To Go, 141
Susurrus Spa, 45
Swartz Bay Wharf, 149
Sweet Retreat, 231
Syrens Lounge, 48

Index

T

Tea on the Quay, 141
Teddy Bear's, 63
Teezer's, 197
Telegraph Harbour, 81
Telegraph Harbour
    Marina, 81
Thai Sisters Café, 197
The Bay Pub, 105
The Boater's Exchange,
    157
The Doctor's Office, 231
The Galley, 182, 185
The Galley Dock &
    Buoys, 179
The Garden Eatery, 95
The Grand, 105, 109
The Hungry Clam, 231
The Keg, 143
The Kitchen, 197
The Latch, 171
The Muffin Mill, 95
The Naked Bean, 231
The Phoenix, 127
The Place Bar & Grill,
    231, 237
The Rumrunner, 161, 166
The Stand, 38
Theo's Family Restaurant,
    161
Thetis Island, 81
Thetis Island Community
    Dock, 82

Thetis Island Marina, 83
Thetis Island Pub, 83, 84
Thistle's Café, 105, 109
Thrifty Foods, 63, 167
TJ Beans, 63
Tod Inlet, 85
Transfer Beach Grill, 127,
    130
Tree House Café, 63, 70
Troller's, 141
Tru Value Foods, 27
True Grain Bread, 105
Tsehum Harbour, 167
Twisted Sisters, 95

U

Udder Guy's, 105
Utopia Bakery Café, 96

V

Van Isle Marina, 167
Vern's Bayside, 198
Vesuvius, 71
Vesuvius Public Wharf,
    72
Vesuvius Village Store,
    74
Vinny's Ristorante, 231,
    238
Vita's Wildly Delicious,
    181, 186
Vortex, 181

W

Water Taxi Service, 207
Waterfront Confections,
    141
Wesley Street Café, 143,
    148
West Beach, 217
West Beach Resort, 218
West Beach Store, 219
West Sound, 221
West Sound Marina, 221
Westcott Bay Orchards,
    239
Westsound Cafe, 223
Whale Museum, 225
Whaler Bay, 15
Whaler Bay Public Dock,
    17
Wigwam, 127
Wild Fennel, 27, 30
Willow Street Café, 96,
    99
Winter Cove, 77

Y

Yellow Point Cranberry
    Farm, 123

Notes